Interpreting the Constitution

INTERPRETING THE CONSTITUTION

Erwin Chemerinsky

PRAEGER

New York
Westport, Connecticut
London

Library of Congress Cataloging-in-Publication Data

Chemerinsky, Erwin.
Interpreting the constitution.

Bibliography: p.
Includes index.
1. United States—Constitutional law—Interpretation and construction. 2. Judicial review—United States. I. Title.
KF4550.C43 1987 342.73′023 87-2484
347.30223
ISBN 0-275-92674-5 (alk. paper)

Library of Congress Catalog Card Number: 87-2484
ISBN: 0-275-92674-5

First published in 1987

Praeger Publishers, One Madison Avenue, New York, NY 10010
A division of Greenwood Press, Inc.

Printed in the United States of America

The paper used in this book complies with the Permanent Paper Standard issued by the National Information Standards Organization (Z39.48-1984).

10 9 8 7 6 5 4 3 2 1

To my sons,
Jeffrey and Adam—
May you live in a world where there
truly is liberty and justice for all.

Contents

Preface

The debate ranges on over the proper method of constitutional interpretation. In the popular arena, there have been recent speeches by the attorney general attacking the approach of liberal Supreme Court justices and replies by some justices defending their methodology.[1] In the scholarly literature, the flood of books and articles on judicial review continues.[2] In Supreme Court opinions, interpretive approaches are often openly discussed and frequently decisive in explaining the results in particular cases. A dramatic example is the Court's refusal last year to find constitutional protection in the right to privacy for consensual adult homosexual activity.[3] The Court justified its conclusion with a methodological claim about the inappropriateness of judicial protection of rights not clearly stated or implied in the Constitution.[4]

This book is part of the ongoing debate. It is written with the hope of changing the focus of the debate, clarifying the issues, and advancing an alternative vision of the role of the Constitution and the Court in our society. A central theme of the book is that the debate over judicial review has focused on the wrong questions. Much of the current discussion about constitutional interpretation has centered on how to reconcile judicial review with democracy defined as majority rule.[5] But, as I argue in Chapter 1, such a definition of democracy is neither descriptively accurate nor normatively desirable. Many aspects of U.S. government, most notably the Constitution, are intentionally antimajoritarian. The concept of majority rule is of little help in defining the role of an antimajoritarian institution—the federal judiciary—or in determining the meaning of an antimajoritarian document—the Constitution.

Likewise, much of the current debate has focused on a way to achieve objective, value-free judicial decision making.[6] But the legal realists long ago taught that judges have inherent discretion in deciding cases, especially in interpreting an open-textured document such as the Constitution. Exercise of judicial discretion is inescapably affected by justices' values. No one is surprised when Justices Rehnquist and Brennan come to opposite conclusions even though both are committed to upholding the Constitution and both are conscientiously performing their duties.

Thus, a major focus of this book is critical, suggesting that much of the recent literature on constitutional interpretation is misfocused. Efforts to devise a method of judicial review that is consistent with majority rule or that eliminates discretion are doomed to fail. Chapter 1 details criticism of the focus of the ongoing debate and hence explains why I chose to write yet another examination of constitutional interpretation and judicial review.

This book also attempts to offer an alternative agenda for debate. The central question is, How should meaning be given to the provisions of the United States Constitution? Questions of the responsibility and role of particular institutions are important, but such questions should be considered only in the context of answering the larger inquiry.

The logical starting place for deciding the proper method of interpreting the Constitution begins with the question: Why should U.S. society be governed by a constitution at all? Constitutional interpretation is instrumental—it exists to accomplish the purposes of the Constitution. Logically, then, analysis should begin by considering why it is desirable to have government controlled by a written constitution. By ignoring this question and simply assuming the authoritative status of the Constitution, the current debate neglects a question that reveals a great deal about the proper method of constitutional interpretation. Chapter 2 addresses why society should be governed by a constitution, concluding that the U.S. Constitution serves the dual function of protecting deeply embedded values—separation of powers, equality, individual liberties—from the political process, and of serving as a powerful symbol unifying the country.

The purposes of the Constitution are especially important in answering two key questions that determine how it should be implemented: First, should the meaning of the Constitution evolve or remain static? And second, if its meaning should evolve, should the evolution be only by amendment or also by interpretation? The latter question is the key issue in much of the current popular and scholarly debate over judicial review. The "originalists," on the one hand, contend that the Constitution's meaning is limited to that which is clear from the text or intended by its drafters.[7] They argue that any change in the meaning of the Constitution must come through the amendment process. The opposing view, advanced by "nonoriginalists," is that the Court may protect values not stated or implied in the Constitution. Nonoriginalists contend that the Constitution should evolve by interpretation, not only by amendment.

Yet relatively little attention has focused directly on this question of whether the Constitution should evolve by amendment or interpretation. To answer the question, it is necessary to decide first how important it is that the Constitution's meaning evolve; only then can it be decided which method of evolution is best.

Chapter 3 focuses on the question of whether the Constitution's meaning should remain static or evolve, and Chapter 4 considers the issue of whether the evolution should be by interpretation or amendment. I conclude that the functions of a constitution, both in safeguarding fundamental values and in serving as a unifying symbol, can be attained only if the Constitution evolves through interpretation.

If it is established that the Constitution should evolve by interpretation as well as by amendment, the next question becomes, What institution(s) should have responsibility for that interpretation? All officeholders take an oath to uphold the Constitution, and all institutions of government interpret the Constitution. Members of Congress and state and local legislatures must make constitutional determinations in deciding whether to vote for a bill. A governor or president needs to evaluate constitutionality in deciding whether to sign or veto a proposed law. Thus, the question really is, Which branch of government, if any, should be authoritative in interpreting the Constitution? Chapter 5 addresses this question. I conclude that for numerous reasons the judiciary should have the final say (absent a constitutional amendment overturning its decision) over the meaning of the Constitution.

If the Court is to interpret the meaning of the Constitution, and if the meaning of the Constitution can evolve such that the Court is not limited to what the Framers intended, is there any limit on the interpretive process? Are there any restraints on the Court, and if so, what are they? Much of constitutional scholarship has been preoccupied with attempting to find an interpretive model that limits judicial discretion. Chapter 6 addresses these questions, arguing that inherently constitutional interpretation is, and should be, an indeterminate, open-ended process. By *indeterminacy*, I simply mean that there is no single correct answer to the vast majority of constitutional questions presented to the Court. Conscientious justices will inevitably come to differing conclusions about the meaning of specific constitutional provisions and their application to particular situations. It is futile to search for a model of constitutional decision making that is objective or discretion free.

Furthermore, I argue that if the Constitution is to serve its functions of protecting fundamental values and unifying society, the judiciary *should* have substantial discretion in determining the meaning of specific constitutional provisions. I recognize, of course, that discretion can be used for good or ill, and there is a risk of judicial discretion being used to frustrate social improvements and progress. Nonetheless, as developed in Chapter 6, I believe that, on balance, judicial discretion in constitutional interpretation is a good thing that will advance society. The chapter concludes by focusing on the objection that open-ended review risks judicial tyranny, describing why the foes of judicial activism substantially overstate the risks of judicial protection of constitutional values.

As is evident from the discussion above, I am doing more in this book than criticizing the current debate and suggesting an alternative agenda for discussion; I am advancing my views about the role of the Constitution in society. My central conclusion is that it is desirable for society to have an institution such as the Court, which is not popularly elected or accountable, to identify and protect values that it deems sufficiently important to be constitutionalized and safeguarded from social majorities. I believe that the most important difference between a statute and the Constitution is that it is much harder to change the Constitution. Because of this immunity from easy alteration, the Constitution contains principles that should be relatively immune from majoritarian decision making. The structure of government is placed in the Constitution to prevent centralization of power, especially in times of crisis. Fundamental rights and protection of minorities are preserved through a constitution that is not easily altered and by a federal judiciary that is relatively insulated from political pressures.

But the Constitution only provides a sketch of how government should be structured and describes rights and protections only in general terms. Throughout this book, I argue that it is desirable to have a constitution written in fairly abstract language enshrining widely shared fundamental values about the proper structure of government and the rights of individuals. It is left for each generation to impart specific meaning to these deeply embedded abstract values.

I contend that the purposes of a constitution—especially protecting cherished values and safeguarding members of minority groups—can be best achieved by a judiciary with broad discretion in interpreting the Constitution. U.S. society is better off because the Supreme Court ordered desegregation of the South, applied the Bill of Rights to the states, decided that the Constitution protects the right of parents to control the upbringing of their children, compelled the reapportionment of state legislatures, held that people have a right to privacy, required the appointment of counsel in criminal cases, and prevented discrimination against disfavored groups such as women, aliens, and illegitimate children. I do not deny the risk of misguided judicial decisions, such as the infamous Supreme Court decisions earlier in this century frustrating social progress and the New Deal. Rather, I argue that, on balance, the benefits of decisions upholding individual liberties, enforcing separation of powers, and advancing equality outweigh the costs of the decisions that history later regards as mistakes.

I am not espousing a radical call for reform. Quite the contrary, I am simply defending what the Court has done throughout U.S. history. Time and time again for 200 years, the Court has explicitly recognized the discretion it possesses in interpreting the Constitution. The process of judicial decision making always has been, and should be, open-ended, with the Court interpreting all constitutional provisions, based on contemporary values.

The Constitution is society's best hope for safeguarding its most cherished values from the excesses of the democratic process. The judiciary, because of its political insulation and its method of decision making, is best suited to apply the Constitution to specific situations and articulate its meaning. By this theory, the judiciary is not given license to assume control of all U.S. government. Rather, the judiciary is given authority over one important aspect of it: the protection of those values deemed so important that they are enshrined in the Constitution.

Chapter 7, the final chapter, concludes by considering objections to this approach. I focus on the frequent claim that if the Court's review is open-ended, the legitimacy of the Court will be undermined. The threat of loss of judicial credibility is unsupported by any empirical or historical evidence and is belied by continued legitimacy despite decades of openly nonoriginalist decisions.

I realize that my theory about constitutional interpretation and judicial review only raises more questions. What values should be protected by the Constitution and the Court? What is the proper allocation of power under the Constitution? What is the appropriate content of terms such as *liberty*, *equal protection*, *freedom of speech*, and the like? I do not pretend to offer full or even partially developed answers to these questions. Although inchoate answers are implied throughout the book, each of these inquiries—questions about what the good society should be and how we should get there—is beyond my scope here. In this effort, I am content to focus on the method of constitutional interpretation and leave for others and perhaps my future writings to elaborate on the more profound and fundamental questions. To a large extent this book is foundational; if my argument is accepted, then the focus for constitutional law should be over what values are worthy of constitutional protection and how abstract values should be given specific meaning and applied to particular situations.

Thus, this is a book about how the Constitution should be interpreted and especially about the judiciary's role in that process. Although certainly I hope to persuade readers of the merits of my conclusions, at the least I seek to convince them that these are the right questions to ask. Hopefully, even those who disagree with my conclusions about the proper role of the Constitution and the courts in society might be persuaded that the grounds of the debate should be changed and perhaps find the agenda for discussion suggested here to be useful and clarifying.

Coincidentally, this book is published in the year of the Constitution's Bicentennial. I am not so presumptuous to think that I can resolve questions that have remained open for 200 years. I have little doubt that if U.S. society is governed by this Constitution for 200 years more, in 2187 many of these same questions about constitutional interpretation and judicial review will still be debated. I do not see the impossibility of resolution of the debate as an indication of its futility. Quite the contrary, its intractability should caution us to beware of those who proclaim that they have the one true way of interpreting the Constitution.

More important, the inability to resolve questions of methodology is a strong indication that the debate really is about substance, not procedure. During the 1930s it was the conservatives who were championing judicial activism, and it was the liberals, frustrated with the Court's invalidation of progressive legislation, who were crying for restraint. More recently, conservatives, disliking the Warren Court's advancement of individual freedoms and social equality, have attacked the Court's method and tried to develop models of review that would limit such liberal decisions in the future. Liberal academics have tried mightily to develop theories of judicial review that defend the modern Court's protection of freedom and equality.

In other words, when judges and scholars are arguing over the method of judicial review, what they are really arguing about is what constitutes the ''good'' society and how it can best be achieved. These are the questions that people always have and always will argue about. The debate over constitutional interpretation is just a small part of that all-important ongoing discussion.

Acknowledgments

A portion of Chapter 1 was previously published in the *Texas Law Review*, and I am grateful for their permission to reprint this material.

My work on this book benefited greatly from the assistance of many friends and colleagues. First, I wish to acknowledge an exceptionally talented group of research assistants: Patty Carellos, Vincent Gonzales, Richard Mandelbaum, Effie Massry, Clayton Thomasson, and especially, David Bartholomew. Alvin Hui and Mel Ilomin painstakingly checked the accuracy of the citations.

Second, I want to thank Kathy Abrams, Larry Alexander, Richard Craswell, George Lefcoe, Michael Perry, Sharon Rush, Jeffrey Shaman, Larry Simon, David Slawson, and the participants at a faculty workshop at the University of Southern California Law Center for their very helpful comments and suggestions on an earlier draft of this manuscript. I am particularly grateful for the very detailed comments I received from Scott Bice, Dan Conkle, Ron Garet, Louis Kaplow, William Marshall, Tom Morawetz, Stephen Siegel, and Michael Shapiro. Without a doubt, this book would be better if I had followed even more of their advice.

Finally, and most important, I want to thank my wife, Marcy Strauss, without whose ideas and editing this manuscript would be much worse, and without whose support and encouragement this book would not have been possible at all.

Interpreting the Constitution

1 Why Another Essay on Constitutional Interpretation and Judicial Review?

The current obsession of constitutional law scholarship—whether activist judicial review can be reconciled with majoritarian democracy—is hardly new.[1] The controversy has reemerged as a result of attacks by conservative critics on recent Supreme Court decisions that protect rights neither mentioned in the Constitution's text nor intended by its Framers.[2] Judges and scholars such as William Rehnquist, Robert Bork, and Raoul Berger contend that the principle of majority rule is violated if judicial decisions are based upon values that are not stated or implied in the Constitution.[3] They argue that democracy requires unelected judges to defer to the decisions of elected officials unless there is a clear violation of the rights protected by the Framers of the Constitution.[4]

A number of prominent scholars have responded to this attack on the legitimacy of judicial review with theories designed to reconcile the Court's activist decisions with majority rule. Commentators such as Jesse Choper, John Hart Ely, and Michael Perry accept the premise of the critics of judicial review—that decisions in a democracy must be subject to control by electorally accountable officials—but maintain that their theories demonstrate why the Court can act to protect values not explicitly mentioned in the Constitution.[5] These authors' works have spawned numerous responses and even entire symposia examining whether judicial activism is appropriate in a democratic society.[6] The controversy has been characterized as a debate between the "originalists," who believe that the Court must confine itself to norms clearly stated or implied in the language of the Constitution, and "nonoriginalists," who believe that the Court may protect norms not mentioned in the Constitution's text or its preratification history.[7]

In this chapter, I argue that this debate over the legitimacy of judicial review is misdirected, futile, disingenuous, and dangerous. The debate is misdirected because it starts with a premise—all decisions in a democracy should be subject to control by politically accountable institutions—that is neither justified nor justifiable. U.S. democracy does not, and should not, correspond to a purely procedural definition of democracy as majority rule. The Constitution purposely is an antimajoritarian document reflecting a distrust of government conducted entirely by majority rule. The Constitution protects substantive values from majoritarian pressures, and judicial review enhances democracy by safeguarding these values.

The current debate is futile because if democracy requires that all value choices be subject to control by electorally accountable officials, then nonoriginalist review, by definition, is not acceptable in a democracy. Judicial review is inherently antimajoritarian; unelected judges are overturning policies enacted by popularly elected legislatures. No model of judicial review can justify nonoriginalist judicial review if it begins with the premise that all decisions must be subject to control by electorally accountable officials.

The contention that judicial review is undemocratic is disingenuous at best. None of the critics of Supreme Court activism suggest that all judicial review should be eliminated. Yet *any* judicial decision that overturns a policy enacted by a popularly elected legislature is antimajoritarian; even judicial review based on the intent of the Framers is, by the critics' criteria, undemocratic. The originalists' only justification for allowing even limited judicial review is that it is functionally necessary to uphold the Constitution. However, if a functional justification for originalism is sufficient to outweigh the principle of majority rule, a functional justification should also be sufficient to sustain nonoriginalism. Because the originalist critics are willing to sacrifice majoritarian decision making to achieve their goals, their reliance upon democratic theory as the basis for their attack on nonoriginalism is both inconsistent and hypocritical.

Finally, the current debate is dangerous because the defenders of judicial review accept the critics' definition of democracy and thereby legitimize the claim that judicial review is unjustified unless it is made consistent with majority rule. The inevitable failure to reconcile nonoriginalist judicial review with this definition of democracy undermines the legitimacy of countless Supreme Court decisions, including those protecting privacy,[8] desegregating schools,[9] upholding the rights of women,[10] safeguarding freedom of speech,[11] and requiring that the states comply with the Bill of Rights.[12] None of these decisions can be justified by the text of the Constitution or the intent of its Framers.[13] In fact, because many of these decisions advance *democracy* as that term is commonly understood, the loss of these rulings would be dangerous according to the standards and values of all in the debate.

This chapter describes why the current debate over the legitimacy of judicial review is misguided. The first section describes the attack on nonoriginalist judicial review and the responses by the defenders of nonoriginalism. The second section of the chapter explains why the debate is misdirected—why both the attack and the defense focus on the wrong questions.

THE CURRENT DEBATE

Virtually all participants in the debate over the legitimacy of judicial review begin with the premise that democracy requires that decisions be subject to control by majority rule. Michael Perry, for example, begins his analysis by briefly stating that majority rule is the controlling premise in a democratic society.

> We in the United States are philosophically committed to the political principle that governmental policymaking—by which I mean simply decisions as to which values among competing values shall prevail, and as to how those values should be implemented—ought to be subject to control by persons accountable to the electorate.[14]

Similarly, John Hart Ely spends little time defining what he means by *democracy* even though his book is described as an attempt to reconcile judicial review with "democratic theory."[15] At the beginning of his book, Ely simply postulates that rule by the majority "is the core of the American governmental system."[16] Perry and Ely are typical in defining democracy as majority rule. There are countless examples of commentators who begin their analyses like a recent scholar writing about constitutional interpretation:

> I claim that the United States is a democratic polity. By this I mean that . . . the nation is meant to be ruled by the majorities of its citizenry.[17]

Thus, the debate over the legitimacy of judicial review begins with the almost universally accepted premise that democracy requires that decisions be made by institutions and individuals who are accountable to the electorate.[18]

It is important to recognize that democracy is defined in purely procedural terms, as the method of adopting policies, not even partially in substantive terms, as the values that a democratic society desires, such as equality or freedom of expression. The underlying assumption is that government in a democracy should fulfill the preferences of its citizens "either directly by vote of the electorate or indirectly by officials freely elected at reasonably frequent intervals."[19] It also should be noted that throughout the debate the term *democracy* is used interchangeably with phrases such as "majority rule" or "electorally accountable policy-making," although none of these concepts is defined with any precision.[20] At the very least, the participants in the current debate over judicial review can be criticized for their superficial consideration of the meaning of democracy and majority rule. Although the political science literature on the concept of democracy is voluminous, most constitutional scholars discussing democracy and judicial review simply begin with a short definition of *democracy*, seldom more than a few paragraphs.

Conservative critics of judicial review argue that permitting courts to strike down legislative actions based on the judiciary's interpretation of the Constitution violates the democratic principle of majority rule.[21] If democracy is defined in purely procedural terms as a requirement that only electorally accountable officials make decisions, judicial review is undemocratic in two ways. First, the Supreme Court is obviously not a democratic institution by this definition because the justices have lifetime appointments and are not directly accountable to the electorate. Second, Court action thwarts the will of the majority by overturning policies enacted by officials popularly elected and democratically accountable. Alexander Bickel termed this tension between judicial review and majority rule the "counter-majoritarian difficulty,"[22] and it is this difficulty that is the center of the debate over the legitimacy of judicial review and the obsession of constitutional law scholarship.[23]

Similarly, if the definition of majority rule is phrased slightly differently as a requirement that all decisions be subject to electoral control, judicial decisions violate this principle because the electorate cannot overturn judicial decisions, directly or indirectly. Unless, of course, the possibility of reversing a decision by constitutional amendment is sufficient to constitute electoral control—in which case, all judicial constitutional decisions are consistent with majoritarianism. However, both proponents and critics of activist judicial review reject the amendment process as insufficient electoral control—although, again, they do so without developing a theory for determining what degree of electoral control is sufficient to meet their definition of democracy.

Conservative critics argue that nonoriginalist decisions are illegitimate because they allow judicial choices to overturn legislative and executive policies. Raoul Berger, for example, contends that "activist judicial review is inconsistent with democratic theory because it substitutes the policy choices of unelected, unaccountable judges for those of the people's representatives."[24] Judge Robert Bork similarly notes that a "Court that makes rather than implements value choices cannot be squared with the presuppositions of a democratic society."[25]

Most defenders of activist judicial review accept the legitimacy of the conservatives' attack and explicitly admit that nonoriginalist judicial review only can be justified if it can be reconciled with majority rule. For example, Daniel Conkle begins his article that seeks to justify nonoriginalist review by observing that "the ultimate validity of any theory of judicial review depends on reconciling such review with the principle of majoritarian consent."[26] Similarly, Perry, at the outset of his widely reviewed book, writes:

> [M]y strategy is not to reject the principle [that decisions in a democracy be subject to control by electorally accountable officials], but, on the contrary, to accept it as a given and then to defend judicial review—in particular, constitutional policymaking—as not inconsistent with the principle.[27]

Thus, the current debate centers around a syllogism advanced by the critics of judicial review. The critics' argument can be summarized as the following deduction:

Major premise: All value decisions in a democracy must be subject to control by electorally accountable officials in order to be legitimate.

Minor premise: Nonoriginalist judicial decisions are value choices made by an institution that is not subject to control by electorally accountable officials.

Conclusion: Therefore, nonoriginalist judicial decisions are illegitimate.

The defenders of nonoriginalist judicial review do not challenge the critics' major premise. Instead, they respond at the level of the minor premise, trying to rescue judicial review by developing a model of court action that does not involve impermissible judicial value imposition. For example, Ely argues that judicial review that attempts to make the political process work by reinforcing representational values is consistent with democracy and does not violate the major premise.[28] Perry argues that under his approach nonoriginalist review by the Supreme Court does not violate the major premise because Congress has the authority to restrict the Supreme Court's jurisdiction.[29] As such, the entire debate focuses on whether it is possible to deny the minor premise of the syllogism and develop a model of judicial review that is consistent with a requirement that all decisions be controllable by electorally accountable officials.

THE MISGUIDED CURRENT DEBATE

The current debate is misdirected, first, because its major premise is based on an unjustified and incorrect definition of democracy, in purely procedural terms, as majority rule. Thus, the defenders of judicial review have committed a crucial error in conceding the major premise of the syllogism. Second, if the major premise is true, then all judicial review, originalist and nonoriginalist, is illegitimate because it all involves decisions by an unelected judiciary displacing choices of elected officials. Therefore, either all judicial review is illegitimate or the major premise is false. Finally, the current debate is misdirected because it fails to provide any method for constitutional interpretation. The debate has focused entirely on the role of the judiciary, which obscures the real question of how meaning should be given to the Constitution. In fact, the role of the judiciary only can be decided in the context of the larger inquiry.

I emphasize that I am not arguing that majority rule is unimportant nor denying that it is one component of a correct definition of democracy. Instead, the analysis which follows establishes that it is wrong to define democracy solely as majority rule, and incorrect to begin with the premise that judicial review must be reconciled with democracy defined in purely procedural terms.

The Syllogism's Major Premise Is False: Democracy Does Not Require That All Decisions Be Subject to Control by Electorally Accountable Officials

As described above, the current debate begins with the premise that society's commitment to democratic government requires that decisions be subject to control by electorally accountable officials. It is important to recognize that this premise is postulated entirely as an axiom. No attempt has been made by any of the commentators to develop a political or moral theory defending this definition of democracy. Perry, for example, writes: "I accept as a given [the principle that] . . . policymaking must be electorally accountable. . . . The principle of electorally accountable policymaking is axiomatic."[30] Perry, although perhaps more explicit than many scholars, is typical in that he simply posits, without any defense, the major premise that decisions in a democracy must be subject to control by majoritarian processes.

In fact, none of the commentators makes any attempt to define what they mean by "electorally accountable policy-making." At what point can a government official be regarded as electorally accountable? How frequent must the elections be in order for an official to be regarded as truly electorally accountable? Are senators sufficiently electorally accountable despite their six-year terms? Is a lame-duck president an electorally accountable official? How indirect might the control be for the officials to still be regarded as electorally accountable? Are members of the president's Cabinet to be deemed electorally accountable? What degree of control by electorally accountable officials is sufficient? Is the possibility of a constitutional amendment to overturn a Supreme Court decision sufficient to make the judiciary an institution that is subject to electoral control? Is the power of the executive to disregard and refuse to implement judicial decisions enough to create control by an electorally accountable institution?

At the very least, there is no basis for an axiomatic definition of democracy. Political scientists offer many alternative definitions and conceptions of democracy. No one can claim authoritative status as the only proper or legitimate definition. Political scientist Martin Edelman writes:

> There is considerable disagreement about what democracy means and implies. . . . Too often proponents of democracy defend their position on the comforting, though erroneous, assumption that it represents *the* American political theory. . . . Neither the Constitution nor the development of American political thought can serve as an authoritative basis for any theory of democracy.[31]

In fact, if any definition of democracy can claim axiomatic status, it clearly is not a definition of democracy as majority rule. A definition can be justified in two possible ways. One is descriptive—that the definition correctly describes the U.S. system of government. The alternative is to argue normatively that regardless of what exists the definition describes what should be the system. Descriptively, it is incorrect to define democracy as a commitment that all decisions be made by majority rule, and normatively, a purely procedural conception of democracy as majority rule is not desirable.

U.S. government cannot be described as dedicated to always maximizing the preferences of the majority. For example, society is committed to protecting many substantive values that it is unwilling to allow the majority to violate or ignore. Society will not allow the legislature to torture or persecute minorities, no matter how much pleasure the majority might derive from such behavior. Similarly, society is committed to protecting free exercise of religion and freedom of speech, even if it means ignoring the majority's preference for suppression. As Justice Robert Jackson explained in *West Virginia Board of Education v. Barnette*:

> One's right to life, liberty, and property, to free speech, a free press, freedom of worship and assembly, and other fundamental rights may not be submitted to vote; they depend on the outcome of no elections.[32]

Society in the United States is as much committed to certain substantive values as it is committed to the importance of majority rule. These few examples of important substantive values reveal the inadequacy of the purely procedural definition of democracy as majority rule that underlies the debate over the legitimacy of judicial review. In fact, if one looks up *democracy* in *Webster's*, the first definition listed is: "a state of society characterized by tolerance to minorities, freedom of expression and respect for the essential dignity of the human individual, with equal opportunity for each to develop freely to his fullest capacity."[33] The justifications for democracy developed by many political scientists emphasize its desirability as a system of government that best protects basic liberties and most ensures equality.[34]

Furthermore, a description of democracy as majority rule is not what the Framers of the Constitution intended. The Framers feared tyranny by the majority and explicitly rejected a system of government of unchecked majority control. Hannah Arendt observes that the "Founding Fathers tended to equate rule based on public opinion with tyranny; democracy in this sense was to them but a new fangled form of despotism."[35] The records of the Constitutional Convention are filled with statements, such as that of Elbridge Gerry, expressing a need to avoid the "excess of democracy."[36] James Madison, who is regarded as particularly influential in the drafting and ratification of the Constitution, was especially distrustful of majorities and wanted to create what he termed a "republic," not a purely majoritarian democracy.[37] Robert Dahl explains:

> Madison, in particular, wished to erect a political system that would guarantee the liberties of certain minorities whose advantages of status, power, and wealth would, he thought, probably not be tolerated indefinitely by a constitutionally untrammeled majority.[38]

The fact that the Framers of the Constitution did not want to create a government based entirely on majority rule is important because originalists are committed to interpreting the Constitution in accord with the Framers' intent.

Therefore, the originalists' own methodology compels them to abandon their purely procedural definition of democracy as majority rule.

Perhaps the clearest illustration of the inaccuracy of a purely procedural definition of democracy is the actual manner in which U.S. government is structured and functions. In countless ways, government activity and structure does not reflect a definition of democracy as majority rule and electorally accountable policy-making. For example, because all states have two senators regardless of their population, senators representing states with much less than half the population can enact laws, and senators representing a substantial majority of the population are often powerless to act.[39] A minority of senators has the power to block the ratification of treaties and the appointment of public officials, like judges and ambassadors. A bill favored by a majority of the people and a majority of Congress might be defeated by a filibuster or vetoed by the president. In fact, the United States Senate was originally intended to represent states and not citizens. Senators were not made electorally accountable until 1913, when popular election of senators replaced selection by state legislatures.

Nor does a purely majoritarian conception of democracy describe the executive branch of government. A second-term president cannot run for reelection because of the Twenty-second Amendment to the Constitution. A lame-duck president is not an electorally accountable official or subject to electoral control. Even the selection of the president through the electoral college is antimajoritarian. A minority of the population, as little as 25 percent, has the power to elect a president because electors are not allocated entirely on the basis of population, and because states must cast all their electoral votes for one candidate. Moreover, there are many key executive officials who are not electorally accountable. Members of the Cabinet, and especially members of independent regulatory agencies whom the president cannot easily remove, are unelected and only indirectly accountable to the people.

Perhaps the clearest example of the inaccuracy of describing democracy in the United States in procedural terms is the power of the judiciary. Since *Marbury v. Madison* in 1803, the Supreme Court has had the power to invalidate legislative acts.[40] From the earliest days of the Republic, the Court has used a nonoriginalist mode of review in protecting rights not stated or implied in the Constitution.[41] This fact is important because it reveals that U.S. society has never required that all decisions be made by electorally accountable officials.

Finally, the very existence of a Constitution refutes a description of democracy as completely majoritarian. The Constitution identifies some matters—the structure of government and certain core values—that the majority cannot change except through an elaborate amendment process. All government officials take an oath of office to uphold the Constitution, which means that in certain instances they must disregard the preferences of the majority in order to comply with the Constitution.[42]

In sum, a definition of democracy as majority rule, as a commitment that all decisions be subject to control by electorally accountable officials, cannot be defended on the grounds that it accurately describes the system of government in the United States. Our government combines majoritarian and nonmajoritarian features. Protecting freedom of speech and upholding the rights of minorities are as much a part of U.S. democracy as are regular elections to ensure political accountability.

Alternatively, the major premise of the current debate—that decisions in a democracy must be made by electorally accountable officials—might be defended normatively. That is, it could be argued that regardless of the system that currently exists, majorities should be able to control all government decisions. Of course, this would mean that the definition of democracy as majority rule could not be stated as an axiom; it would need to be defended by a normative theory. No such theory has yet been offered in the debate.[43]

Moreover, it is unlikely that such a theory will be persuasive or accepted. At the most basic level, always maximizing the majority's short-term preferences should be deemed unacceptable because some things—the treatment of minorities and fundamental rights—should be protected from majority rule. As will be explained in more detail in Chapter 2, it is desirable for society to limit the majority's ability to discriminate against minorities or to violate basic human and political rights. The Constitution should be regarded as an antimajoritarian document that accomplishes exactly this result of insulating some matters from majoritarian control. As such, it is hardly objectionable that judicial review enforcing an antimajoritarian document is also antimajoritarian.

Furthermore, even superficial inquiries into political and moral theory reveal the normative bankruptcy of a purely procedural definition of democracy. In evaluating the proper normative definition of democracy, it is necessary to ask the basic question, Why is democracy a desirable system of government? While an answer to this question is complex and beyond the scope of this discussion, an examination of the question is revealing. Democracy might be defended because of its intrinsic value, that is, the intrinsic value that exists in allowing citizens to participate in government. Democratic also is likely to be defended in instrumental terms as best promoting certain accepted values. For example, Henry Mayo's classic work *An Introduction to Democratic Theory* identifies a number of reasons why democracy is desirable.[44] Mayo notes the ability of democracy to resolve disputes peacefully and to promote the noncoercive exercise of government authority, its ability to preserve individual autonomy and liberty, and its ability to maximize equality and justice.[45] Many other scholars defend democracy in similar instrumental terms as advancing values that are almost universally accepted in U.S. society.[46]

This literature reveals a key flaw in the current debate over judicial review. If democracy is desirable because it advances certain values, then the proper definition of democracy is the one that best maximizes the selected goals. Defining democracy in purely majoritarian terms provides minimal protection of these values because the majority would be allowed to trample the central values. For example, if democracy is preferred because it maximizes liberty, then pure majority rule that risks substantial deprivation of important liberties is not the correct definition of democracy. The proper definition must include substantive values. Less abstractly, if democracy is defended in instrumental terms of maximizing certain values, then judicial review that safeguards those values enhances democracy. In other words, judicial review may be antimajoritarian, but it is not a deviant institution.[47] To the contrary, it can be defended as an excellent means for protecting precisely the values that democracy is designed to further.

The current debate is flawed because it gives majority rule precedence over all other values. Judicial review has been viewed as a means that must be reconciled with the ultimate end of electorally accountable policy-making.[48] But if it is accepted that democracy, and even majority rule, are in large part instrumental as means to other ends, then judicial review is appropriate because it helps to achieve those goals. If democracy is a desirable system of government because it best ensures equality and promotes individual autonomy, then judicial review is an important feature of such a system because it helps to achieve these ultimate ends.

An alternative normative inquiry into the meaning of U.S. democracy is to ask why the values embodied in the Constitution are worth caring about. Moral and political theorists have developed sophisticated justifications for why equality is important,[49] why individual rights should be protected,[50] why the government should be structured with a separation of powers.[51] My task is not to repeat these arguments. Rather the point is that society values many things in addition to majority rule. To focus exclusively on reconciling judicial review with majority rule is to forget other core values and especially to ignore the Court's ability to advance and protect other basic values. The arguments advanced for equality, and rights, and separation of powers are arguments for why democracy normatively should be defined as more than "majority rule."[52]

It might be argued that the term democracy should be limited to meaning majority rule, and the other values should be included as part of an overall definition of good government.[53] But even then my point remains valid: it is incorrect to focus solely on majority rule in evaluating judicial review because there are other values which must be taken into account.

Moreover, these other substantive values are and should be part of the definition of democracy. As explained above constitutional scholars begin with the premise that judicial review must be reconciled with democracy.[54] Democracy is accepted as the core concept of the governmental system. If democracy is defined solely as majority rule, then the concept of majority rule will have unjustified psychological and rhetorical primacy over other important values. The best approach is to adopt a much richer definition of democracy, one that includes the core governing values which political and moral theorists have justified.[55] Majority rule is one of these, but not the only one.

What all this establishes is that democracy cannot be defined, descriptively or normatively, in purely procedural terms as requiring that all decisions be subject to control by electorally accountable officials. This conclusion has enormous implications for the debate over judicial review. First, it reveals that the major premise of the debate is incorrect: majority rule is not the exclusive guiding principle for U.S. government. Judicial review therefore cannot be criticized simply because it is antimajoritarian; and the whole notion of the "counter-majoritarian difficulty" is based on an incorrect definition of U.S. government. As such, it is misguided and unnecessary to focus on how to reconcile judicial review with majority rule. Although majority rule is valued, so is the antimajoritarianism inherent in the existence of a constitution and judicial review. The values inescapably conflict, and it is wrong to say that the latter is inappropriate unless it achieves the former, majority rule.

Second, the rhetorical force of the attack on activist judicial review is derived from the claim that it is undemocratic. It is hard to imagine a more damning criticism of a practice in our society than the accusation that it is antidemocratic. The charge itself creates a presumption against the practice. The originalists' attack on judicial review employs this attack by claiming that all noninterpretive review is antidemocratic and invalid. Defenders of judicial review unfortunately fell for this ploy and have devoted their efforts to the task of reconciling judicial review with majority rule. Once it is demonstrated that democracy is not synonymous with majority rule, and judicial review is not per se antidemocratic, the rhetorical force of the criticism is removed.

Finally, this discussion has demonstrated the importance of including substantive values in the definition of democracy. Judicial review enhances democracy because it is a vehicle for maximizing protection of those substantive values. Although no attempt has been made to define democracy, it is clear that any accurate and desirable definition must include substantive as well as procedural values. It is incorrect to define democracy so that it is synonymous with majority rule or a requirement that all decisions be subject to control by electorally accountable officials. U.S. democracy includes regular elections to ensure government accountability, but it is also includes protecting cherished values, such as speech, association, and privacy, and safeguarding minorities. In short, the current debate is fundamentally misdirected because it begins with a premise that is unjustified and unjustifiable.

The Attack on Judicial Review Is Disingenuous: All Judicial Review Is Antimajoritarian

If the major premise of the syllogism is true, and all decisions in a democracy must be subject to control by electorally accountable institutions and individuals, then *all* judicial review, originalist or nonoriginalist, is illegitimate. All judicial review involves unelected judges invalidating the actions of electorally accountable officials. This means that attackers of judicial review must either argue for the elimination of all judicial review or abandon the major premise of their argument.

I contend, therefore, that no theory can reconcile judicial review with majority rule. To establish this conclusion, first, I will examine those theories that purport to achieve such a reconciliation. After demonstrating their failure to define a model of judicial review that is consistent with complete majority rule, I will argue that even originalist review is inconsistent with majority rule. The conclusion that emerges is that all judicial review is antimajoritarian, so that it is hypocritical and disingenuous to single out any particular method and criticize it for being *antidemocratic* (in the sense in which the critics use that term).

The Defenders of Judicial Review Fail to Reconcile Judicial Review and Majority Rule

If democracy requires that values be chosen by electorally accountable officials, judicial review by unelected judges cannot be reconciled with a purely procedural definition of democracy. Either the commitment to majority rule or the commitment to judicial limits on majoritarian decisions must be sacrificed. The theories of Michael Perry and John Hart Ely—probably the two most prominent and widely discussed current theorists who attempt to reconcile nonoriginalist judicial review with democracy—demonstrate this conclusion. Neither scholar's theory succeeds in preserving both majority rule and activist judicial review.

Consider first Perry's defense of nonoriginalist review. Perry argues that nonoriginalist review is essential to elaborate and enforce individual rights that were not constitutionalized by the Framers and to protect these rights from government interference.[56] He contends that the "function of non-interpretive review in human rights cases is prophetic"; it should "advance moral evolution" by creating a dialogue that is directed toward finding correct moral and political values.[57] Although Perry advances persuasive reasons in support of nonoriginalist review, these reasons only demonstrate why majority rule is not completely trustworthy. Perry's arguments in favor of nonoriginalist review do not reconcile judicial review with majority rule.

So how does Perry attempt to make nonoriginalism consistent with his definition of democracy? He says that "the legislative power of Congress . . . to define, and therefore to limit, the appellate jurisdiction of the Supreme Court and the original and appellate jurisdiction of lower federal courts" preserves majority rule.[58] Congress, a democratic body, can control the courts through the power to restrict federal court jurisdiction and thus can preserve both judicial review and democratic principles. This undoubtedly is the heart of Perry's theory; he admits that "if in fact Congress did lack such a power, I would not know how to defend noninterpretive review in terms consistent with the principle of electorally accountable policymaking."[59]

Perry's theory fails to achieve his goal of ensuring both majority rule and nonoriginalist judicial review. He is caught by the same dilemma that he tries to resolve: either restrictions on federal court jurisdiction do not overturn or otherwise effectively stymie Supreme Court decisions—in which case, majority rule is lost—or these limits on jurisdiction do have the effect of reversing the Court's policy choices—in which case, noninterpretive judicial review is sacrificed.

Consider the first possibility, that Supreme Court decisions would remain valid constitutional law despite subsequent exercise of the congressional power to limit federal court jurisdiction. Restricting court jurisdiction does not, by itself, overrule prior judicial decisions.[60] For example, an act of Congress that prevents federal courts from hearing cases that involve abortion[61] or school prayer[62] would not alter Supreme Court precedents that create a right to abortion or ban school prayers. The Supreme Court's decisions would remain the law, and both Congress and the states would be obligated to uphold them.[63] Instead of reversing prior Court decisions, restrictions on federal court jurisdiction would freeze these decisions because the Court would have no opportunity to modify its earlier holdings.[64] As a result, the Court's antimajoritarian decisions would remain unchanged, and restrictions on jurisdiction would not protect majority rule.

The second possibility is that Congress and the states might ignore Supreme Court precedents in areas from which jurisdiction subsequently had been withdrawn, in which case majority rule would be preserved at the expense of judicial review. If Congress could overturn precedents by limiting jurisdiction, the Court's decisions would survive only as long as a majority of Congress agreed with them.[65] Judicial review as a check on majoritarian tyranny is illusory if the majority can overrule Supreme Court decisions any time that it wishes.

Most commentators, including Perry, recognize that the probable consequence of limiting federal court review would be widespread disregard of earlier decisions,[67] especially because the purpose of jurisdictional restrictions is to change the law substantively.[68] To allow such legislation would effectively overturn specific Supreme Court decisions. It would, in fact, subvert the entire constitutional structure.[69] Congress would have the power to enact unconstitutional laws, for example, that prohibit abortion or that permit school prayer, and could exempt these laws from federal court review. In effect, this power would overrule *Marbury v. Madison*[70] because the judiciary would no longer be able to rule on the constitutionality of federal statutes if Congress wanted to prevent such review. Similarly, the core constitutional concept of federal supremacy would be lost, because state courts, with Congress's permission, could disregard Supreme Court decisions. If Congress were to restrict the Supreme Court's jurisdiction, states could ignore Supreme Court precedents with impunity and make state law supreme over federal. The Supreme Court could no longer ensure state compliance with the Constitution in those areas in which Congress had restricted federal court jurisdiction. The notion of a national constitution with uniform meaning throughout the country would be lost.[71]

Perry might respond that these criticisms are overstated because he would not allow Congress to proscribe originalist judicial review.[72] The theory advanced in his book only permits Congress to restrict jurisdiction in nonoriginalist areas, where the Constitution is silent. For a number of reasons, this distinction does not answer the criticisms. First, Perry concedes that almost every major Supreme Court decision in the past 30 years has been nonoriginalist and therefore within Congress's power, in effect, to overrule.[73] Because very few of the Court's constitutional decisions are originalist, the fact that Congress could not reverse originalist decisions hardly protects judicial review. If nonoriginalist review is essential, as Perry claims, it is unsatisfactory to allow it to exist at the sufferance of Congress.

Second, if Congress can assert majority rule to limit nonoriginalist review, why cannot Congress assert the same definition of democracy to limit originalist decisions? Perry says that Congress may restrict the Court's jurisdiction in areas where nonoriginalism is followed. If, however, majority rule is the dominant value, Congress should have the power to limit the Court across the board. Article III's "exceptions clause," which arguably authorizes restrictions on jurisdiction, does not distinguish between originalist and nonoriginalist review.[74]

Third, even if one assumes the validity of Perry's point that Congress can limit only nonoriginalist review, the distinction between originalist and nonoriginalist decisions is hardly clear. The Court could circumvent jurisdictional limits by labeling its decisions *originalist*, and Congress could impose restrictions by terming the areas *nonoriginalist*.[75] Constant tension between these branches of the federal government would result. As Lawrence Sager observes, even if a "majoritarian check on the Court would be desirable, it must still be recognized that the control of jurisdiction by Congress is an utterly wretched device to serve that end."[76]

In response to these criticisms of his approach to reconciling judicial review and majority rule, Perry might argue that Congress would rarely, if ever, use its power to restrict federal court jurisdiction.[77] This misses a key point: If Congress does not use its power to restrict jurisdiction, then there is no majoritarian control over the judiciary. Moreover, in light of the numerous bills now pending in Congress to restrict federal court jurisdiction, it is not at all certain that such laws will not be enacted.[78] In fact, thus far the "scholarly consensus" that such restrictions on jurisdiction are unconstitutional has been a "political force [keeping] . . . Congress from enacting such legislation."[79] If theories such as Perry's are accepted, they may increase the likelihood that laws restricting jurisdiction will be enacted.

My goal has not been to prove that it is unconstitutional for Congress to limit federal court jurisdiction as a means of changing the substantive law. There already exists ample literature detailing many reasons why such restrictions on jurisdiction are unconstitutional.[80] Rather, my point is that regardless of their constitutionality, restrictions on federal court jurisdiction cannot reconcile judicial review with majority rule. Either precedents will be followed—in which case, majority rule is thwarted—or the decisions will be ignored—in which case, judicial review as a check on majority tyranny is lost.

Consider next Ely's attempt to devise a model of judicial review that does not violate the major premise of the syllogism, that is, that allows popularly elected officials to make all value decisions. Unlike Perry, whose theory attempts to reconcile all nonoriginal judicial review with majority rule, Ely argues that only one type of nonoriginalist review is permissible. Ely argues for what he terms a "participation-oriented, representation reinforcing approach."[81] He concedes the major premise of the syllogism, admitting that the Court usurps democratic rule if it imposes substantive values, but he contends that his theory allows the

Court to avoid making such value choices.[82] Under Ely's approach, the sole purpose of constitutional review is to create a fair process, either by providing "procedural fairness in the resolution of individual disputes" or by "ensuring broad participation in the processes and distributions of government."[83] Ely maintains that because his theory allows the Court to avoid making value choices, it "is not inconsistent with, but on the contrary (and quite by design) entirely supportive of, the underlying premises of the American representative democracy."[84]

Ely, like Perry, is trapped by the very dilemma that he tries to resolve: he cannot have both judicial review and a definition of democracy as majority rule. Under Ely's theory, the Court either will impose substantive values—in which case, majority rule is lost—or will defer to legislative policy choices—in which case, judicial review is meaningless. To demonstrate this dilemma, it is useful to consider how specific constitutional provisions are treated under Ely's theory.

First, how would Ely's approach deal with the numerous constitutional provisions protecting substantive rights? For example, the Constitution prevents impairment of the obligations of contracts, protects the free exercise of religion, prohibits the government from establishing religion, bans the taking of private property without just compensation, and prohibits cruel and unusual punishment. These constitutional provisions do not concern the process of government, as Ely defines it,[85] but rather constitute clearly substantive rights that the Constitution prevents government from infringing upon.[86] These constitutional rights present Ely with a dilemma. He can contend that the Court should refuse to enforce these provisions because none of them relate to the process of government—in which case, judicial review of key constitutional provisions is lost—or he can allow the Court to interpret the meaning of these provisions—in which case, majority rule is denied as courts overturn legislative decisions to protect these rights.

Ely seems to choose the latter alternative, for in a number of places, he demonstrates how his process-based theory protects substantive values, such as the right to travel.[87] Yet this seems to be exactly the kind of antimajoritarian value imposition that Ely opposes. In protecting the right to interstate travel, the Court would strike down legislation on the basis of a right not mentioned in the Constitution.[88] The Court's imposition of values is the same under Ely's theory as it is under the nonoriginalist model; only the justification differs.

Moreover, under Ely's expansive definition of process, virtually every constitutional issue can be phrased in procedural terms that justify judicial review. For example, even the decision that the state cannot restrict a woman's right to an abortion[89]—viewed by Ely as the height of judicial value imposition[90]—can be justified under a process-oriented model. Applying Ely's definition of equal protection,[91] the Court could find that laws that prohibit abortion deny to a minority, the poor, a service available to the majority who can afford to travel to states or countries where abortion is legal.[92] Pressure from vocal special-interest groups blocks the democratic process and necessitates court action to ensure protection of the minority. Although this argument may not be the strongest case for legalized abortions, it illustrates how the Court can cast almost any decision in procedural terms.[93]

Second, even in dealing with those constitutional provisions that are process based, Ely does not avoid the need for the Court to make substantive value judgments. If the Court defines what is a fair process, policies enacted by majoritarian institutions are overruled; if the Court must defer to legislative determinations of fairness, judicial review is nonexistent. Ely chooses the first alternative. He permits the judiciary to determine what is a fair process.[94] But it is impossible for the Court to decide what is "fair" or "just" representation without making substantive value judgments.[95] For example, at what point is malapportionment of state legislatures so egregious that it is unconstitutional?[96] There is no way to decide this issue without a substantive theory of democracy;[97] thus, the Court inevitably must substitute its judgment for that of the popularly elected legislature.

Furthermore, in deciding whether an adjudicatory process is fair, the Court must make the same choices that it would under the nonoriginalist approach. For instance, deciding whether the Fifth Amendment mandates free counsel for criminal defendants[98] or whether suspects in criminal investigations should be given *Miranda* warnings[99] requires the Court to define and balance individual rights against society's interest in apprehending criminals. Ely's definition of democracy demands that politically accountable legislatures perform such balancing. Nonetheless, Ely states that under his process-oriented model the Court would decide these issues because they relate to the fairness of the criminal process.[100] What criteria would the Court use in choosing which values have priority? As Ely offers no alternative to the justices' using their own values, ultimately his approach is no different from the nonoriginalist methods that he criticizes.

Ely contends that his theory is consistent with democracy even though judges overrule the majority's policy choices because democracy requires proper representation and fair processes.[101] This argument, however, reveals a shift in his definition of democracy. If democracy is defined in procedural terms as a requirement that value choices be made by electorally accountable officials, then judicial reversals of legislative decisions are inconsistent with majority rule, regardless of the content of the Court's decisions. To justify allowing judicial review to create a fair process, Ely must adopt a definition of democracy that includes substantive values such as fair representation and just adjudication. While this latter definition may be preferable, it is different from the definition of democracy as majority rule that Ely begins with and that he seeks to reconcile with judicial review. Although the content of the Supreme Court's decisions may further the representation of all in society, "the *process* of judicial review is not democratic because the Court is not a politically accountable institution."[102] Thus, even judicial review that is "representation-reinforcing" inevitably involves judges using their values to displace legislative decisions.

Finally, consider Ely's theory in relation to the equal protection clause of the

Fourteenth Amendment. An unequivocal commitment to majority rule requires acceptance of the reality that majorities frequently persecute minorities. Judicial protection of minorities is inherently antimajoritarian because the Court is thwarting the will of popularly elected legislatures.[103] While Ely is certainly correct that protecting minorities is indeed a crucial function of the Court, its desirability does not make it democratic. Again, unless democracy is redefined to include a substantive value—here equality—judicial protection of minorities is inconsistent with democracy.[104]

Furthermore, the Court must make substantive value judgments in determining what is equal.[105] Deciding what people are alike and deserve to be treated alike requires some substantive basis for comparison. For example, Ely argues that laws discriminating against blacks are invalid because they are based on "prejudice," but those prohibiting homosexuality might be justified because they are based on "moral judgments."[106] However, all who are discriminated against, including homosexuals, claim that the basis for their persecution is prejudice, and all who discriminate claim a moral basis for their actions.[107] In sum, any judicial review under the equal protection clause is inconsistent with the premise that requires that all decisions be made by majority rule.

The conclusion is not that the justices should ignore participational values. Ely persuasively argues that these are among the most important values that the Court protects. But Ely's theory fails to reconcile nonoriginalist review with his definition of democracy because the Court still overturns the decisions of popularly elected officials based on its own substantive value judgments.

Ely and Perry are not alone in their failure to accommodate both majority rule and nonoriginalism.[108] If democracy is defined as requiring that all value choices be subject to control by electorally accountable officials, no theory can ever justify nonoriginalism.[109] The question is formulated in a way that makes an answer logically impossible: a requirement that all policy decisions be made by majority rule precludes unelected judges from ever making value choices.

Conservative critics rejoice in this conclusion, contending that it establishes (assuming the truth of their major premise) the illegitimacy of nonoriginalism. However, if one examines originalism, it is clear that it is every bit as antimajoritarian as nonoriginalism.

Originalist Judicial Review Is Inconsistent with a Requirement That Decisions in a Democracy Be Subject to Control by Electorally Accountable Officials

Originalists claim that originalist judicial review is legitimate in a democracy but that the Court usurps democratic rule when it decides cases based on norms not stated or implied in the written Constitution.[110] But why is not all judicial review, including originalist review, improper, as it all involves unelected judges overturning policies enacted by electorally accountable officials? Why is the necessary and logical implication of the originalists' argument never drawn, that *Marbury v. Madison*[111] should be overruled and that the majority, through popularly elected legislatures, should have the final say on the meaning of the Constitution?

Originalists try to answer this question by invoking the distinction between originalism and nonoriginalism. They claim that an originalist methodology merely applies the Constitution's values, whereas a nonoriginalist one requires that unelected judges impose their own values. Of course, this argument is problematic because all decision making, including originalism, allows discretion and involves judicial value imposition. History is inevitably ambiguous, requiring judges to make value judgments in interpreting the historical record.[112] Furthermore, because formalism is impossible, value judgments inevitably arise in applying the law to new situations.[113] Although originalism often involves less judicial value imposition, it is incorrect to pretend that any model of judicial decision making can be so formalistic as to end all judicial discretion.

Even assuming, however, that originalism could somehow avoid judicial value judgments, judicial review still is not democratic because any ruling overturning decisions by popularly elected officials is, by definition, undemocratic. Although the Court may follow the Constitution, it still thwarts majority will and therefore is illegitimate by the originalists' definition of democracy whenever it strikes down legislative or executive policies.

Originalists may answer that the Framers of the Constitution intended that their choices be followed and thus that the Court is obligated to do so.[114] This claim is premised on highly questionable history and logic. As Alexander Bickel observed, the "authority to determine the meaning and application of a written Constitution is nowhere defined or even mentioned in the document itself."[115] There is great dispute about whether the Framers intended judicial review,[116] and there is no historical basis for concluding that the Framers intended to constitutionalize any particular theory or interpretation.[117] Furthermore, it is circular to say that because the Framers intended that we follow their intent, we are obligated to do so.[118] There must be some substantive theory explaining why it is appropriate to interpret the Constitution according to the Framers' intent.[119]

More important, even if the Framers intended that the Court adhere to the Framers' expectations, and even if this obligates it to do so, judicial review is still antimajoritarian. Judges applying the Framers' intent are striking down statutes enacted by popularly elected legislatures, based on the desires of men who lived two centuries ago. If originalists criticize activist judicial review for being rule by nine "Platonic guardians,"[120] is not following the Framer's intent rule by a small group of long-dead guardians? Furthermore, why should we believe that the Framers, a group of white landowning males who were not representative of their society, better reflect current majority wishes than does the United States Supreme Court?[121] The point is a simple one: Judicial review is antimajoritarian even if it strictly adheres to intended constitutional norms.

Originalists often answer that originalist judicial review is democratic because the people consented to the adoption of the Constitution.[122] First, factually it is wrong to say that the people ever consented to the Constitution because less than

5 percent of the population participated in the ratification process.[123] More important, it is erroneous to say that since the people ratified the Constitution, originalist review is democratic, because not a person alive today—and not even most of our ancestors—voted in its favor.[124] Democracy is defined by originalists to require decisions by *current* majorities;[125] majority rule does not exist if society is governed by decisions of past majorities that cannot be overruled by a majority of the current population.[126]

Originalists try to circumvent this argument by contending that the failure of subsequent generations to change the Constitution indicates an implicit consent to its authority.[127] In other words, by tacitly consenting to the Constitution, we agree to be ruled by it; thus, its originalist application is democratic. This argument assumes that a failure to amend the Constitution indicates contemporary majority approval of the document. Even, however, if a majority opposed a constitutional provision, that majority could not change the Constitution unless the reform were favored by the supermajority necessary to enact a constitutional amendment (two thirds of both houses of Congress and three quarters of the state legislatures). Thus, the absence of a constitutional amendment does not mean that a majority supports the document as it stands.

More important, by arguing that the absence of amendment reflects consent of the majority, originalists concede the legitimacy of all nonoriginalist judicial review. If the failure to amend the Constitution constitutes democratic consent, then the failure to overrule nonoriginalist Supreme Court decisions by constitutional amendment implies consent to those decisions.[128] The originalist argument that consent based on silence accords with democratic principles forfeits the entire debate to the nonoriginalists because this analysis indicates that there has been social approval of all Supreme Court decisions except the few that have been overruled by constitutional amendment.[129]

Ultimately, the originalists' argument cannot be defended without a clearer definition of the meaning of democracy and majority rule. The underlying question is whether democracy permits current majorities to bind and limit future majorities. Can a society committed to democratic principles but fearing ill-advised decisions reflecting the passions of the moment constrain its ability to change certain policies in the future? Can a society desiring to enshrine basic values make it more difficult for future majorities to overrule them? Such limits on decision making are inconsistent with a simple definition of majority rule. Unless originalists refine their definition of majority rule to allow such constraints, it is impossible for them to account for the existence of the Constitution, much less develop a theory for its interpretation.

Thus, all judicial review, originalist and nonoriginalist, violates the premise that decisions in a democracy must be made by majority rule through electorally accountable officials. This conclusion has major implications for the debate over the legitimacy of judicial review. Now originalists must either argue that all judicial review should be eliminated and *Marbury v. Madison*[130] overturned, or claim that some types of judicial review are so important that they justify sacrificing the principle of majority rule. If the critics argue the former, the debate shifts completely and becomes a dispute over whether constitutional judicial review is ever desirable. Presumption in such a debate will rest with those who are defending a practice that has existed for almost 200 years. Instead of attackers of judicial review having the rhetorical initiative by claiming that Court decisions are inconsistent with democracy, now they must make a normative argument as to why all judicial review is inappropriate and why *Marbury v. Madison* should be overruled.

Alternatively, originalists can argue that some types of Court decisions are so important that they justify sacrificing majority rule. Again, notice how the debate shifts. The appropriate question then becomes, What values are so important that the Court should protect them from social majorities? This is a question of crucial importance and is exactly what should be debated. Notice, however, that by agreeing that some values are so fundamental as to justify judicial overruling of majoritarian decisions, the attackers of judicial review are forced to abandon their major premise. No longer can they claim that all decisions in a democracy are illegitimate unless made by electorally accountable officials because they have admitted that some decisions should be made by the Court.

In other words, by demonstrating that all judicial review is inconsistent with a requirement for decisions by electorally accountable policymakers, critics of judicial review are compelled either to attack all judicial review or to abandon their major premise. Either move enormously helps the defenders of judicial review and radically changes the nature of the debate.

The critics of judicial review have not tried to argue that all judicial review should be eliminated. Instead, they have tried the latter approach, contending that originalist judicial review is necessary to uphold the Constitution. They explain that the Constitution should be followed and compliance with the document necessitates judicial review.[131] Of course, the questions then become: Why not trust the legislature to preserve the Constitution? Why allow antimajoritarian review? Moreover, if majority rule is the highest value in a democracy, why should a legislature feel bound to the Constitution at all? Shouldn't it be able to follow the wishes of the majority? The originalist argues at this point that the Constitution is so important that the majority should not be able to disregard it.

This argument does not reconcile originalist judicial review with majority rule. To the contrary, it rests on the premise that the Constitution is more important than majority rule. This argument for judicial review is a functional one, based on the need to protect certain values from majoritarian decisions. Simply put, originalist review is supported not because it is consistent with majority rule, which it obviously is not, but because constitutional government is deemed more important than majority rule.

But if originalists are willing to sacrifice majority rule, are they not disingenuous in criticizing nonoriginalists for being antimajoritarian? As all judicial review is antimajoritarian, to argue against particular models based on majoritarian principles is pointless. If a functional justification can support originalist review, the only question is whether there is an equally compelling functional justification for nonoriginalist review. In fact, the functional justification for nonoriginalist review is identical to a primary reason offered for originalist review: the need to protect certain crucial values from majoritarian decision making.

In other words, once we agree that constitutional values are more important than majority rule, we abandon the major premise of the current debate, and the question becomes, Which values should be protected from the majority? The concept of majority rule obviously provides no answer to this question and supplies no reason to prefer originalist values over nonoriginalist ones.

Thus, demonstrating that all judicial review is antimajoritarian is important because it establishes that the major premise of the current debate is incorrect, that the focus on majority rule is misguided, and that what we really should be arguing about is which values should be constitutionally protected.

The Current Debate Fails To Provide a Method For Constitutional Interpretation

The current debate is misguided because it focuses entirely on the role of the judiciary and it derives the appropriate method of constitutional interpretation from the definition of the judicial role. This approach is completely backward: the method of judicial review should be a function of the chosen method of constitutional interpretation, not the reverse.

Originalists have concentrated on attacking the legitimacy of specific nonoriginalist Court decisions. Their focus has been on limiting judicial review by contending that the Court should protect only values clearly stated in the Constitution or intended by its Framers. Originalists argue that the judiciary may not act unless there is a clear indication of an original intent to constitutionalize disapproval of the practice in question. Judge Robert Bork contends:

> Where the constitutional materials do not clearly specify the value to be preferred, there is no principled way to prefer any claimed human value to any other. The judge must stick close to the text and the history, and their fair implications, and not construct new rights.[132]

Similarly, originalist William Van Alstyne writes:

> If the meaning of a clause cannot be established without recourse to meta constitutional appeals (or arguments of mere policy), that fact merely provides reason and straightforward explanation of the judicial conclusion that the challenged act of Congress cannot be said to fail to square with the constitutional clause invoked by the litigant who relied upon it.[133]

What is important about these two quotations, which are typical of the originalist position, is that they focus entirely on the method the judiciary should use in interpreting the Constitution. The emphasis is on judicial conduct and not on the general and more important question of how the Constitution should be interpreted. Either the latter question is completely ignored or the method of constitutional interpretation is treated as a by-product of the definition of the proper judicial role.

At the very least, this is undesirable because regardless of the judicial role, there is a need to determine the proper method for Congress, the president, and state governments to use in interpreting the Constitution. All government officers take an oath to uphold the Constitution, and they need to know how to go about interpreting it. When a legislator decides whether to vote for a law restricting the right to abortion, the legislator must evaluate its constitutionality even if the Court could never rule on the subject under an originalist methodology. When the president has to decide whether to veto a law of questionable constitutionality, or evaluate the constitutionality of possible executive conduct (for example, whether to impound congressionally appropriated funds), the chief executive must interpret the Constitution.

Furthermore, under current justiciability doctrines, there are certain matters where the political branches of government have the final say over the meaning of the Constitution.[134] The Supreme Court has ruled that certain subjects pose a political question and therefore are not for the courts to review. For example, generally the Court has treated foreign policy as a political question and has refused to review the constitutionality of such executive decisions.[135] Especially in those instances where the Court is not involved, the chief executive and Congress need to interpret the Constitution. Often the decisions are in areas of crucial importance: Was the Vietnam War constitutional? Is the War Powers Resolution constitutional?

In fact, the originalist definition of the judicial role expands the need for constitutional interpretation by the political branches of government. Under originalism the Court is only involved where the Constitution is clear. In all other instances the decisions are left to the legislature and the executive. The absence of a Court decision does not release the political branches of their obligation to follow the Constitution. They need some method for interpretation.

The current debate is flawed because it has focused exclusively on the judicial role and has not provided any method of constitutional interpretation by the other branches of government. The originalists' obvious response to this criticism is that the other branches of government should also follow an originalist methodology.

First, this response reveals the misdirection of the current debate. Originalists justify originalism solely on the ground that if the judiciary uses any other methodology, it is usurping decisions of majoritarian institutions. This argument obviously does not justify why a majoritarian institution should use an originalist methodology. A completely different argument would need to be advanced to justify why the political branches should follow originalism. However, by deriving the method of constitutional interpretation from their concern over the proper judicial role, originalists simply assume that originalism is justified for constitutional interpretation by all institutions and individuals. This is not to say that it is impossible to defend originalism as a proper method of interpretation by all parts of government; rather, the point here is that the antimajoritarian nature of judicial review at most argues for originalism in court decision making. Another theory must be advanced to justify the use of originalism by the politically accountable branches of government.

Second, as will be argued in more detail later, originalism is an especially undesirable method of interpretation if it is used by all branches of government for all decisions. The Constitution contains many gaps. If all branches of government are bound by originalism, and only may act if there is express constitutional authorization, no one can act in many instances. For example, consider the question, What institution in U.S. government can recognize foreign governments? Article II does not give the recognition power to the president. Neither does Article I nor Article III give this power to Congress or the courts, respectively. An originalist methodology would lead to the conclusion that no one in government has the power to recognize foreign governments.[136]

Nor is this example unique. For instance, what branch of government has the authority to remove Cabinet officials from office? This question is hardly academic—it led to the impeachment of Andrew Johnson.[137] Article II gives the president appointment powers but not removal powers. Article I does not give Congress removal powers. Does this mean that from an originalist perspective no one can remove Cabinet officers?

There are endless examples. An originalist methodology limiting the involvement of one branch of government might work, but originalism cannot be easily defended as a method for all constitutional interpretation.

Finally, originalism leads to hopeless indeterminacy when used by the other branches of government. If the Constitution is silent, should the absence of a prohibition be regarded as an authorization, or should the silence be regarded as a lack of authority? For example, does the president have the inherent power to invoke executive privilege? This question has been extremely important throughout U.S. history and was critical in determining whether President Richard Nixon would stay in office.[138] Article II of the Constitution does not mention anything about executive privilege. Does the silence mean that the president has no constitutional authority to claim executive privilege? Or does the absence of a prohibition of executive privilege mean that it exists?

The point of this discussion is to establish that it is necessary to determine the proper method of constitutional interpretation, and that originalism cannot be uncritically chosen as the appropriate methodology. The current debate is flawed because it focuses on just the judicial role and makes no attempt to ascertain how the Constitution should be interpreted.

An inquiry into the proper method of constitutional interpretation will reveal a great deal about the appropriate judicial role. Unfortunately, this inquiry has not occurred because of the misguided focus on reconciling judicial review with majority rule.

WHAT THE DEBATE OVER CONSTITUTIONAL INTERPRETATION SHOULD BE ABOUT

Thus far in this chapter I have argued that there is a need for additional analysis of the proper method of constitutional interpretation because the debate in the current literature is fundamentally misdirected. As I have just argued, the central question to be answered is, How should meaning be given to the provisions of the United States Constitution? Questions of the responsibility and role of particular institutions are important, but such questions should only be considered in the context of answering the larger inquiry.

The remainder of this book suggests an alternative agenda for debate and presents arguments about the proper role of judicial review in interpreting the Constitution. The focus for discussion should be on questions such as: Why should society be governed by a constitution? Should the Constitution evolve or remain static? If the Constitution evolves, should the evolution be by interpretation or only by amendment? Who should be the authoritative interpreter of the Constitution? What constraints exist on judicial constitutional interpretation? Each of these questions is addressed, in turn, in the succeeding chapters.

2 Why Should U.S. Society Be Governed by a Constitution?

Constitutional interpretation is the process of giving meaning to specific constitutional provisions in order to resolve controversies confronting government.[1] As such, constitutional interpretation is an instrumental process; it exists to accomplish the goal of implementing the Constitution in particular situations. There is, of course, an underlying question: Why should the Constitution be followed at all? That is, why should the Constitution be regarded as authoritative?[2] There is nothing inherent to a written constitution that answers these questions. For example, the Constitution could be treated like the Declaration of Independence and viewed as a rhetorical document with no governing authority. Or the Constitution could be viewed as an initial blueprint for government, a starting place, that future governments could follow or ignore as they saw fit.

Virtually all the discussion about constitutional interpretation has ignored this question and simply assumed the authoritative status of the Constitution. Henry Monaghan explains this omission.

> The authoritative status of the written Constitution is . . . an incontestable first principle for theorizing about American constitutional law. . . . For the purposes of legal reasoning, the binding quality of the constitutional text is incapable of and not in need of further demonstration. It is our master rule of recognition.[3]

Monaghan does not explain why it is impossible and unnecessary to inquire why society chooses to be governed by a constitution. Identifying the reasons the Constitution is regarded as authoritative is of enormous value in determining the proper method of constitutional interpretation. For example, if society regards the Constitution as authoritative because the Framers are thought to have been divinely inspired, then constitutional interpretation will consist of trying to learn and follow the Framers' intent. In other words, under this view, the Framers are looked to because they are regarded as having possessed unique wisdom and even having communicated God's will.[4] By contrast, if the Constitution is regarded as authoritative because of the perceived need for an antimajoritarian document to protect minorities from majority tyranny, then the appropriate method of constitutional interpretation is the one that best protects minority rights. The general point is explained by Larry Simon: "That which is valued or believed to be good about a constitution is the (or a) source of its authority, and interpretive methodology is derived accordingly."[5]

A full inquiry into the reasons for having an authoritative constitution would itself be a lengthy treatise. However, even a preliminary examination of the reasons why society should be governed by a constitution is useful in determining the proper method of constitutional interpretation. The analysis in this chapter is the basis for the conclusions drawn in subsequent chapters as to the need for constitutional evolution, the desirability of evolution by interpretation, and the appropriate allocation of institutional responsibilities. The first section of this chapter explores why U.S. society should be governed by a constitution (1) in order to protect the structure of government and fundamental rights from social majorities and (2) because a constitution is a powerful symbol uniting society. The second part of the chapter briefly examines countries that are governed without a constitution and shows how the absence of a constitution in these places is based on assumptions that are incongruous with fundamental values and norms in the United States.

THE VALUES OF CONSTITUTIONAL GOVERNANCE

In thinking about why it is desirable to have a constitution, it is important to recognize that government and society could exist without one. Great Britain, for example, has no written constitution. If there were no constitution, society would structure government through informal agreements and by statutes adopted by the institutions accorded lawmaking authority. There likely would be some initial informal agreement creating the institutions of government, and then those institutions would determine both the procedures of government and its substantive enactments. For example, the Framers of U.S. government could have served as the initial legislature and, in that capacity, devised a structure of government embodied in a statute that could be altered by subsequent legislatures.

The absence of a constitution does not mean that individuals would possess no rights. Rather, an individual's rights would be embodied in statutes or would arise from common-law decisions of the courts (assuming that the society chose to accord such powers to its courts). Of course, even with a constitution, many rights are found in statutes, (e.g., the rights contained in the Civil Rights acts),[6] and others arise entirely from the common-law decisions of courts (e.g., rights against private deprivations of liberty and property found in tort law).[7]

How does U.S. government differ from this because it has an authoritative constitution? First, a constitution that only can be amended through an elaborate and difficult process is much harder to change than are statutes. Whereas legislative enactments could likely be modified by majority rule of subsequent legislatures,[8] the U.S. Constitution can only be altered by action of two thirds of both houses of Congress and by ratification of three quarters of the states. The difficulty in amending the Constitution is reflected in there being only sixteen amendments in the almost 200 years since the adoption of the Bill of Rights. Second, a constitution is symbolically different from all other laws.[9] It is regarded with special reverence and thought of as foundational for U.S. government.[10] It is not just another statute.

The obvious question is, Why should a society generally committed to majority rule choose to be governed by a document that the majority cannot alter? Although, as explained in the first chapter, majority rule is not synonymous with democracy, certainly it is an important component of democracy in the United States, and there is a general commitment to the proposition that the people should govern. Laurence Tribe poses the question:

> Why a nation that rests legality on the consent of the government would choose to constitute its political life in terms of commitments to an original agreement—made by the people, binding on their children, and deliberately structured so as to be difficult to change.[11]

Why should past generations, long dead, continue to govern us through a document written for an agrarian slave society? Noah Webster observed that "the very attempt to make perpetual constitutions, is the assumption of a right to control the opinions of future generations; and to legislate for those over whom we have as little authority as we have over a nation in Asia."[12] The Constitution is a powerful antimajoritarian symbol—a statement that there is much that a simple majority of society cannot, and should not, change.

There are two major reasons why society should be governed by an authoritative constitution. First, such a document creating the structure of government and enshrining fundamental rights achieves desirable goals; it prevents dictatorship, lessens the likelihood of tyranny, maximizes protection of minorities, and best ensures safeguarding of individual rights. Second, and less commonly recognized, an authoritative constitution, written in sufficiently abstract terms that virtually everyone in society agrees with its provisions, serves as a powerful unifying symbol for society.

The Constitution as a Limit on Majoritarian Decision Making

It is hardly original or profound to observe that a constitution exists to prevent tyranny by the majority, protecting the rights of the minority from oppression by social majorities. Historians have long observed that fear of despotism animated the Framers in drafting the U.S. Constitution.[13] Rebelling against what they perceived to be the tyranny of the king of England, and fearing all exercises of power, the Framers desired a limited government. In fact, the first government the Framers created under the Articles of Confederation was found to be much too limited, with the national government lacking essential powers, such as the ability to issue currency and regulate commerce.[14]

In drafting the Constitution, therefore, the Framers wanted to create a government with the necessary authority but structured in such a way as to limit its ability to inflict injury or act tyrannically. A constitution specifying fixed terms in office for elected officials and detailing procedures for regular elections helped prevent dictatorships and ensured the government's accountability to the people. The fact that the terms of office and procedure for elections were specified in the Constitution meant that current officeholders and could not simply enact a law lengthening their terms or canceling the elections.

Likewise, the Constitution specified the limited powers of each branch of government and created a system whereby generally two branches needed to act for anything to occur. Enacting a law requires congressional passage and presidential approval (or a congressional supermajority to override a veto). Enforcing a law requires executive prosecution and judicial conviction. Again, the effect is to prevent any branch of government from asserting absolute authority. A constitution ensures that this structure cannot be easily changed, especially in times of crisis when there is a tendency toward government by dictatorship.

Furthermore, the Constitution safeguards basic liberties from social majorities, providing additional protection for political minorities. For example, Article I of the Constitution prohibits Congress or the states from enacting ex post facto laws—laws punishing people for acts that were legal when committed—and bills of attainder—laws singling out individuals for punishment. Ex post facto laws and bills of attainder were viewed as important tools used to persecute political enemies of ruling governments.[15] Article I also prevents Congress from suspending the writ of habeas corpus, a crucial vehicle for protecting those who are unjustly imprisoned.

Additionally, Article I requires that all expenditures be pursuant to an act of Congress, limiting the ability of any group to spend money for its own benefit. Article I, section 10, prohibits any state from impairing the obligation of contracts, reflecting a fear that a legislature responsive to the majority of society, who are debtors, would act to harm the minority, who are creditors.[16] Furthermore, Article III of the Constitution states that all trials must be by jury; trial by a jury of peers was regarded as a safeguard against sanctions imposed by despotic rulers.

If these protections of individual liberty were placed just in statutes, a tyrannical government could overrule them. Although the assurance of electoral accountability through regular elections and the checks imposed by other branches of government provide some protection against tyranny, these limits were viewed as inadequate. What if a majority of society favored the despotic actions because the oppression targeted an unpopular group? Electoral accountability provides inadequate protection to the minority because support from the majority is sufficient to support the oppressing government. And if the majority controls both the legislature and the executive, checks and balances offer relatively little protection. To provide an additional safeguard should such majority tyranny occur, individual rights were placed in the Constitution. In the face of a tyrannical majority, at least the minority would be assured by judicial enforcement of the Constitution that there would not be ex post facto laws, bills of attainder, or confiscatory taxes, and no matter what, there would be the protection of writs of habeas corpus and trial by jury.

In fact, during the ratification process, many colonies expressed concern that the text of the Constitution inadequately protected individual rights. Fearing government power, some colonies insisted that a Bill of Rights be added to the Constitution.[17] In accord with this demand, the first Congress proposed, and the states ratified, amendments to the Constitution that ensured protection of crucial shared values such as freedom of speech, press, and religion; protection against unreasonable searches and seizure; the right to trial by jury in criminal and civil cases; freedom from self-incrimination; a prohibition of cruel and unusual punishment; assurance that life, liberty, and property would not be taken without due process of law; and a guarantee that property would not be taken for public purposes without just compensation. The protection of property was not of incidental concern. There is strong evidence that the Constitution was viewed as a way to protect the landowning minority from actions by the majority to confiscate their wealth and property.[18] By enshrining rights in an authoritative constitution, immune to easy modification by social majorities, the Framers thought they were providing crucial protection of political minorities and unpopular groups.

So a constitution represents an attempt by society to limit itself to protect the values it most cherishes. A powerful analogy can be drawn to the famous story of Ulysses and the Siren.[19] Ulysses, fearing the Siren's song, which seduced sailors to their death, had himself bound to the ship's mast to protect himself from temptation. Ulysses's sailors plugged their ears with wax to be immune from the Siren's call, whereas Ulysses, tied to the mast, heard the beauty of the song but was not harmed by it. Despite Ulysses's pleas for release, his sailors followed his earlier instructions and kept him bound and unable to heed the Siren's song. His life was saved because he recognized his weakness and protected himself from it.

A constitution is society's attempt to tie its own hands, to limit its ability to fall prey to weaknesses that might harm or undermine cherished values. A constitution, like Ulysses's instructions to his sailors, is a precommitment to a set of commands. Jon Elster writes that precommitment is a way of protecting oneself against imperfect rationality; "[b]inding oneself is a privileged way of resolving the problem of weakness of will; the main technique for achieving rationality by indirect means."[20] This binding, or precommitment, is a way of "achieving by indirect means the same ends as a rational person could have realized in a direct manner."[21] Because individuals and groups are seldom perfectly rational, and frequently irrational by their own standards, they hedge against their weakness of will with precommitments to people, ideas, and institutions.

To make this less abstract, society binds itself in a constitution to protect its most important values from the threats that history shows are posed by the passions, pressures, and irrationalities produced by crises and public events. Each society has certain values that it regards as fundamental. For example, since the earliest days of U.S. history, this society has valued public participation in government decision making. There has always been widespread belief in the desirability of a representative democracy and the power of the people to govern through regularly scheduled elections and by speaking out to influence the course of government decision making. There likewise has been deep concern for protecting the individual from arbitrary government power. The colonial experience and earlier English history teach the need to protect against abuses such as ex post facto laws, forced self-incrimination, and cruel punishments.

Ideally, U.S. society would always honor and protect these values, making precommitment, binding ourselves to the mast of the Constitution, unnecessary. History teaches, however, that there are Sirens' songs that seduce nations away from even their most prized values. Crises—economic, political, and military—cause pressure for expedient solutions often at the expense of deeply held beliefs. Often, one reaction to crisis is a desire to centralize power in a strong leader—an action that risks dictatorship. Another reaction to turmoil is to suppress freedoms. Dissenters, for example, frequently are prosecuted during times of war or political upheaval. During World War I and more recently during the McCarthy era, individuals were convicted and sentenced to long jail sentences for quite harmless utterances.[22] Moreover, crises often lead to a desire to find scapegoats and to the persecution of minorities. Hitler's "final solution" was devised during Germany's severe postwar depression. U.S. internment of Japanese-Americans during World War II evidences how even a strong commitment to freedom can give way during a perceived crisis.

History teaches that the passions of the moment can cause people to sacrifice even the most basic principles of liberty and justice. A constitution is society's attempt to protect itself from itself. The Constitution enumerates cherished values—guarantees of political participation, individual rights, protections from the government—and makes change or departure very difficult. Thus, like Ulysses, society knows there is a Siren and through a constitution ties its hands to help resist a song that might cause short-term desires to triumph over long-term interests.

Although the analogy between the Constitution and Ulysses is appealing, there is a problem with it. Ulysses tied his own hands; through a constitution society binds future generations. Or phrased differently, one might respond to all of the above discussion by saying that it only explains the reasons for the initial adoption of the Constitution; it does not justify why society should continue to be governed by it. The Framers of the Constitution feared their least rational moments and wanted to protect their values by binding themselves in a constitution. But this does not justify our continued governance by the document. The fact that the Framers desired an authoritative constitution says nothing about why modern society should have one. There must be reasons for following the Constitution apart from the fact that men who lived 200 years ago thought it a good idea to be governed by it.

One response is that modern society, too, fears the Siren's song and wants a constitution to bind itself to, to ensure protection of fundamental values. The same motives that inspired the drafting and ratification of the Constitution—the fear of the effects of short-term impulses in decision making—remain and justify the continued existence of a constitution. The widespread regard for the Constitution and the absence of any call for its abolition, or even for a major overhaul, indicate the ongoing belief in the desirability of an authoritative constitution.

Although this argument of the continuing acceptance of the Constitution has great force, it is not enough to simply assert that the Constitution should be regarded as authoritative because the people of current generations seem to consent to it. Because changing the Constitution is extraordinarily difficult, requiring supermajorities of many separate institutions, it is not possible to assume that the majority does consent to the Constitution just because they continue to be governed by it. Even if the majority objected to it, change would be impossible until the vast majority of society shared their views. It is possible that the absence of objections to the Constitution reflects a realization of how difficult it would be to have it eliminated as a part of U.S. government. More likely, there truly is a widespread acceptance of the desirability of the Constitution and a sense that it is good for society to continue to be governed by it.[23]

The existence of a constitution can be justified by establishing that there are values which should be entrenched in society and made difficult to ignore or overrule, and by demonstrating that a constitution is an effective vehicle for protecting these values. Political and moral theories support the existence of such values. For example, there is a voluminous body of literature developing many different theories justifying the existence and protection of individual rights.[24] The essence of the concept of individual rights is that they serve as "trumps" over majoritarian decision making.[25] My task here is not to justify the existence of rights or even to recount some of the many rights theories which have been developed. Rather, my point is that if one begins with the premise that individual rights should be protected from government interference (and I recognize that not all do), then a constitution can be defended as a means for entrenching these values and protecting them from infringement.[26]

Likewise, if one accepts the arguments of political and moral philosophers that equality is a value which should be honored and promoted by government, then a constitution is a way of enshrining and advancing that value. Again, my task is not to justify equality or even to begin the difficult task of defining it.[27] Instead, the claim is that if one starts with the premise that equality matters—for example, that government should not arbitrarily discriminate against social minorities—then one wants a vehicle for ensuring that the value is not disregarded. Placing the value in a constitution which is made deliberately difficult to change, and providing for enforcement of the value by an institution which is not directly accountable to the people is one way to safeguard and foster equality.

Therefore, a constitution is desirable if one begins with the premise that there are values which should be safeguarded from majoritarian decision making. The response to this is that it only justifies a constitution if the document enshrines the correct values, those that are indicated by the chosen political or moral theory. In other words, my argument is that a constitution is justified if one believes that there are values worthy of enshrining and that theorists defend the existence of such values. But the constitution, then, is desirable only if it protects the values which justified its existence in the first place. What if the constitution protects the wrong values? There are a wide array of political and moral theories justifying many different values. Can the existence of a constitution be justified without demonstrating that it protects the right values? A constitution would be undesirable if it entrenched disapproved values. For example, a constitution which provided that one race would be slaves to another would be undesirable. As such, it cannot be assumed that just because there are values worthy of protection that the constitution necessarily protects them or that the existence of the constitution is necessarily desirable.

Several responses are possible. One is to argue that there is something inherent to the process of constitution drafting that inclines it toward the right values. But I am not sure why this would be true. Constitutions are usually drafted at times of social crises, such as after a successful revolution, and are usually the product of negotiation. Although it is possible to hypothesize that constitution drafting is a call to reflection about basic values and therefore likely to lead to a document reflecting the moral reality or the deep consensus, I know no way to prove this to be true.

An alternative response is to argue that the benefits of the chance that the Constitution will provide pre-commitment to the right values justifies the risk of the possibility that society will commit itself to the wrong values. As to choosing between no protection of values from social majorities or risking protection of the wrong values, it is better to choose the former. Again, though, proof seems difficult without an explanation for why constitutions are more likely to protect the right rather than the wrong values.

I can see two responses that are more likely to be successful, one particular to the U.S. Constitution and the other abstract concerning constitutions in general. The former approach would be to establish that the U.S. Constitution protects the right values, that is, to develop a political or moral theory to justify the values which are contained within that document. If values such as freedom of speech, equal protection, separation of powers, freedom against self-incrimination, and the others within the Constitution are justified as correct—that is as worthy of protection from majoritarian infringement—then the existence of a document protecting them can be defended. The argument would not be that all constitutions are meritorious, but instead, merely that one containing these values is desirable. My task here is not to justify each of these values, but instead to note that there is ample literature defending each of these norms and to postulate that if one accepts the existence of these justifications, then the existence of the U.S. Constitution is desirable as a way of protecting the values it contains.

Alternatively, the social contract theories developed by John Rawls provide a possible solution to this problem and explain the continued legitimacy of the Constitution.[28] The argument is that if at any moment the members of society were forming a government, and none knew what his or her position would be under the new government, it is likely that they would create an authoritative constitution to limit government and ensure their protection, should they end up as political minorities. In other words, the desire for a constitution is not limited to those who actually participated in the initial creation of government. Rather, a constitution reflects an ongoing desire to ensure protection of minorities and fundamental rights.

To demonstrate this conclusion, imagine that a group of people were getting together to create a government and all lacked knowledge as to their status and place under the new government. No one would know if he or she would be powerful or powerless, rich or poor. This situation is what Rawls termed the "original position."[29] It is useful in considering how a group of people might want to constitute government because it serves to identify what rational deliberations, excluding considerations of individual self-interest, would produce.[30] Individuals acting from behind the veil of ignorance do not know their individual places in society (class, position, social status) or even their individual assets and abilities (intelligence, strength). What the parties do know are all the general facts about human society—the principles of economics, the history of political affairs, the basis of social organization, and the laws of human psychology.[31]

It is rational and likely that such a group of individuals would want to use a constitution to structure a government. These individuals would want to create a government to provide them with the benefits and services that they will want to receive from government (e.g., military protection, protection of interstate free trade, etc.) At the same time, they would want to make sure that government had limited powers to inflict injury upon them. A constitution would let them create a government with the powers to provide the benefits, but with limits, so as to control government and minimize the chance of harm.

For example, all the individuals likely would fear that if they end up being in the powerless group in society, those in power could establish themselves as dictators with unlimited authority. Thus, there would be a desire to create the structure of government in a constitution that would be followed and could not be changed by those in power in order to make sure that dictatorial power would never exist. Furthermore, these creators would want to specify procedures for changing government officers to ensure that if they are the political minority, they would have the chance to become the majority. In other words, the individuals creating the government would want to enshrine in a constitution the mechanism of political change to ensure that they could not be permanently disenfranchised. A constitution, with control over government and resistant to change, is an ideal mechanism for limiting the powers of government to minimize the likelihood of future governments imposing substantial harms.

Similarly, all the people creating government are likely to agree to certain basic values, at least when stated abstractly. For example, all might agree that freedom of expression is a good thing. They would fear, however, that future governments might eliminate freedom of speech. Therefore, to protect this shared value they would include it in such a constitution before any knew who would benefit from suppression of speech and who would lose.

In short, it is completely rational for a group of people acting from behind the veil of ignorance to create a constitution to limit government powers and protect themselves from possible injury. To protect themselves, the creators would want an authoritative constitution that would control future government actions. Not knowing whether they will be the majority or the minority, individuals would want to ensure their own protection, should they be in the minority. Thus, the heuristic of the veil of ignorance explains why those framing the government would create a constitution protecting minority rights, notwithstanding a general commitment to rule by the majority. A constitution allows government by majority rule but also provides protection against tyranny by the majority.

A number of objections might be raised to this analysis. First, it might be argued that it is wrong to assume that people will create a constitution to protect themselves from future governments. Instead, why would not individuals acting from behind the veil of ignorance gamble that they would be the ones in power and create a government with the ability to enrich them, both financially and in the ego rewards that unlimited power could provide? Individuals reasoning in this way would believe that what they would gain from such a government if they were in power outweighs what they could lose from a despotic government if they were among the powerless. As P. A. Boynton asks, "The question then is whether or not the 'take no risks' policy which is adopted by parties in the original position . . . should be regarded as the inevitable outcome of rational choice exercised under conditions of the veil of ignorance?"[32]

In answering this objection, consider the thought process of a rational person deciding whether it is better to create a government with limited powers or a potentially despotic government. A person acting from behind the veil of ignorance would realize that it is more likely that he or she would be more powerless than powerful because there are always more people in society, especially despotic societies, who are powerless. Moreover, the harms of a despotic government are potentially enormous—loss of life, absence of all freedoms, maldistribution of wealth. As such, the small chance of being in power would have to promise enormous rewards to justify individuals taking the risk of creating a government with the power to inflict such large harms.

Second, the above analysis can be challenged by objecting to the concept of the veil of ignorance. There are many possible bases for such objections,[33] with one of the most important being that the veil of ignorance inevitably leads to the selection of liberal principles of justice, and hence it is a tool deducing ideologically biased principles. According to Milton Fisk, the use of the veil of ignorance separates individuals from their real condition as social beings who define and understand themselves primarily in terms of group or class interests.[34] As a result the veil of ignorance forces individuals to adopt the uniquely liberal values of individual liberty and freedom, contradicting the claim that the veil of ignorance is a value-neutral instrument used to ensure fairness and rational deliberations.[35]

This is a powerful criticism but one that can be answered in a number of ways. One response is to concede the criticism and simply to argue that the veil of ignorance heuristic justifies the existence of a constitution and the protection of personal liberties in a society committed to the liberal premise that the individual is the basic unit of society. Since society both in 1776 and now accepts this premise, the objection does not undermine the claim that in U.S. society a constitution should exist to protect the individual. The criticism does reveal, however, why the above argument does not justify the existence of the Constitution for those who dispute the basic liberal ideology that the individual should be the most important consideration in society.[36] In fact, the Rawlsian argument begins with the basic assumption that people behind the veil of ignorance would choose a principle of political equality and majority rule and then perceive the need for protecting minority rights. Again, the point is that Rawls's social contract theory justifies the existence of a constitution only if basic principles of liberal ideology are accepted.

I do not want to rely too heavily on this brief argument from Rawls. It is, however, one way of explaining the desirability of a Constitution in a society committed to rights and equality.

Thus, I have argued that the Constitution reflects a precommitment to basic values, that it was desirable for the Framers of U.S. government to adopt such a document, and that society continues to need such an authoritative text protecting fundamental values. Several implications follow from this analysis. First, it is desirable for society to have an authoritative constitution to prevent tyranny and protect minorities and fundamental values. Society should be governed by a constitution not because the Framers intended it but because the current needs of the people are served by an authoritative constitution. Second, this analysis reinforces the argument made in the previous chapter that society's exclusive concern is not with majority rule; the concept of democracy must be defined to include substantive elements such as protecting the rights of the minority. Thus, as argued in the previous chapter, it is wrong to criticize judicial review for being antimajoritarian because, by definition, the application of an antimajoritarian document is antimajoritarian.

Furthermore, once it is decided that the purpose of a constitution is to protect some things from the majority, the questions becomes, What matters are so important that they must be protected from the majority.[37] This question inevitably is an inquiry into political and moral theory: What values are so important that a majority of society should not be able to infringe them? What processes of decision making are best for identifying and protecting these values?

Thus far I have tried to elaborate a defense for the traditional explanation for the existence of an authoritative constitution: the need to protect the minority from the majority by structuring government and enshrining rights in a document that is controlling and difficult to change. In subsequent chapters, I will explain why this conclusion necessitates a constitution that evolves by judicial interpretation.

The Constitution as a Unifying Symbol

There is another, much less frequently discussed, justification for an authoritative constitution. A constitution written in terms sufficiently general and abstract that almost everyone can agree to them provides enormously important symbolic benefits for society. The U.S. Constitution is written in very broad language. For example, the statement of rights in the Constitution includes phrases such as "freedom of speech," "unreasonable searches and seizures," "due process of law," "cruel and unusual punishment," and "equal protection of the laws." Even provisions of the Constitution dealing with the structure of government are written in general terms. For example, the president is given the power to serve as "Commander in Chief"; Congress is accorded authority "to regulate commerce . . . among the several states"; the judiciary is given the power to decide "cases and controversies."

In part, the Framers chose to write the Constitution in such general terms because it was easier to gain agreement both at the Constitutional Convention and during the ratification process to these more abstract concepts than it would have been to gain acceptance of more specific provisions.[38] The Framers undoubtedly recognized that they could not anticipate all the events and situations that might require constitutional coverage. General constitutional language allows adaptation to exigencies that could not be foreseen.

More important, from a contemporary perspective, the general phrasing of the Constitution allows virtually everyone in society to agree to its contents. Political scientists have long demonstrated that there is widespread social consensus to rights stated in abstract terms but no agreement as to specific applications.[39] A classic study by J. Prothro and C. Grigg found:

> [C]onsensus can be said to exist among the voters on the basic principles of democracy when they are put in abstract terms. The degree of agreement on these principles ranges from 94.7 to 98.0 percent, which appears to represent consensus in a truly meaningful sense. . . . On the generalized principles . . . the agreement transcends community, educational, economic, age, sex, party, and other common bases of differences in opinion. . . . When these broad principles are translated into more specific propositions, however, consensus breaks down completely.[40]

The research of Herbert McCloskey and Alida Brill provides numerous examples to support this conclusion.[41] For example, 97 percent of the U.S. public responded affirmatively when asked: "Do you believe in freedom of speech?"[42]

However, the study found that as "soon as one moved from questions about freedom of speech in the abstract to questions about the exercise of speech in particular situations, the level of support drops off sharply."[43] McCloskey and Brill explain:

> [F]ewer than 60 percent of the mass public in our sample would grant freedom of speech to people who are intolerant of the opinions of others. . . . Only 49 percent would uphold the right of individuals to express certain opinions if the majority voted to ban those opinions. Even fewer would permit foreigners who criticize our government to visit or study here. . . . Only 18 percent would permit the American Nazi party to use the town hall to hold a public meeting, and only 23 percent would grant a group's request to use a public building to denounce the government.[44]

McCloskey and Brill report similar findings for every constitutional right: almost unanimous consensus to the abstract right and tremendous disagreement as to virtually every particular.[45]

Thus, the Constitution is written in sufficiently abstract and general language so that virtually everyone in society can agree to its provisions. The Constitution serves as a "condensation symbol"—its ambiguity allows each person to believe that his or her specific conception is embodied in the general language.[46] Such a document, which is believed in by almost all citizens, serves a number of essential purposes.

First, the Constitution serves as a unifying device, increasing the legitimacy of government and specific government actions. Areas of agreement are placed in the foundational document that creates the government. The government has greater legitimacy because people believe in the document that creates the political institutions. Furthermore, the specific actions of the government will have increased legitimacy, and will be respected and complied with despite disagreement, because the process of government is accepted.[47] This legitimacy is especially important in times of crisis because the Constitution provides a source of social stability, and the acceptance of the Constitution provides confidence that problems can be handled from within its structure.[48]

The widespread consensus that the Constitution is desirable provides a powerful symbol that unites the country. Thomas Grey observes that the Constitution "has been, virtually from the moment of its ratification, a sacred symbol, the potent emblem (along with the flag) of the nation itself."[49] Similarly, historians report that the ratification of the Constitution had exactly this unifying effect.

> In the early days of the American republic, citizens revered the Constitution because it symbolized a nation united in its pursuit of democracy, egalitarianism and material progress.[50]

> The rhetoric of national unity marked the beginning of Constitution worship. The people rejoiced that the disunity of the confederation had been turned into the unity of the Constitution. . . . [A]ll parties had become rival worshippers in the cult of the Constitution which proved the greatest stabilizing force in the new government.[51]

Throughout U.S. history the Constitution has served as an important unifying symbol, providing an "overarching sense of unity even in a society otherwise riddled with conflict."[52] Of course, claims about legitimacy are empirical, and the answers provided here are impressionistic, not quantitative. Yet the absence of any serious cries to substantially reform or eliminate the Constitution in 200 years is powerful empirical support for its social legitimacy.

The Constitution's importance as a unifying symbol is explained by Max Weber's theory of the concept of a nation.[53] Weber said that three factors lead to the existence of a nation and a sense of national unity. First, there needs to be some objective common factor shared by all the people. Second, this common factor needs to be something that is valued within the society and that produces a feeling of solidarity. Finally, this solidarity needs to find expression in political institutions.[54] The U.S. Constitution meets all three criteria: it is a common factor shared by all citizens; it is valued; and it is the basis for government institutions. Thus, not surprisingly, the Constitution has long been regarded as a primary source of national unity.[55]

It is important to emphasize that the Constitution is able to perform these legitimizing and unifying functions only because it is written in general language about which almost everyone agrees. Laurence Tribe explains:

> The value of the Constitution as an evolving repository of the nation's core political ideals and as a record of the nation's deepest ideological battles depends significantly on the limitation of its substantive content to what all (or nearly all) perceive to be fundamentals; a document cluttered with regulatory specifics could command no such respect.[56]

For example, almost all state constitutions are drafted in much more specific language than the United States Constitution.[57] One consequence is that state constitutions are accorded much less respect and relatively frequently have been replaced in their entirety.[58] It is easy to understand why state constitutions change much more rapidly than the United States Constitution. To amend a state constitution requires action of only one legislature. Modifying the federal Constitution requires approval of both houses of Congress and three quarters of the state legislatures. The frequency of change of state constitutions in comparison with the U.S. Constitution is thus revealing of the importance of a stable document in producing legitimacy. Tribe continues: "The cluttered and rapidly changing contents of state constitutions may partially explain why even the most enduring and fundamental provisions of these documents rarely command the respect routinely paid to federal constitutional guarantees."[59]

A second major benefit of a constitution written sufficiently abstractly so that almost everyone agrees as to the language is that disagreement within society is channeled to minimize its potential destructiveness. Areas of agreement are at the center of society, so that disagreements occur in the context of consensus as to the nature of the government and basic values. Dialogue is possible because there are shared values; disagreement is over the specific content of agreed-upon provisions.[60]

A general constitution thus enables government to overcome potentially destructive forces. A constant problem for all governments is that individuals will act for their personal gains even though the effects of their actions are detrimental to the whole of society.[61] Consequently, there is the danger that individuals in power will attempt to use their authority to perpetuate their advantages, even though such actions would have net negative effects for society.[62] At the same time, those who are losers under such a system have no incentive to remain loyal to the existing system, which fails to meet their needs and perhaps even disenfranchises them. The losers' best protection is to find a way to overthrow the existing system as soon as it is feasible to do so.

A general constitution overcomes these destructive forces. Because the document is general, it does not create permanent winners or losers. The losers can believe in the document because it does not enshrine their powerless status. They subscribe to the values in the document and can believe that they will become winners tomorrow. Winners believe that the document is desirable because they are ahead under it. The losses that result either are the product of extraconstitutional factors, and hence no reason to oppose the document, or are the result of interpretations of the document, in which case the interpretation is attacked, not the document.

Put less abstractly, those who are disadvantaged in society continue to accept the legitimacy of the government because they continue to believe in the fairness of the Constitution. They believe that the Constitution creates a structure of government that protects them and that provides an opportunity for them to advance. Because they subscribe to the basis of the system, they do not constantly reevaluate their support for the government. Charles Elder and Roger Cobb explain:

> No system is likely to be able to withstand the test of a constant and self-interested evaluation of its performance on the part of all or even most of its members. If most people were constantly engaged in the process of weighing the personal costs and benefits involved, it is doubtful that much in the way of collective political action would be possible. However, most persons are not inclined to expend the time, energy, and effort required by such a calculus. Loyalty is tendered as much on the basis of long-standing affective sentiments toward the symbols of the system as it is from any short-term satisfactions derived from the immediate allocation of material or symbolic benefits. This more basic support [arises] in the form of emotive ties to the basic symbols of the system.[63]

In essence, the ambiguity of the Constitution perpetuates a real-world veil of ignorance as people and groups that look to the Constitution see no indication from it as to whether in the future they will be powerful or powerless. If they are the minority, they will want the protection of the Constitution and its assurance that they will have the chance to become the majority. Thus, there is continued support for the Constitution and the processes of government it creates. A general constitution allows all individuals to believe that their personal benefits from the system exceed their costs.[64] However, as discussed later in this chapter, it must be recognized that this legitimacy and acceptance could be thought of as a negative if people accept undesirable situations and do not adequately work to improve things because of false assumptions about what the Constitution can provide.

Furthermore, a constitution written in abstract language helps society mediate the tension between a social desire to bind itself to prevent harmful decisions and a desire to permit change and flexibility. There is an inherent conflict between a desire for precommitment to lessen the chance of errors and a desire for freedom to choose to achieve desirable results in particular cases. A constitution written in general language allows society to have some of both: precommitment to basic values but with the opportunity for future generations to interpret them to achieve just results in specific situations and for particular times. Though, of course, this could produce the worst of both worlds, instead of the best.

This analysis establishes that it is desirable to have an authoritative constitution not only to protect minorities but also to reap the enormous benefits that flow from the existence of a widely supported foundational document. Subsequent chapters will develop the implications of this conclusion for constitutional interpretation. For example, the fact that the Constitution is written in general terms ensures that it cannot be applied to yield determinate results in particular cases. Inevitably, its general language will not provide clear answers to most constitutional controversies.[65] General statements of ''principle necessarily leave their specific implications open to future debate.''[66] Interpretation is necessary to apply abstract areas of agreement to specific situations where there is disagreement. It is futile to search for a method of constitutional interpretation that leaves no discretion and deductively applies the Constitution to yield determinate, objectively correct results.[67]

Moreover, the desirability of a constitution sufficiently general as to be supported by widespread consensus has important consequences for the manner of constitutional evolution. As will be argued in Chapter 4, it is undesirable for the Constitution to evolve solely through amendments because if every modification of the document required an amendment, the document would be cluttered with divisive specifics. The Constitution would lose its constitutive function.

As alluded to above, some might object that the unifying function of the Constitution is undesirable. They could argue that in light of the above analysis that the Constitution deceives the losers in society's power struggles into accepting a system that is to their detriment. The claim is that the losers are falsely led to believe that they can win in the future, that the Constitution creates an open system, and that their interests are being protected. Ultimately, the conclusion of this criticism is that the Constitution gains unity but at the price of divisiveness that might help those inadequately served under the current system.

This argument cannot be lightly dismissed or easily answered. Responding to this objection raises basic questions: Are the losers in the current political system better off within it than they would be under the alternatives? Is society as a whole better off with the existing system? These inquiries raise foundational questions, obviously beyond the scope of this book, about the desirability of the U.S. system of government. At this juncture, I simply wish to acknowledge my assumption and recognize that my analysis is premised on the desirability of such features of U.S. government as majority rule, desire to protect minorities, and liberal ideologies such as those emphasizing individuals and their rights. Ultimately, the question is, Would more people be better off, on balance, with a radically different system of government? Accepting axiomatically the desirability of the U.S. political system and its commitment to liberty and to equality, to majority rule and to protecting minority rights, the Constitution is invaluable in allowing society to protect its values.

SOCIETIES WITHOUT CONSTITUTIONS

The analysis in this chapter makes it seem as if the existence of an authoritative constitution is almost inevitable. Such a conclusion would explain why most constitutional commentators have simply assumed that the U.S. Constitution is controlling. Yet what is troubling about this conclusion is that it ignores the fact that most countries do not have an authoritative constitution.[68] Therefore, in concluding the discussion of why it is desirable to have a constitution, it is worth considering why a society might choose not to have such a controlling document.

Why would a society choose to be governed without the legal limits that a constitution imposes on government? The analysis in this chapter suggests that the absence of a constitution likely reflects one of two situations. One is that there is sufficient consensus in society about basic values and sufficient trust in the majority and its representatives to make a constitution unnecessary. In other words, the society believes that individuals possess rights, but it believes a constitution is unnecessary to protect those rights because the majority can be trusted. Alternatively, the absence of a constitution might reflect the belief that there is no need to protect the individual from the state because the individual possesses no rights or powers apart from the state. If the state is regarded as all powerful, it would be inconsistent to have an authoritative constitution limiting the government. The former description explains the absence of a constitution in Great Britain; the latter explains the absence of an authoritative constitution in the Soviet Union.[69]

Great Britain, despite its long history of commitment to individual rights, has no written constitution.[70] Unlike the United States where the Constitution is authoritative, in Great Britain, Parliament is the final source of legal authority.[71]

The doctrine of parliamentary sovereignty accords Parliament authority to enact any law. J. A. Jalowicz explains:

> It is well known that Great Britain, of which England forms part, has no written Constitution. The doctrine of the Supremacy of Parliament is fully established, there is no higher law than an Act of Parliament and it is impossible for any one Parliament to bind its successors.[72]

No authoritative document limits Parliament. Nor do individuals possess any rights that they can assert as a defense to an act of Parliament.[73] Theoretically, Parliament could pass a law to prevent the conviction of a favored individual, or even to overturn a conviction already reached by the judiciary.[74] One commentator described the extent of Parliament's authority by saying that it "is a fundamental principle with English lawyers that Parliament can do everything but make a woman a man, and a man a woman."[75]

The absence of a constitution in Britain can be understood as reflecting trust in Parliament. The strong tradition of concern for individual rights provides the basis for confidence in the majority. The fear and distrust of government power that, in part, explains the U.S. Constitution seems less prevalent in Great Britain. Nevil Johnson explains:

> Britain [is] . . . different from other mature political societies [because of an] . . . extraordinary and basically unbroken continuity of traditional political habits. The uniqueness of the British Constitution is to be found in the fact that it has erected that very insight into a dominant feature of the Constitution itself. It appears to eschew rules and principles so far as possible, proclaiming instead that the rights and procedures which it claims to protect have their security and continuance in particular political habits and understandings and only there.[76]

Thus, the absence of a constitution reflects social consensus and trust in Parliament. Interestingly, in recent years, there have been increasing calls for the creation of an authoritative constitution.[77] Commentators have argued that there no longer is sufficient commitment to traditional values and beliefs, nor sufficient consensus as to how power should be exercised, to provide adequate protection of civil rights or ensure the survival of a particular form of government.[78]

By contrast, the absence of an authoritative constitution in the Soviet Union reflects not trust in the majority but rather a belief that the state is above the law.[79] Although there is a Soviet constitution, it imposes little in the way of actual restrictions on the government's powers. Olympiad S. I. Ioffe and Peter B. Maggs explain:

> [W]hile Common Law in the United States can be called the system of legal constitutionalism, and Civil Law in West Germany assumes the name of the system of the legal state (*Rechtsstaat*), Socialist Law in the USSR, in contrast, appears as a system of legal restrictions supported by the state which is itself legally unrestricted.[80]

Marxist doctrine dictates that the individual is liberated only through the liberation of the masses.[81] When the interests of the masses coincide with the individual's claims, there is no problem; but when they conflict, the masses' interests must prevail.[82] Accordingly, it would be inconsistent to have an authoritative constitution to limit the majority or to protect the individual from the state.

The Soviet Union does have a written constitution detailing numerous individual rights. For example, the Soviet Constitution grants freedom of speech, freedom of the press, and freedom of assembly.[83] However, the constitution states that these rights are to be exercised "in accordance with the peoples' interests and with a view to strengthening the socialist system."[84] Thus, the state is accorded full authority to override any rights contained in the constitution, and individuals have no right to challenge the decisions of the state. In other words, it is the state that is authoritative, not the constitution.

This brief examination of the British and Soviet systems reinforces the conclusion that an authoritative constitution is desirable and necessary in the United States. The assumptions of neither the British nor the Soviet system are applicable in the United States. In the United States, as already explained, there is widespread consensus only as to abstract statements of rights.[85] There is no tradition of legislatures protecting rights, and no basis for trust that government will protect the rights of the minority. To the extent that the absence of a constitution requires trust in government, the United States needs a constitution because from the earliest days of the Republic there has been fear of tyranny by the majority. In addition, it must be remembered that the number of government units, including federal, state, and local entities, is well into the tens of thousands. Each needs to be controlled to prevent infringements of basic values.

Furthermore, the assumptions of the Soviet system are directly contrary to the philosophical underpinnings of U.S. society. In the United States, there is a belief that individuals possess rights and that the individual deserves protection from the wishes of the masses. Unlike the Soviet Union, which puts the state above the law, in the United States a preeminent concern is limiting the power of the state to prevent tyranny.

In other words, what this analysis demonstrates is that the absence of a constitution would be inconsistent with basic aspects of U.S. society. The examination of the British and Soviet systems reinforces the conclusions of this chapter: that an authoritative constitution is desirable to guard fundamental rights, to ensure protection of minorities, and to provide a powerful unifying symbol. Hence, the best method of constitutional decision making is the one that accomplishes these objectives.

3 Should the Constitution Evolve or Remain Static?

A key issue in the dispute over the proper method of constitutional decision making is whether the meaning of the Constitution is fixed and permanent or whether it can change and evolve. Advocates of judicial restraint frequently articulate the former static position. They frequently quote Thomas Cooley's statement, in his famous treatise on the Constitution: "The meaning of the Constitution is fixed when it is adopted and it is not different at any subsequent time."[1] There are similar declarations from the United States Supreme Court. For example, in *South Carolina v. United States*, in 1905, the Court stated: "The Constitution is a written instrument. As such, its meaning does not alter. That which it meant when it was adopted it means now."[2]

In contrast, those who believe that the Constitution should evolve evoke the famous words of Chief Justice John Marshall, in *McCulloch v. Maryland*: "[W]e must never forget that it is a Constitution we are expounding. . . . [A constitution] intended to endure for ages to come, and consequently, to be adapted to the various crises of human affairs."[3] Contemporary scholars such as Robert Bennett thus argue, "[I]t is the expectations of each succeeding generation, interacting with evolving notions of public policy, that matter."[4]

The debate over whether the Constitution should evolve or remain static actually poses two distinct, although certainly interrelated, questions. One issue is that described above: Is—and should be—the Constitution subject to change? The second question is, If the Constitution is to evolve, how should such evolution occur? Usually, the latter inquiry concerns whether the meaning of the Constitution should evolve by interpretation or only through the amendment process.

It is extremely important to recognize that these are two separate questions. First, the distinction matters for the sake of clarity. Although scholars frequently express the view that the meaning of the Constitution should remain static,[5] what they most likely are saying is that the Constitution should be altered only through amendment. No one appears to take the position that all changes in the document, even by amendment, should be impermissible. In other words, those who argue for a static Constitution are not arguing, as their language makes it seem, that the Constitution should never be changed. Rather, they are taking a position as to how modification should occur. However, their phrasing of the issue inevitably evokes responses explaining why the Constitution should evolve.[6] The two sides of the debate do not address each other because they fail to realize that there are two separate questions at issue.

Second, it is important to treat the two questions separately because there truly are two distinct questions worthy of examination. Virtually all modern U.S. scholars would concede that there needs to be some mechanism for changing the Constitution.[7] The Constitution includes a provision specifying the procedure for amendment, thus making it seem irrelevant to ask whether the Constitution should be immune from change.

However, it is possible to imagine a society choosing a document that is permanent and not subject to any change, or at least that identifies particularly important provisions and specifies that these clauses may not be revoked or amended. For example, the constitutions of West Germany and Brazil expressly state that the division of power between the national and local governments is not subject to amendment.[8] Morocco's constitution states that it may not be amended to eliminate the monarchy or Islam as the official religion.[9] Nations that have experienced foreign occupation often have provisions limiting amendment in the case of future foreign invasion. For example, the constitution of the French Fourth Republic, adopted in 1946 in the wake of liberation from Nazi control, prohibited amendment of the constitution ''in case of occupation of all or part of the metropolitan territory by foreign force.''[10] The current French Constitution, adopted in 1958, continues this prohibition, forbidding amendment ''when the integrity of the territory is in jeopardy.''[11]

In fact, even the United States Constitution specifies certain matters that could not be changed, even by amendment. Article V, which details the amendment process, states: ''Provided that no Amendment which may be made prior to the Year One thousand eight hundred and eight shall in any Manner affect the first and fourth Clauses in the Ninth Section of the First Article; and that no State, without its consent, shall be deprived of equal Suffrage in the Senate.'' Article I, section 9, clause 1, prohibits Congress from prohibiting the importation of slavery until 1808; and Article I, section nine, clause four, stated, ''No Capitation, or other direct, Tax shall be laid, unless in proportion to the Census or Enumeration herein before directed to be taken.''

Thus, it is conceivable that a society might choose to have unalterable constitutional provisions. The decision for permanence might reflect a political compromise necessary for ratification, such as the provisions in the U.S. Constitution mentioned above. Alternatively, a society might prohibit amendment if it believes it has found certain enduring truths that it wants to protect from heretics. An example of this would be a constitution that expressly declares the religion for the society.[12] A permanent, unalterable constitution also could reflect a society that fears change and greatly values the stability that it believes a static constitution provides. Accordingly, it is necessary to consider not only how a constitution should evolve but also whether it should evolve or remain static.

Finally, and most important, it is important to consider the reasons why a constitution should evolve in order to decide the manner by which such evolution should occur. In other words, if it is established that it is crucial that the U.S. Constitution should evolve, then the second question becomes an instrumental inquiry of how to best accomplish evolution. Specifically, once it is accepted that it is essential that the Constitution should evolve, then it is relatively easy to establish that the evolution should occur through interpretation and not just by amendment. If the Constitution could change through amendment only, virtually no evolution would occur.

Therefore, this chapter addresses the first question: Should the Constitution evolve or remain static? The following chapter addresses the second question, How should evolution occur? That is, should evolution be by interpretation or only by amendment? Subsequent chapters consider who should interpret the Constitution and how they should go about accomplishing that task.

IS THIS EVEN AN ISSUE? THE INEVITABILITY OF CONSTITUTIONAL EVOLUTION

As a preliminary matter, it might be argued that I have posed a nonissue in asking whether the Constitution should evolve or remain static. It could be argued that the Constitution must inevitably evolve because it is impossible to find the static meaning of a written document. The argument is that it is impossible for a contemporary Court, or any other institution, to interpret a document except from the perspective of its own society, and that the infusion of such modern perspectives, by definition, is a form of evolution. In fact, this argument also answers the second question of how evolution should occur; the process of constitutional decision making inevitably requires the Court (or other institutions) to give meaning to the document, and this process ensures evolution by interpretation. Thus, advocates of judicial activism claim that evolution by interpretation is inevitable, and it is misleading to even pose the questions as I stated them. I would welcome such a conclusion because ultimately I seek to establish that the meaning of the Constitution should evolve by interpretation, and this argument provides support without even considering the two questions I posed.

The argument that contemporary interpretation is inevitable is a strong one. It is well established that the words of a document can rarely be given determinate meaning because of the inherent vagueness and ambiguity of language.[13] Many literary critics argue that there is no correct interpretation of any text, that all interpretations are a reflection of context and the beliefs of the interpreter.[14] Sanford Levinson explains that "all language is read against a background of . . . shared understandings, purposes, and assumptions that can, at any given instant, defeat the apparently precise ink on the page."[15] Thus, Stanley Fish argues that inherently interpretation is "not the art of construing, but the art of constructing."[16]

In fact, this is not a new argument. John Marshall expressed the same thought almost 170 years ago.

> Such is the character of human language that no word conveys to the mind, in all situations, one single definite idea; and nothing is more common than to use words in a figurative sense. Almost all compositions contain words, which, taken in this rigorous sense, would convey a meaning different from that which is obviously intended.[17]

This indeterminacy is especially apparent in phrases like "due process of law" or "equal protection." Because, as argued in the previous chapter, the Constitution is written in general language to which almost everyone can agree, there is no determinate, specific meaning for most constitutional provisions. Even the constitutional language that appears more specific is indeterminate. For example, Justice Hugo Black often endorsed a literal interpretation of the First Amendment, declaring, "I read 'no law abridging freedom of speech' to mean no law abridging."[18] But as Owen Fiss points out, this phrase is hardly unambiguous: "Does 'speech' embrace movies, flags, picketing and campaign expenditures? What is meant by 'freedom'?"[19] Furthermore, does the language that "Congress shall make no law" mean that the executive can infringe upon freedom of speech? Similarly, when the Constitution speaks of "Commerce . . . among the several States,"[20] does that mean commerce between the states (interstate commerce),[21] or does it mean commerce among, within, the states (including interstate and intrastate commerce)?[22] Does the term *commerce* refer to all business activity or just one stage of business relating to sales, distinct from mining, manufacturing, and production?[23] A final example, and my favorite, is provided by Paul Brest: does the requirement that the president be a "natural born" citizen prohibit those born by Caesarean section from being president?[24] Or, expanding Brest's example, because the term *natural birth* has a fairly definite meaning these days, does the Constitution prevent anyone from being president whose mother received an anesthetic during childbirth? A culture that believed such individuals to be inferior obviously could interpret the language in this way.

Such constitutional provisions are the rule, not the exception. What constitutes a "declaration of war"? What are the president's powers as "Commander-in-Chief"? What is a "high crime or misdemeanor" for purposes of impeachment? What is a "republican form of government" under Article IV of the Constitution? What is the "establishment" of religion? What is an "unreasonable search and seizure"? The examples go on and on.

Decision making applying the Constitution to specific situations inevitably requires interpretation, and interpretation inherently reflects the values of the interpreter. Thus, the two questions posed at the beginning of this chapter are answered: The Constitution, if it is to govern society, will evolve by interpretation.

Proponents of the view that the Constitution should be either static or evolve only through amendment might try to rescue their position by arguing that ambiguities in language should be resolved by recourse to the intent of the document's drafters. The method attempts to follow the traditional practice of statutory construction; that is, when the text of a statute is unclear, its meaning should be determined by the intent of the drafters as indicated by its preadoption history. According to this argument, the Constitution's meaning is limited to that which its Framers intended. Those who argue against any constitutional evolution would contend that the document's meaning is fixed at the time of its enactment, and that all application is to be governed by the Framers' purposes. Thus, modern values are irrelevant and may not be added to the document by interpretation or amendment. More commonly, the argument made is that the meaning of the Constitution is limited to what the Framers intended, and that the only legitimate form of evolution is through constitutional amendment.[25]

However, even assuming that the Framers' intent should guide modern constitutional interpretation (an issue discussed in the next chapter), there is not an unambiguous, knowable Framers' intent that can be found to resolve constitutional questions. Instead, the process of determining the Framers' intent inevitably is a process of interpretation that is affected by contemporary values. Therefore, again, it must be concluded that the Constitution will evolve by interpretation.

The initial indeterminacy problem stems from an inability to determine who the Framers were. That is, which group's intent should be authoritative in applying the Constitution? The process of ratification included not only Congress and the drafters of a provision but also the states. John Wofford explains:

> [I]f we are really searching for the states of mind of those responsible for the presence in the Constitution of a particular provision, it is hard to understand why we should be particularly concerned only with those who drafted the provision or supported it actively. Responsibility is more widely distributed; in order to become part of the Constitution, the provision had to be accepted by the Philadelphia Convention or by the Congress, and then ratified by the states acting either through legislatures or through special conventions. Yet, to admit the relevance of such a large number of states of mind is to set forth a task virtually impossible to fulfill.[26]

In other words, the interpreter must make a choice as to whose intent will count—a question for which there is no determinate, correct answer.

Furthermore, even if a particular group is chosen as authoritative for purposes of constitutional decision making, it is impossible to state the group's intent without engaging in an interpretive process. Undoubtedly, different members of the group had varying and perhaps conflicting reasons for adopting a particular constitutional provision.[27] Some of the purposes might have been articulated, but others might not have been expressed. To decide which expressions are authoritative and which are not is, of necessity, a process of choice and interpretation. Social choice theorists demonstrate that it is usually impossible to construct a set of social preferences out of the preferences of individual members of a group.[28] Again, the conclusion is that there is not a concrete and knowable intent of the Framers waiting to be found;[29] there exists only a process of interpretation to determine meaning.

Additionally, even if the group is determined, and even if somehow a collective intent could be found, the historical materials are too incomplete as to support authoritative conclusions. Jeffrey Shaman explains that the "Journal of the Constitutional Convention, which is the primary record of the Framers' intent, is neither complete nor completely accurate. The notes for the Journal were carelessly kept and have been shown to contain several mistakes."[30] As Justice Robert Jackson eloquently remarked, "Just what our forefathers did envision, or would have envisioned had they foreseen modern conditions, must be divined from materials almost as enigmatic as the dreams Joseph was called upon to interpret for Pharoah."[31] For example, virtually the entire record of what occurred at the Constitutional Convention consists of James Madison's notes. William Crosskey makes a persuasive case that there is a "possibility that this testimony may have been, not inadvertently, but deliberately, false and misleading as to what the various members had said."[32]

Finally, even if all the above problems were surmounted, it is possible that the interpreter would discover that for some provisions the Framers did not have any specific intent. Especially as to the provisions written in open-textured language, it is quite likely that the Framers meant for these provisions to gain meaning from experience and application.

Thus, basing decisions on the Framers' intent does not avoid the need for interpretations, and such interpretations will inevitably be influenced by modern values and circumstances. This conclusion should not be surprising because historiographers long have recognized that "what [history] yields is heavily dependent upon the premises of its users."[33] The famous historian R. G. Collingwood, in his classic work *The Idea of History*, argues:

> History means interpretation. . . . [W]e can view the past, and achieve our understanding of the past, only through the eyes of the present. The historian is of his own age and is bound to it by the conditions of human existence. The very words which he uses . . . have current connotations from which he cannot divorce them. . . . History is what the historian makes.[34]

In other words, "history is always an interpretation,"[35] and that interpretation cannot be completed without being influenced by modern values.

My point is not, as the argument is often made, that originalism is impossible because of these historiographical difficulties.[36] Rather, I contend that it is impossible for someone to claim that there should be an authoritative Constitution that does not evolve by interpretation. The very process of applying the Constitution of necessity requires interpretation, and that interpretation, either of the language or of the drafters' intent, will be influenced by modern values. In other words, once it is decided that a constitutions should govern—and especially a constitution written in very general language—then, of necessity, the document will evolve by interpretation. Furthermore, as will be discussed in a later chapter, the above analysis refutes any claim that originalism permits value-free interpretation or allows judges to find objective, determinate solutions to constitutional problems.[37]

It is tempting at this point to conclude that I have answered both the questions posed at the beginning of this chapter and have established that the Constitution should evolve, rather than be static, and that such evolution is inevitably by interpretation, not just amendment. Unfortunately, such a conclusion goes farther than the proof allows. All I have demonstrated is that it is impossible to have a static authoritative constitution; some interpretation, influenced by modern values, will occur. But originalists can concede this and argue that taking this as a given, whenever possible the Constitution should be given its original meaning, as that can be best determined, and such meaning should not change once found, or at least not change without constitutional amendment. For example, everyone would agree that the Framers did not intend to give Congress the power to regulate interstate radio waves because the Framers did not know that such a thing exists. Therefore, an originalist would argue that the Constitution does not authorize such regulation and that such regulation is impermissible (at least until there is a constitutional amendment). Another example: the originalist would say that although the equal protection clause of the Fourteenth Amendment is ambiguous, there is virtually universal agreement that its drafters did not have as their purpose guaranteeing equal treatment of women.

Thus, although the ambiguity might prevent determinacy in many decisions, there are some where original meaning can be established. To conclude that determinacy is usually impossible does not prove that it is always impossible. Furthermore, decision rules could be created that would result in greater determinacy. For example, it could be stipulated at the outset who will be considered the Framers and what record will be taken as authoritative and that interpretations remain fixed and cannot be overruled. Although none of these devices secure determinacy, they would reduce the indeterminacy.

Therefore, while a static Constitution, or one that evolves only by amendment, is impossible, there are still important differences between the originalist and the nonoriginalist. If the originalist and the nonoriginalist agreed that the Fourteenth Amendment did not, at its inception, apply to protect women from discrimination, the former would conclude that it is impermissible for it to apply to women today, whereas the nonoriginalist could reject that conclusion. At the very least, originalists and nonoriginalists accord the judiciary differing degrees of discretion in determining the meaning of constitutional provisions.

Accordingly, it still is necessary to address the two questions posed at the beginning of this chapter so as to choose between the differing conclusions of originalists and nonoriginalists in instances where they interpret the historical record similarly. Also, it is desirable to examine these questions because thus far I have demonstrated only that descriptively it is impossible to have a static constitution; I have not yet established that normatively it is desirable that the Constitution evolve by interpretation. It is important, however, to keep in mind constantly that the originalist cannot argue that the Constitution should be permanently fixed or unchangeable until amendment. Both originalists and nonoriginalists must accept the desirability of a Constitution that evolves by interpretation.

The Desirability of Constitutional Evolution

The first question can then be restated a bit more precisely: Should the goal be, to the greatest extent possible, a static, unchangeable Constitution, or should the goal be an evolving Constitution? I contend that achieving the purposes of the Constitution, described in the previous chapter, requires that the Constitution evolve. Although I doubt that many would argue that the Constitution should be permanently fixed and not change even by amendment, nonetheless it is useful to explore why evolution is crucial. I contend that if it is accepted that the meaning of the Constitution must evolve, then it follows—as the next chapter argues—that the Constitution must evolve by interpretation and not just by amendment. I do not ascribe to originalists the position that the Constitution is fixed and unchangeable. Many who term themselves "moderate originalists" even allow modification by interpretation. The point here is to establish the importance of constitutional evolution.

Earlier I argued that an authoritative constitution is desirable as a way to protect minorities and fundamental rights from the majority and because of the social values to having a general, unifying constitutive document. Because society changes over time, a constitution can perform these functions only if it, too, evolves. The easiest examples to support this conclusion come from the need for the Constitution to evolve in light of technological change. Technological advancements necessitate a process of constitutional evolution if the Constitution is to succeed in protecting minorities and basic rights from the majority.

For instance, if society were truly committed to a static Constitution, "cruel and unusual punishments" would be only those punishments that the Framers meant to prohibit. The Framers obviously did not intend to outlaw the use of electric shocks as a form of torture because they did not know of that form of punishment. Therefore, a static Constitution would not forbid the use of electric shocks under the Eighth Amendment's prohibition of cruel and unusual punishment. The majority of society could totally circumvent the Framers' intent of outlawing cruel and unusual punishment by simply substituting this new form of torture for that which the Framers did intend to outlaw. The result is that the goal of society protecting itself from cruel and unusual punishment at the hands of despotic rulers is not achieved because the despots can shift to new, even worse forms of punishment not anticipated by the Framers. If the value embodied in the Constitution is to be upheld, it must evolve to include new technological threats.

The intuitive response to this argument is that cruel and unusual punishment need not be limited to the specific list of tortures the Framers knew about; the list can be expanded to include similar modern threats. However, this argument concedes the argument that I seek to establish in this chapter—that the meaning of the Constitution should evolve, that the Constitution should not be completely static. The position that the Constitution states basic concepts that contemporary society applies by using its own conceptions is one that explicitly allows the meaning of the Constitution to be adapted to modern circumstances and concerns.[38]

The example of cruel and unusual punishment is representative, not atypical. If the First Amendment is limited to what the Framers meant it to apply to, Congress could censor the broadcast media in any way it wished because the Framers did not intend to protect expression over radio and television.[39] The goal of ensuring protection of a right, freedom of speech, from the majority cannot be achieved without evolution to reflect technological change. If the Fourth Amendment is limited to what it applied to at the time of its ratification, government could use wiretapping in any way it wanted. The very values that the Constitution was intended to safeguard could be infringed upon, and the Constitution provides no protection unless it evolves.

Similarly, the institutional arrangements that the Constitution was designed to preserve would be lost without evolution. For instance, the Constitution reflects a belief that the national government must have authority to regulate commerce among the states. There is strong evidence that one of the primary objections to the Articles of Confederation, and therefore one of the main purposes of the new Constitution, was to create a national economy that the federal government could regulate.[40] However, if the Constitution's meaning was fixed at the time of its drafting, commerce cannot be deemed to include any modern method of transportation. Therefore, Congress would lack authority to regulate any commerce by motorized vehicle. In light of the obvious importance of cars, trucks, and planes to modern commerce, a truly static Constitution could not preserve the institutional arrangement that the Constitution was designed to create. Likewise, Congress would lack power to fund an air force because the Framers could not conceive of such a branch of the armed forces or even to buy computers because they were unknown at the time of ratification.

It is not just technological advances that require constitutional evolution. Changes in social arrangements and especially in social values require an evolving Constitution. A comparison of society in 1787 with that of 1987 reveals not only physical changes, but moral ones as well. One hopes that these changes reflect moral progress—that society has grown more egalitarian, more compassionate. At the very least, descriptively, basic values such as privacy and equality have somewhat different content today than they did 200 years ago. As Alisdair

MacIntyre wrote in his famous book *After Virtue*, "evaluative expressions we use have changed their meaning. In the transition from the variety of contexts in which they were originally at home to our own contemporary culture, 'virtue' and 'justice' and 'piety' and 'duty' and even 'ought' have become other than they once were."[41]

It is likely that most would agree that the meaning of particular values evolves. As such, the meaning of values in the Constitution should not be static. The Constitution should protect values that are fundamental now, not those that were important 200 years ago. In 1787, slavery was acceptable, women were disenfranchised, notions of free speech and due process were limited. Without the possibility for evolution, the Constitution would be confined to anachronistic beliefs. If the Constitution does not evolve, it will contain values that are universally rejected by society. A document that sanctions slavery and counts a slave as only three fifths of a person for purposes of representation would be repugnant in modern society. The Constitution cannot serve as a unifying document if it contains provisions that the vast majority of society deem unacceptable.

Likewise, over time society may be concerned with the need to protect additional groups that it previously had discriminated against. U.S. society originally excluded women from virtually all aspects of civic life: women could not vote; married women could not own property or hold public office.[42] Social values have evolved, and if the Constitution is to achieve its goal of protecting minorities from the majority, there is a need for the Constitution to evolve to protect additional groups from the majority.[43] There must be some way for the Constitution to evolve to reflect contemporary moral judgments that particular groups are in need of protection from social majorities.

Finally, moral evolution requires the protection of additional rights deemed fundamental. The goal of a constitution is to protect fundamental rights from the majority. The list of rights deemed fundamental will change as morality evolves and society changes. For example, privacy might come to be regarded as fundamental and needing of protection. If the Constitution is to serve its purpose of protecting fundamental rights, it must be able to evolve to include this value.[44] Nor does it respond to this point to say that society can protect a right by statute if a majority come to regard it as fundamental. If a right is regarded as being as important as those protected in the Constitution, society will want to include it in the Constitution so as to protect it from future infringements. Again, the conclusion is that the Constitution must be amenable to change.

I am not arguing at this point that the Constitution should be *interpreted* to include modern values. The proper manner of evolution, be it by interpretation or amendment, is addressed in the next chapter. The point here is just that constitutional evolution is required if the Constitution is to succeed in its objective of protecting minorities and their rights and if it is to serve as a unifying document.

I recognize also that there is a danger that constitutional evolution could undermine the protection of minorities, rights, and the structure of government.

The opportunity for evolution risks releasing the bonds of pre-commitment that a constitution provides. There is no reason to assume, absent justification, that evolution will necessarily be positive and not negative.

Yet, the point of the above discussion was that absent evolution the Constitution will not succeed in achieving its purposes. Evolution, although risking greater harm, also offers the possibility of success. Later, in Chapter 6, I explain why, over the long term, changes will more likely be positive than negative.

There is another argument that achieving the goals of the Constitution requires evolution. If the Constitution cannot evolve, at some point it will become so outmoded that it will be completely discarded and a new constitution written. An evolving document can adapt. The clearest example of this is that our society continues to be governed by a constitution written for an agrarian slave society. If the Constitution cannot adapt by evolution, it will become progressively less relevant and even more objectionable. A nonevolving constitution will not protect the values or the minorities that the current society cares about. A nonevolving Constitution imposes values thought to be outdated and repugnant to society, such as racist and sexist values. As a result, at some point there will be demands for a new constitution.

The fight over whether and when to rewrite the Constitution will be divisive, as those who are benefiting from the current Constitution will oppose change. Instead of the Constitution functioning as a unifying document, it will be the center of disagreement. Furthermore, the process of drafting a new constitution means that the current majority is writing the document that will govern its society. The majority therefore might write a document that provides it benefits, and the Constitution is then less effective in restraining contemporary majorities and protecting minorities. A constitution that is frequently replaced is less able to serve as a stabilizing force and as a unifying symbol.

An evolving document is preferable because it allows society to undo its mistakes, rather than be permanently governed by them. For instance, early in U.S. history it was decided that the Constitution's method of electing the president and vice president was undesirable; that it was not wise for the vice president to be runner-up in the election for president. An evolving Constitution allowed for the Twelfth Amendment to correct this error in drafting. Likewise, an evolving Constitution can correct what are perceived to be errors in the interpretation that inevitably must occur. An early Supreme Court decision held that Article III of the Constitution permitted states to be sued by residents of other states.[45] The Eleventh Amendment, prohibiting federal court suits against states by citizens of other states or foreign countries, was added to the Constitution to overturn the earlier Court decision.[46] If the Constitution could not evolve, society would be governed by what it overwhelmingly deemed to be an incorrect decision. Although, of course, it must be recognized that evolution risks bad changes. However, the difficulty of constitutional amendments makes it relatively unlikely that many will be added to the Constitution. Historical experience shows that relatively few (perhaps only the prohibition amendment) have been regarded as undesirable. Moreover, in Chapter 6 I explicitly consider why society has relatively little to fear from evolution by judicial interpretation.

All this establishes that it is desirable, even essential, that the Constitution be amenable to some form of change. Originalists cannot argue against this conclusion, at least in the context of the current debate. Recall that the originalists' major premise is that decisions in a democracy should be made by majority rule. If the Constitution cannot evolve, then the majority of society has no ability whatsoever to govern itself in areas where the Constitution regulates. A permanent, unalterable constitution exacerbates the countermajoritarian difficulties of having a constitution. If there is no evolution, current majorities are confined to be ruled by the past. An originalist who starts with the premise of majority rule would have to reject a constitution that is incapable of evolution.

Thus, it is imperative that the Constitution evolve. This conclusion is particularly important because of its relevance to the next question: How is such evolution best accomplished?

4 Should the Constitution Evolve by Interpretation or by Amendment Only?

The analysis thus far has demonstrated that many aspects of the current debate between originalists and nonoriginalists are useless in providing a basis for choosing between these competing paradigms of constitutional decision making. For example, the argument that constitutional decision making must be consistent with majority rule, the primary argument offered in favor of originalism,[1] is based on an incorrect definition of democracy. Furthermore, because both originalist and nonoriginalist judicial review are antimajoritarian, the principle of majority rule provides no basis for choosing between the paradigms. Similarly, it has been demonstrated that the claim that originalism is value neutral is incorrect because originalism inevitably is indeterminate and allows the interpreters' values to influence the decision-making process.[2]

What, then, is the real difference between originalists and nonoriginalists? When all the misleading claims are brushed aside, the key distinction is that originalists believe that the meaning of the Constitution should be changed only by amendment, whereas nonoriginalists permit meaning to evolve by interpretation. Of course, what was established at the beginning of the previous chapter must be emphasized again: the process of giving meaning to specific provisions and applying the Constitution under an originalist approach would inevitably require interpretation that would be influenced by modern values. Taking this as a given, the question is, When the meaning of a constitutional provision is identified, can that meaning be changed by interpretation or is the meaning fixed until a constitutional amendment is enacted?

Originalists such as Raoul Berger, Robert Bork, and William Van Alstyne explicitly state that they believe that amendment is the only legitimate means for constitutional evolution.[3] These commentators argue that the Constitution cannot be deemed to protect a particular right unless it is clear that the Constitution's drafters intended to protect such a right. Judge Bork, for example, writes that "where the constitutional materials do not clearly specify the value to be preferred, there is no principled way to prefer any claimed human value to any other."[4] In such instances the Constitution should be regarded as providing no answers to the constitutional question, and the matter left to the majority of society to resolve as it deems appropriate.

In a recent article, William Van Alstyne develops a similar originalist argument.[5] Van Alstyne argues that constitutional decision making should be governed by Justice Owen J. Roberts's famous statement in *United States v. Butler*:

> When an act of Congress is appropriately challenged in the courts as not conforming to the constitutional mandate, the judicial branch of government has only one duty—to lay the article of the Constitution which is invoked beside the statute which is challenged and to decide whether the latter squares with the former.[6]

Van Alstyne argues that unless it is clear that a specific matter does not square with the Constitution, it should be regarded as constitutional.[7]

Therefore, commentators such as Judge Bork and Van Alstyne take the position that the Constitution only applies to that which it was originally intended to include. Nothing else violates the Constitution until and unless the document is amended. So, for example, if it is clear that the Framers of the Fourteenth Amendment did not intend to guarantee equality for women, it is illegitimate to apply the equal protection clause to invalidate gender classifications. From the originalist perspective, only a constitutional amendment could impose a constitutional limit on sex-based discrimination.[8]

Similarly, if there is no clear intent of the Framers to desegregate schools or protect the right of women to have access to contraceptives or abortion, the Constitution does not justify decisions invalidating laws segregating schools or prohibiting abortions.[9] Unless the Framers intended to outlaw a practice, the Court has no authority to declare legislative or executive acts unconstitutional, and the legislature and executive can implement their policies without concern that they are violating the Constitution. Again notice that although originalists usually state their conclusions in terms of judicial powers, constitutional decision making is engaged in by all branches and levels of government. The question of which branch of government should be the ultimate arbiter of the meaning of the Constitution is a distinct question that is addressed in the next chapter.

In contrast to the originalists, nonoriginalists believe that the Constitution's meaning is not limited to what the Framers intended; rather, the meaning and application of constitutional provisions should evolve by interpretation.[10] Nonoriginalism allows constitutional interpretation to include norms and values not expressly intended by its Framers. The fact that the Framers did not intend to prohibit gender discrimination or apply the Bill of Rights to the states is irrelevant to the nonoriginalist in deciding what the Constitution means.

Hence, the key difference between the originalist and the nonoriginalist is whether the Constitution should evolve only by amendment or whether it should also be capable of change by interpretation. This central question has received little direct attention because the debate over constitutional interpretation has focused on misleading questions, such as whether nonoriginalism can be reconciled with majority rule.

Actually, the above discussion is somewhat misleading because there are not only two choices in constitutional interpretation: originalism and nonoriginalism. Originalism, as it is described above, is a rather extreme position and many who call themselves originalists take a more moderate approach, allowing some evolution by interpretation. Likewise, there are many different nonoriginalist theories; a point developed in detail in Chapter 6. Yet, because so much of the debate has been framed in originalist, nonoriginalist terms, it is worth analyzing these paradigm models before considering alternatives.

The analysis in this chapter is divided into three major sections. The first considers the arguments that have been advanced in favor of originalism and explains why they are inadequate. The second section presents a normative justification for why the Constitution must evolve by interpretation if it is to achieve the purposes of a constitution described in Chapter 2. Finally, the third section considers ways in which originalists might try to rescue their paradigm, especially by changing it to allow room for evolution by interpretation. This final section examines in detail the less extreme versions of originalism, such as "moderate originalism," which allow for some evolution by interpretation.

THE ORIGINALISTS' ARGUMENT

To the extent that there has been any discussion of the question of whether evolution should be by amendment or interpretation, originalists have tried to argue that their position is true by definition. They have claimed that it is inherent to a written document that any changes must be brought about by amendment.[11] Such an axiomatic approach is unpersuasive and inadequate because there is nothing inherent to the Constitution that says anything about how its meaning should evolve.

The current debate is a dispute between two major alternative ways for giving a constitutional provision meaning: one focuses on the original intent of the provision (to the extent that such intent is knowable); the other allows the Court to interpret the provision from the perspective of modern values. Again using the example of gender discrimination and the equal protection clause, one view is that the equal protection clause does not apply to sex-based classifications because the Framers did not intend such application; the other view is that it can be applied to gender classifications because of current judgments about the inappropriateness of sexism. Certainly, either side can claim that it provides the true and correct way to understand the Constitution. What is needed are arguments as to which is the preferable method for interpreting the Constitution. There is nothing inherent to the Constitution that answers this question, and it is simply question begging and poor argumentation to claim that either approach is a priori true. The defense of either approach requires normative arguments; neither side can win by stipulation. Larry Simon explains: "There is no intrinsically legal or constitutional answer to the question how should the Constitution be interpreted. The evaluative standards must come from the external perspective of political and moral theory."[12]

To illustrate how much the defense of originalism has featured question begging, consider the arguments of a number of prominent originalists. Henry Monaghan argues, for example, that the process of interpretation requires that the purposes of a document's drafters have authoritative status. Monaghan writes:

> A distinction is sometimes posited between textual analysis and original intent inquiry such that only the constitutional text and not parole evidence can be examined to ascertain constitutional meaning. But any such distinction seems to be entirely wrong. All law, the Constitution not excepted, is a purposive ordering of norms. Textual language embodies one or more purposes, and the text may be understood and usefully applied only if its purposes are understood. No convincing reason appears why purpose may not be ascertained from any relevant source, including its 'legislative history.'[13]

The problem with Monaghan's argument is that he assumes that the purposes that motivated a provision are authoritative and then simply argues that the Framers' intent is controlling because it is evidence of purpose. But the entire question is whether, in constitutional interpretation, the goal is to find the intended purposes behind a provision or whether modern society can supply its own meanings and purposes. In other words, Monaghan is correct that the Framers' intent is relevant if the goal is to find original purposes. This argument, however, begs the key question of whether originalism or nonoriginalism is the appropriate paradigm—that is, whether the Constitution is limited to the Framers' intent until it is amended or whether modern society can interpret provisions from its own perspective.

Phrased slightly differently, there are at least two ways to view the Constitution's language. One way is to conclude that a constitutional provision must be given its original meaning until it is amended. The other way to interpret a provision is to construe its language without reference to the Framers' intent, allowing it to evolve based on modern applications of the Constitution's values.[14] From this perspective, the language of the Constitution is a vessel that can be filled with new meanings through interpretation. The difference between these two approaches is the choice between originalism and nonoriginalism. Monaghan offers no reason why the former is preferable.

Another example of argument from definition is the contention of Walter Benn Michaels that "any interpretation of the Constitution that really is an interpretation of the Constitution . . . is always and only an interpretation of what the Constitution originally meant."[15] Michaels concludes, based on his definition of the term *interpretation*, that "there is no such thing as non-originalist modes of interpretation."[16] Michael's argument is simply a tautology: he defines *inter-*

pretation as requiring originalism and therefore concludes that only originalism is a legitimate method of interpretation.

Nor is there any reason to accept Michaels's definition unless he provides a normative defense for that method of constitutional decision making. He does not explain why his definition of *interpretation* is preferable to a definition that says that *interpretation* is the process of giving meaning to a provision based on modern values. Michael Perry makes exactly this point in response to Michaels.

> But why should we accept [Michaels's] . . . stipulation? As a matter of ordinary language, 'interpretation' has no single, canonical meaning. Like many other words, 'interpretation' is used in more than one way. The search for what the author intended is one sense, but not the only one.[17]

If Michaels is making an argument about how the Constitution should be given meaning, he must develop a normative argument; he cannot establish the proper methodology by definition.

It is possible that Michaels is making a much more limited point that nonoriginalism should not be termed *interpretation*, as that term usually connotes a process of finding authorial intentions. If this is what Michaels is saying, he is not making an argument against nonoriginalism; rather, he is only saying that for the sake of clarity nonoriginalism should be termed something other than *interpretation*, such as " 'constitutional application' or 'evolution' or 'extrapolation' or 'meaning giving.' "[18] Although other literary critics challenge Michaels's restrictive definition of *interpretation*,[19] the key response is that the choice of terminology is completely irrelevant. Regardless of what the process is called, what matters is whether the Constitution can evolve other than by amendment, and this question cannot be answered except by developing normative arguments.

Yet another example of a tautological defense of originalism is Edward Melvin's recent claim that the oath of office that judges take compels them to follow an originalist methodology.[20] Melvin writes that "when a judge takes his oath to uphold the Constitution he promises to carry out the intention of the framers."[21] Taken literally, this statement is incorrect: judges, like all public officials, only swear to uphold the Constitution; judges do not take an oath to any particular view of constitutional decision making.[22] The oath of office only can be viewed as mandating originalism if a normative argument is made that judges uphold the Constitution only if they are originalists in their decision making. Melvin offers no such argument as to why constitutional evolution by interpretation should be viewed as inconsistent with the oath of office. Melvin's argument is a tautology: he defines the oath of office as requiring originalism, and on the basis of his definition, he concludes that nonoriginalism is impermissible.

Perhaps the most important example of question begging by originalists is their attempt to invoke the Framers' intent as a justification for originalism. Raoul Berger, for example, argues that the Constitution's meaning must remain static until there is an amendment because that is what the Framers intended in drafting the Constitution. Berger states, "The Framers did not leave us in the dark on this score; by Article Five they confided the power to amend to the people and not to the judges."[23] Similarly, Judge Bork argues that the meaning of the Constitution cannot be changed by evolution because "not even a scintilla of evidence supports the argument that the framers and the ratifiers of the various amendments intended the judiciary to develop new individual rights, which correspondingly create new disabilities for democratic government. . . . If the framers really intended to delegate to judges the function of creating new rights by the method of moral philosophy, one would expect they would say so."[24]

This argument is circular. It says that the Framers' intent is authoritative because the Framers intended their intent to be authoritative.[25] Because the difference between originalism and nonoriginalism is whether the Framers' intent is controlling until the Constitution is amended, it is question begging to try to resolve the issue by looking to the Framers' intent. To avoid circularity, there must be some substantive theory, some normative argument, justifying why it is appropriate to interpret the Constitution according to the Framers' intent.

Furthermore, there is strong evidence that Raoul Berger and Judge Bork are incorrect—that the Framers did not intend their intent to be controlling. Many scholars have argued persuasively that in choosing to write the Constitution in general language the Framers meant for the Constitution to evolve via interpretation and to "gather meaning from experience."[26] For example, Gerald Lynch concludes that "the framers of particular constitutional provisions intended to leave particular questions of interpretation for future development by the courts."[27]

An examination of the Framers' jurisprudence further supports the view that they expected the meaning of the Constitution to evolve. The Framers believed that individuals possessed natural rights, and that the purpose of government, as expressed by John Locke, was to protect the rights that individuals possessed in the state of nature.[28] The Framers did not see it as necessary to enumerate the rights they believed to be natural.[29] The Framers recognized that courts would articulate natural law principles in the process of deciding cases. Robert Clinton explains that "the articulation of concepts of natural law rested principally with the judges. As seen through [the Framers'] . . . eyes, the judges of the day were 'discovering' natural law."[30] Thus, the Constitution's protection of natural rights was intentionally left vague, and it was knowingly left to the judiciary to specify the particular meaning of the rights.

In a recent article titled "The Original Understanding of Original Intent," H. Jefferson Powell demonstrates that the Framers did not intend their views to control future constitutional interpretation. Powell concludes:

> It is commonly assumed that the 'interpretive intention' of the Constitution's framers was that the Constitution would be construed in accordance with what future generations could gather of the framers' own purposes, expectations, and intentions. Inquiry shows that assumption to be incorrect. Of the numerous hermeneutical options that were available in

the framers' day—among them the renunciation of construction altogether—none corresponds to the modern notion of originalism.[31]

At the very least, this undermines the originalists' tautological claim that the Framers' intent should be followed because they intended their intent to be followed. More important, if it is true that the Framers intended for the Constitution's meaning to evolve, then originalism self-destructs as a method of constitutional decision making. Originalism requires that the Constitution be interpreted in accord with the Framers' intent. Therefore, if the Framers intended that subsequent generations use a model other than originalism, the originalists' premise forces them to abandon their theory.[32]

My major point thus far has been that most of the defenses of originalism have been tautological and question begging. This is not to say that nonoriginalism is preferable, only that choosing between originalism and nonoriginalism requires a normative analysis of whether the Constitution should evolve by interpretation or only by amendment. Originalists have avoided making such normative arguments; instead, they have attempted to prove their case by definition and stipulation.

There are two other arguments frequently made for originalism that deserve consideration; both are descriptive statements masquerading as normative arguments. First, originalists frequently conclude that their theory is correct because the Supreme Court frequently speaks in originalist terms, actively looking to the Framers' intent.[33] This, of course, is only a description of Supreme Court decision making; it says nothing normatively about the desirability of such an approach. If, however, the originalists were to convert this into a normative argument and contend that for some reason the past method of constitutional decision making should be followed, then the originalists would concede the entire debate to the nonoriginalists because throughout U.S. history the Supreme Court has accepted nonoriginalism.

In numerous decisions, the Court has expressed its rejection of originalism. For example, in *United States v. Classic*,[34] the Court stated:

> [In deciding] whether a particular provision of the Constitution applies to a new subject matter it is of little significance that it is one with which the framers were not familiar. For in setting up an enduring framework of government they undertook to carry out for the indefinite future and in all the vicissitudes of the changing affairs of men, those fundamental purposes which the instrument itself discloses.[35]

Similarly, in *Home Building and Loan v. Blaisdell*,[36] the Court denounced the view that the Constitution is limited to what the Framers intended.

> It is no answer to say that this public need was not apprehended a century ago, or to insist that what the provision meant to the vision of that day it must mean to the vision of our time. If by the statement that what the Constitution meant at the time of its adoption it

means today, it is intended to say that the great clauses of the Constitution must be confined to the interpretation which the framers, with the conditions and outlook of their time, would have placed upon them, the statement carries its own refutation. It was to guard against such a narrow conception that Chief Justice Marshall uttered the memorable warning—'We must never forget that it is a Constitution we are expounding.'[37]

It is hard to imagine a clearer rejection of originalism.

Similarly, in *Brown v. Board of Education*, the Court observed: "In approaching this problem, we cannot turn the clock back to 1868 when the Amendment was adopted, or even to 1896 when Plessy v. Ferguson was written."[38] The Court was even more explicit in rejecting originalism as a method for interpreting the Fourteenth Amendment when it stated in *Harper v. Virginia Board of Elections*:

[T]he Equal Protection Clause is not shackled to the political theory of a particular era. In determining what lines are constitutionally discriminatory, we have never been confined to historic notions of equality, any more than we have restricted due process to a fixed catalogue of what was at a given time deemed to be the limit of fundamental rights. Notions of what constitutes equal protection for the purposes of the Equal Protection Clause *do* change.[39]

The Court has stated frequently that a nonoriginalist methodology is essential in constitutional decision making. Justice Byron White, for example, once remarked:

[T]he Court has not discovered or found the law in making today's decision, nor has it derived it from some irrefutable sources; what it has done today is to make new law and new public policy in much the same way that it has in the course of interpreting other great clauses of the Constitution. This is what the Court historically has done. Indeed this is what it must do and will continue to do until and unless there is some fundamental change in the constitutional distribution of governmental powers.[40]

Nonoriginalism is not a new paradigm. For example, H. Jefferson Powell observes that the Supreme Court's decision in 1973, in *Chisholm v. Georgia*, permitting states to be sued in federal courts, could not be justified under an originalist methodology. Powell remarks that "[i]f the Court had regarded itself as bound by the expectations of the Constitution's framers and supporters, a decision in Georgia's favor would have been warranted."[41] More dramatically, *Marbury v. Madison* is regarded by most commentators as a nonoriginalist decision because the Constitution is silent about judicial review and the Framers' intent is ambiguous at best.[42] There are numerous examples of nonoriginalist decisions throughout the nineteenth century.[43] During this century, almost every major Supreme Court decision, from the repudiated doctrines of the Lochner era through the decisions of the Warren and Burger courts, has been nonoriginalist in its methodology.[44] Jeffrey Shaman expresses it well: "Notwithstanding the orthodox protestations that it is illegitimate for the Court to 'revise' or 'amend' the Constitution, this is in fact what the Court always has done by continually creating new constitutional meaning.''[45]

I am not arguing that this description of the Court's constant nonoriginalism answers the normative question of which paradigm is most desirable for constitutional decision making. Instead, the point is that originalists are plainly wrong when they claim that the Court's occasional originalist rhetoric implies a rejection of nonoriginalism.

The fact that the Court embraced nonoriginalism in its decisions has relevance in choosing between the paradigms only to the extent that knowing current practices determines who has presumption and who has the burden of proof in the debate.[46] In choosing between originalism and nonoriginalism, it is important to keep in mind that this is 1987 and not 1787. The Court does not have the luxury of writing on a blank slate, and any shift in theories of judicial review involves costs. If earlier decisions are inconsistent with the prevailing theory, they can be overruled, but stare decisis will be sacrificed and doctrinal instability will be common. On the other hand, if earlier decisions are allowed to stand, under the new theory the Court might not adhere to them, thus creating inconsistencies in the law.[47] For example, what happens to the right to privacy if a theory is adopted under which the Court cannot protect this right?[48] Are earlier decisions protecting privacy overruled? Or is the right preserved but not applied in future cases, in which case inconsistency is inevitable? This is not to say that the Court is obligated to follow the theory that it has used primarily thus far.[49] Rather, because there are costs in shifting paradigms, a presumption exists in favor of the theory—nonoriginalism—practiced for almost 200 years.

At the very least, this is important rhetorically because thus far in the debate over constitutional interpretation, originalists have presented themselves as advocating the traditional method of decision making and have described nonoriginalists as the challengers who must bear a heavy burden of proof. Nonoriginalists have wrongly been placed on the defensive. It is originalists who are arguing for a major change in the interpretive methodology.

One final argument offered by originalists in favor of their paradigm needs to be considered. Many originalists argue that the fact that the Constitution specifies a procedure for amendment mandates that constitutional evolution occur only through the amendment process.[50] For example, one originalist commentator recently remarked: ''Since the Constitution provides the formal amendment process, to the extent that it remains unamended, it must be interpreted in the original sense.''[51] Correctly put, the issue is whether 200 years of nonoriginalism should be abandoned and originalism adopted as the only legitimate model of constitutional interpretation.

However, the existence of a provision creating a procedure for amendments does not by itself reveal anything about when that procedure should be used or whether the procedure is the exclusive method of constitutional interpretation. A normative argument must be made as to why the existence of an amendment process in the Constitution means that nonoriginalism is illegitimate. No such argument has been presented yet.

I imagine that the claim would be that each part of the Constitution must be interpreted to have independent significance, and any view that makes a provision superfluous is incorrect. The originalist would then claim that nonoriginalism renders the amendment process unnecessary and therefore nonoriginalism is incorrect. There are two major problems with this argument. First, again, it is arguing entirely from a stipulation: why is redundancy to be avoided? To the extent that constitutional evolution is desirable, as demonstrated in the previous chapter, it is advantageous to have multiple, different mechanisms to accomplish change.

Second, the originalists' argument based on the amendment clause is defeated if the amendment process has an independent function under nonoriginalism. If the amendment process accomplishes something that cannot be attained solely by interpretation, then it is not redundant, and nonoriginalism is, by this argument, acceptable. Under nonoriginalism, the amendment process serves as a way to reverse Supreme Court decisions that are viewed by an overwhelming majority of society as unacceptable. In U.S. history the Constitution has been amended four times to overturn Supreme Court decisions.[52] The amendment process can also function to change the procedure of government in situations where the Court has no basis for imposing such modifications by interpretation. For example, the Twenty-second Amendment limits the president to two terms of office, and the Twenty-third Amendment provides the District of Columbia with representation in the Electoral College. It is likely that neither of these changes would have been accomplished through interpretation.

Additionally, the amendment process serves an important independent function of providing symbolic reinforcement of those new matters placed in the Constitution. Constitutionalizing specific values has enormous effect in reinforcing those norms and communicating their importance to society. For example, the post–Civil War amendments prohibiting slavery, ensuring that the states provide equal protection and due process to their citizens, and guaranteeing the right to vote had substantial symbolic effect.

Nonoriginalism does not render the amendment process superfluous. The Constitution's detailing of the procedure for amendments therefore provides no basis for choosing between originalism and nonoriginalism.

Thus far, I have demonstrated only the inadequacy of the traditional defense of originalism. The next step is to present an explanation as to why the Constitution should evolve by interpretation and not just by amendment.

WHY THE MEANING OF THE CONSTITUTION SHOULD EVOLVE BY INTERPRETATION

The Constitution can achieve its purposes, as described in Chapter 2, only if it can evolve by interpretation. If the Constitution is static until amended, as originalists argue, it will fail to provide an adequate check on the majority and it will fail to provide a unifying symbol for society.

Constitutional Evolution Via Interpretation

The previous chapter demonstrates why it is essential that the Constitution evolve in order to achieve its objectives. Constitutional evolution requires change by interpretation; to say that the Constitution may be modified only by amendment is to say there will be virtually no evolution. The cumbersome amendment process, requiring approval by two thirds of both houses of Congress and three quarters of the state legislatures, makes it likely that few amendments will be added to the Constitution. Just 16 amendments have been added in almost 200 years. This means that the Constitution will remain virtually static, failing to evolve to meet the needs of a society that is advancing technologically and morally.

In fact, originalists even admit that the complex amendment procedure makes it highly unlikely that the Constitution will be amended. When the argument is raised that the judiciary's powers are checked by the amendment process, the traditional response of originalists is that this is insufficient because amendments are unlikely and rare. Stephen Carter, who espouses an originalist approach to at least part of the Constitution, recently stated, "In the 1980's, Article V is very nearly a dead letter. The contention that it provides a realistic check on judicial activity is at best wishful thinking, certainly somewhat naive, and at worst disingenuous."[53] Putting aside for the moment the question of whether the amendment process is an adequate check on the judiciary, originalists recognize the near impossibility of amendments. Therefore, a constitution that evolves only by amendments rarely evolves. The conclusion reached in Chapter 3 that evolution is essential dictates the rejection of originalism.

More specifically, the previous chapter argued that unless the Constitution evolves, it will not protect minorities and their rights adequately, and it will not serve to unify society. A few examples illustrate this conclusion and therefore the unacceptability of originalism. For instance, how would an originalist deal with Article II of the Constitution, which refers to the president as "he"?[54] The Framers intended that the president would be male and in fact excluded women from all political participation.[55] Thomas Jefferson once remarked that "were our state a pure democracy there would still be excluded from our deliberations women, who, to prevent deprivation of morals and ambiguity of issues, should not mix promiscuously in gatherings of men."[56] Thus, an originalist interpreting Article II would be compelled to declare unconstitutional the election of a woman as president or vice president until the Constitution was amended.[57] Both the language of the text and the Framers' intent makes clear that the president was intended to be male. If the Constitution were not amended to reflect society's current values—either because it did not occur to people to amend Article II or because such an amendment was politically impossible[58]—then the election of a woman as president or vice president would be unconstitutional. The Constitution would hardly be serving its purpose of protecting a group traditionally discriminated against, and the Constitution's ability to unify society would obviously be undermined, if society were denied its choice for president or vice president.

This example, while dramatic, is not atypical. Under an originalist approach, the federal government would not be under any obligation to treat citizens equally. The equal protection clause of the Fourteenth Amendment only applies to the states.[59] No provision of the Constitution required the federal government to provide equal protection of the laws. The Supreme Court circumvented this limitation by interpreting the due process clause of the Fifth Amendment to impose a requirement that the federal government provide equal protection.[60] This conclusion, however, is nonoriginalist because it is supported by neither the text nor the Framers' intent. The Fourteenth Amendment includes both a due process clause and an equal protection clause. An originalist, therefore, would believe that these clauses have separate meanings. Moreover, there is no indication that the Framers, in drafting the Fifth Amendment, intended it to create a requirement for equal protection.[61]

The conclusion is that under an originalist approach, until the Constitution is amended the federal government could discriminate in almost any way it wanted. The Constitution would not serve its goal of protecting minorities if the federal government were unconstrained by considerations of equality. Moreover, the Constitution would not serve a unifying function if the federal government were allowed to discriminate and the states were prohibited from acting in the identical manner.

The examples are endless. Unless the First Amendment were amended, the president could suppress speech because the First Amendment only says that Congress may make no law. Similarly, Congress could censor speech on radio and television because there was no Framers' intent to apply the First Amendment to these media.

These examples demonstrate that the Constitution must evolve and that interpretation provides a means for the necessary evolution. By interpretation the Court can declare that "he" in Article II should be regarded as a generic reference to all humans and the election of a woman is constitutional. By interpretation the Court can hold that the Fifth Amendment imposes a requirement of equal protection on the federal government. By interpretation the Court can rule that the president must obey the First Amendment and that the broadcast media is protected by the Constitution.

Originalists could respond that there is no inherent reason why the Constitution could not be amended to achieve these results. Certainly, in theory, the Constitution could be amended; however, the relative unlikelihood of amendment makes it inferior as a process of evolution. For example, often the nature of the subject matter makes it unlikely that amendments would be enacted. It is highly unlikely that state legislatures would have approved a constitutional amendment to reapportion state legislatures.[62] Nor is it probable that the legislatures would have approved amendments to apply the Bill of Rights to the states[63] or to desegregate the schools.[64]

Moreover, evolution by amendment is inferior because it is unlikely that society would be willing to devote the energy and resources to amend the Constitution constantly. If all evolution were by amendment, frequent amendments would need to be added to the Constitution. All the examples mentioned thus far, and innumerable more, indicate the large number of places where the Constitution would have to be amended to reflect changes in society. But the cumbersome nature of the amendment process, and the need for approval from so many different institutions, makes it highly unlikely that very many amendments would be ratified. In short, once it is established that the Constitution must evolve, then it follows that evolution should occur through interpretation and not just through amendment.

Furthermore, if amendments were made frequently, the Constitution would lose its symbolic value as a brief, abstract document. If amendments were routine and not exceptional, there is reason to fear that precisely when it matters most, constitutional protections might be eliminated by amendment.

Protecting Minorities and Rights

A second major argument as to why the Constitution should evolve through interpretation is that protection of minorities and their rights requires it. Chapter 2 established that one of the primary purposes of a constitution is to safeguard minorities from the powers of the majority. Chapter 3 established that technological advances often pose new threats to rights, and moral progress creates concerns for new minorities and new rights. If amendments were the only way to change the Constitution, protection against new threats and protection of new minorities and of new rights would require action by a supermajority of the society. In other words the minority would be protected from the majority only if a supermajority of society decided to act. Such a requirement means virtually no protection at all.[65]

Consider a simple example. Social changes made education increasingly important during the twentieth century. Few would doubt that if blacks are to achieve true social equality, education is essential. Nor would many deny that the Jim Crow laws that segregated the South, including its schools, were based on an assumption of the inferiority of blacks.[66] Therefore, equal protection for a crucial minority (both in numerical size and in moral terms, given the history of slavery) required provision of quality education and the elimination of segregation. The Constitution would fail one of its most important purposes if it did not provide this protection for blacks.

However, it is highly improbable that the Constitution would have been amended to declare separate but equal schools unconstitutional or to eliminate the Jim Crow laws. Neither Congress nor the requisite number of states likely would have ratified such amendments. It is highly unlikely that Congress would have enacted legislation to desegregate the South pursuant to its authority under section 5 of the Fourteenth Amendment. Southern senators and representatives had disproportionate influence in Congress, especially during the 1950s and 1960s and likely could have blocked any amendment. During this time, virtually all congressional committees were chaired by southerners, who generally served longer terms because the South was controlled largely by one political party.[67] Given their influence in Congress, and congressional procedures that gave great power to committee chairs, southerners were in a position to prevent any amendment. There is no doubt that they would have used all their influence to thwart an amendment ordering desegregation. In 1956, 96 southern congressmen issued a declaration denouncing the Supreme Court's decision in *Brown v. Board of Education* and calling on their states to "resist forced integration by any lawful means."[68]

Moreover, it is unlikely that states would have ratified such an amendment even if Congress had managed to pass it. Because more than a quarter of the states had laws segregating their schools,[69] it is improbable that three quarters of the states would have voted for an amendment ending segregation. As Edmund Cahn remarked, "As a practical matter it would have been impossible to secure adoption of a constitutional amendment to abolish 'separate but equal.' "[70]

The Constitution needed to evolve to protect blacks and especially to eliminate segregated schools. Evolution only by amendment would not have eliminated segregation. Generally stated, it makes no sense to protect minorities only if a supermajority of society acts. If the Constitution is to achieve its goal of protecting minorities and their rights, it must evolve by interpretation, not just by amendment.

In fact, protecting the value of majority rule and the rights of the majority also justifies constitutional evolution. A powerful example of this is reapportionment. Until the Supreme Court's reapportionment decisions in the 1960s, most state legislatures were malapportioned, giving undue voting strength to rural areas and inadequate representation to more populous areas. It is unlikely that the political process would have corrected this. Those in power as a result of malapportionment were unlikely to vote themselves out of office by redistricting. Only the judiciary, with its power to interpret the Constitution, could remedy this problem.

Preserving the Constitution as a General, Unifying Document

A third major reason why the Constitution should evolve by interpretation is to preserve the Constitution as a general, unifying document. Assuming that I am wrong, and amendments can be added to the Constitution easily, then there would be countless amendments. Article I of the Constitution would need to be amended to give Congress power to regulate modern means of commerce. Article II would need to be amended to specify the president's powers to remove Cabinet officers, recognize foreign governments, and invoke executive privilege, to give just a few examples.[71] The First Amendment would need to be amended to protect television and radio broadcasts from censorship. The Fourth Amendment would need to be amended to limit wiretapping. The Fifth Amendment would need to be amended to prevent coerced confessions and ensure provision of counsel for indigents. The Sixth Amendment would need to be amended to solve the problem of prejudicial publicity, which the Court has tried to handle through interpretations.[72] The Eighth Amendment would need to be amended to prohibit modern forms of torture. The Fourteenth Amendment would need to be amended to ensure equal protection to women, aliens, illegitimate children, and other groups not intended to be protected by the amendment's Framers.[73] Amendment would be necessary to apply the Bill of Rights to the states. The Constitution would have to be amended to protect the right to privacy, the right of parents to control the upbringing of their children, and the right of family autonomy.[74] And this list is only the beginning, a few examples from an almost endless list.

As the Constitution becomes filled with these innumerable amendments, it would lose its value as a general, constitutive document. The more specific the document, the less it could serve as a unifying device for society. When a controversial constitutional decision is made through interpretation, those who disagree with the result can view their loss as hopefully temporary and look forward to reversal in future interpretations. But if the result is enshrined in the Constitution, the chances of change are much less. The unifying value of the document is lost as it contains more and more specific provisions with which some people disagree. Moreover, if the proposed amendments were rejected, the affected group would feel alienated and hopeless. The majority of society publicly decided that the losing group was not deserving of constitutional protection. As this process repeatedly occurred, an increasingly large segment of society would become disgruntled. By contrast, when losses result because of interpretations, it is less of a message of rejection from society and there remains the hope of winning through future changes in interpretations.

A relatively short, general document accomplishes a constitutive function much better than a lengthy, detailed one. People can comprehend a shorter document better, and feel more allegiance to it, than a very long text. John Marshall observed that a Constitution with the "prolixity of a legal code . . . could scarcely by embraced by the human mind. It would probably never be understood by the people."[75] As discussed in a previous chapter, because of their greater degree of detail, state constitutions engender much less respect than does the more general national document. Joseph Long remarked:

> The federal constitution . . . has happily escaped the fate that has befallen the constitutions of the states. Not only are they subject to constant change, but they have long since ceased to be constitutions in a true sense. Instead of embodying broad general propositions of fundamental permanent law, they now exhibit the prolixity of a code and consist largely of mere legislation. No one now entertains any particular respect for state constitutions. It has little more dignity than an ordinary act of legislation.[76]

Laurence Tribe similarly remarked how the "cluttered" nature of state constitutions explains why "they rarely command the respect routinely paid to federal constitutional guarantees."[77]

Preserving a relatively short, general document requires that evolution occur by interpretation. If changes could come about only via amendment, and if amendments did occur, the document would grow enormously in size and specificity. A primary value of the Constitution, as explained in Chapter 2, would be lost.

Interpretation Best Achieves Constitutional Evolution

A fourth major reason why originalism is undesirable is that evolution by interpretation allows experiments, facilitating change and minimizing the risk of errors. Even assuming that both interpretation and amendment could provide the necessary evolution, interpretation is a preferable method of change. If a result attained by interpretation proves undesirable, it is possible to undo the mistake relatively easily. However, if an amendment proves to be a mistake, change is much more difficult. Of course, desirable changes gained by interpretation are more vulnerable than those obtained through amendments.

For example, it is quite possible that at the end of the nineteenth century, society, committed to a laissez-faire mentality,[78] might have been willing to enact a constitutional amendment protecting freedom of contract from legislative interference. The Supreme Court accomplished this result without constitutional amendment, by interpreting the liberty of the due process clause to include freedom of contract.[79] Based on this interpretation, during the Lochner era, the Court struck down almost 200 state laws regulating business and protecting employees and consumers.[80] By the 1930s it was clear that these rulings were a mistake: consumer and worker protection laws were essential.[81] If freedom of contract and equality of bargaining power ever really existed between employer and employee, it clearly was an illusion during the depression when there were millions of people out of work.

In short, by the 1930s it was clear that the Lochner era doctrines were a mistake and needed to be overruled to facilitate economic recovery and social welfare. If liberty of contract were enshrined in the Constitution, change would have required an amendment that business and conservatives might have tried to block. Because the doctrines were a product of interpretation, the change could be accomplished with relative ease in a couple of Supreme Court decisions.[82]

Originalists frequently point to Lochnerism as a classic illustration of the dangers of nonoriginalism. However, would not the error and the damage have been much worse had the principles of Lochnerism been placed in a constitutional amendment?

Furthermore, interpretation allows incremental change, achieving evolution in situations where dramatic changes would not occur. For example, the desegregation of the South was ordered incrementally in a series of decisions. Initially, the Court, in *Missouri ex rel. Gaines v. Canada*, ordered a southern state to provide law school education within its borders to blacks because it provided such education for whites.[83] The Court stated that unless Mississippi provided equal facilities for blacks, they were entitled to admission to the existing segregated school. In a later decision, *Sweatt v. Painter*, the Court held that Texas had to admit blacks to the state law school even though it had recently created a separate law school for blacks.[84] The Court found that the separate facilities were not equal, and therefore blacks had the right to attend the white school. In a subsequent decision, *McLaurin v. Oklahoma State Regents*, the Court held that a state could not require a black admitted to a white school to sit in separate sections of classrooms, library facilities, and cafeterias.[85]

All of these cases preceded *Brown v. Board of Education*, which declared unconstitutional racially segregated elementary and secondary schools.[86] *Brown* was followed by a series of decisions striking down Jim Crow laws requiring segregated beaches, buses, golf courses, and parks.[87] Finally, in 1963 the Court could declare, "[I]t is no longer open to question that a State may not constitutionally require segregation of public facilities."[88] Desegregation occurred incrementally, not through one Supreme Court decision or one amendment.

Political scientists have long believed that incremental change is more likely to occur than radical change.[89] The radical change might not happen at all, or at least not until much later, without the incremental reforms. Each incremental change sways attitudes, making subsequent reforms easier to achieve. It might take years of dissatisfaction and worsening conditions before a radical change occurs. Therefore, with incremental changes, society gains the benefit of each of the changes along the way, rather than gaining no benefit until the radical change. Constitutional evolution by interpretation facilitates incremental changes.

Certainly, incremental change has its disadvantages as well. Radical change often can accomplish things that might never come about incrementally.[90] Also, incremental changes can chip away at rights as much as add to them. Nonetheless, over the long term, progressive changes are much more likely to happen incrementally than all at once. Relatively few radical changes occur in a society. Establishments, vested interests, and inertia all make incremental change the only realistic hope for improvements.

Effective Functioning of Government

A final argument for evolution by interpretation is that it is desirable in order for government to function under a constitution. The Constitution, written as a general document, as a blueprint for government,[91] has many gaps. Many of these have been mentioned previously: no one is given authority to recognize foreign governments; no one is given power to remove Cabinet officials; no one is given the power to rescind treaties; and so on.[92] Originalists, focusing almost exclusively on Court decisions protecting rights, ignore the question of how government is to deal with these gaps.

Given the Constitution's commitment to a limited federal government, an originalist likely would have to say that government only has the authority explicitly provided in the Constitution. Additional authority can be granted to the federal government only by amendment. Therefore, for example, the president cannot remove Cabinet officials because Article II only bestows the appointment power, not removal authority. Likewise, because the removal power is not mentioned in Article I or Article III, neither the legislature nor judiciary possesses such authority. In other words, since the power is not contained in the Constitution, to an originalist it does not exist. No institution or individual would have the authority to remove Cabinet officials.

The degree of inflexibility embodied in an originalist approach could virtually paralyze government. Government needs to do countless things that the Framers could not possibly have imagined. Powell observes that even in the first few years of the country numerous decisions had to be made where the Constitution provided little guidance:

> The establishment of the executive departments, the debates over a protective tariff and a national bank, the consideration of a memorial against the slave trade and of the proper means of handling public debt—all involved the resolution of constitutional authority not plainly answered on the face of the document.[93]

An originalist must concede that without express constitutional authorization government lacks the authority to act until the Constitution is amended. Interpretation, on the other hand, allows the gaps to be filled and permits government to function under a general, constitutive document.

The conclusion that emerges from these arguments is that the Constitution should evolve by interpretation, not just by amendment. Institutions engaged in constitutional decision making are not bound to follow the Framers' intent or the originalist paradigm. The Constitution's purposes are best fulfilled if the Constitution is not limited to the norms stated in the text or intended by its drafters. The interpretation of the Constitution should be an evolutionary process, providing modern meanings for constitutional provisions.

The logical next questions are: Who should have authority to interpret the Constitution? and What constraints should exist on institutions engaged in constitutional interpretation? These questions are addressed in the next two chapters. Before examining these issues, however, it is necessary to consider attempts by some originalists to redefine the paradigm to answer the arguments advanced for nonoriginalism.

ALTERNATIVE MODELS OF ORIGINALISM

In considering originalism, I have focused on the traditional definition, offered by commentators such as Raoul Berger, that the Constitution's meaning is limited to that which is expressed in the text or intended by the Framers. Some, who consider themselves originalists, have developed alternative definitions of originalism that are less rigid and that allow some evolution by interpretation. I contend that either these models are so indeterminate as to be indistinguishable from nonoriginalism or they suffer from all the problems described above of a model that allows the Constitution to evolve only by amendment.

At this point, it is worth trying to clarify the notion of *indeterminacy*. In the simplest sense, indeterminacy exists if there is no single correct answer to a legal question. If judges acting in good faith can come to opposite, equally defensible conclusions, the matter can be labeled indeterminate. To a large extent, originalists defend their methodology by pointing to the indeterminacy and judicial discretion that exists under nonoriginalism.

There is, of course, a continuum of indeterminacy—ranging from judges having relatively few acceptable choices to a much larger set of possible outcomes. The point I make in this section about moderate originalism is that it does not yield determinacy and in fact creates a very large set of acceptable outcomes.

Phrased differently, the conclusion I seek to establish here is that moderate originalists are nonoriginalists if they allow evolution by interpretation and originalists if they do not. This does not imply that all nonoriginalists are the same. As discussed in Chapter 6, there are many different nonoriginalist theories according a range of discretion to constitutional interpretation. Here I simply establish that moderate originalists should be considered nonoriginalists, despite their label, to the extent they allow constitutional evolution by interpretation.

Actually, there are several paradigms that try to position themselves between originalism and nonoriginalism. First, there are paradigms that are termed *moderate originalism*.[94] Paul Brest, who coined the phrase "moderate originalism," states that it is "more concerned with the adopters' general purpose than with their intention in a very precise sense."[95] Whereas strict originalism limits constitutional decision making to what the Framers intended, moderate originalism allows consideration of modern circumstances in interpretation. Because the Framers' intent can be stated at many different levels of abstraction, the distinction between originalism and moderate originalism is not always clear. Ultimately, the difference is that originalism is based on the belief that the specific meaning of a constitutional provision is static until it is amended, whereas moderate originalism endorses the view that the meaning of the Constitution shifts over time.

Two prominent examples of moderate originalism deserve consideration. One, which might be termed *conceptualism*, is developed by Ronald Dworkin. Conceptualism requires the Court to determine the underlying purpose of a constitutional provision and to apply this purpose in developing modern governing principles.[96] Unlike strict originalism, conceptualism does not require that the Court follow the Framers' specific intentions. Instead, the justices are asked to identify the underlying "concept" of a provision and to use it in formulating modern "conceptions" to guide decision making. Each constitutional provision has a core meaning that is static, which the courts apply to modern circumstances. Dworkin explains:

> Suppose I tell my children simply that I expect them not to treat others unfairly. I no doubt have in mind examples of the conduct I mean to discourage, but I would not accept that my meaning is limited to these examples. . . . First I would expect my children to apply my

> instructions to situations I had not and could not have thought about. Second, I stand ready to admit that some particular act that I thought was fair when I spoke was in fact unfair, or vice versa, if one of my children is able to convince me of the latter. . . . I might say that I meant the family to be guided by the *concept* of fairness, not by any specific *conception* of fairness that I had in mind.[97]

Conceptualism is a form of moderate originalism because the Framers' intent is still relevant—their intent provides the concepts; but conceptualism is distinct from strict originalism because the Court can develop its own modern conceptions in deciding cases. Munzer and Nickel observe that the "object of the distinction between [concepts and conceptions] is to justify the claim that the core meaning of the Constitution remains unchanged even when judges diverge from the specific content that the framers would have found there."[98]

First, advocates of conceptualism must provide a normative argument as to why it is the appropriate method of constitutional interpretation. There is nothing that inherently makes it more desirable or more correct than any other approach. The question not answered by Dworkin and other supporters of conceptualism is, What justifies this method of interpretation?[99] Why, for example, should the Framers' concepts—even if they could be identified—govern modern society? Just as originalists must justify why the Framers' intent should guide interpretation, so must conceptualists justify their use of *original intent* and the desirability of their theory for constitutional decision making.

Second, and more important, conceptualism is so completely indeterminate as to be indistinguishable from nonoriginalism. Conceptualism, by definition, allows evolution by interpretation. Judges are not limited because the concept, the Framers' intent, can be stated at a level of abstraction sufficiently general to permit any result. The concept behind any constitutional provision can be stated at several different levels of generality. For example, the equal protection clause may represent the concept that blacks are entitled to treatment equal to whites.[100] It also could reflect the concept that groups that had been enslaved, as blacks were, should receive equal treatment.[101] The clause might mean that discrimination is impermissible against all racial minorities,[102] or that groups that are "insular" political minorities should be constitutionally protected.[103] Most generally, the clause may embody the concept that all discrimination must be justified by some legitimate government purpose.[104] Each is a plausible interpretation of the underlying concept or purpose behind the equal protection clause, and at various times, each has been endorsed by the Supreme Court.

The result in particular cases will likely depend on the level of generality at which the concept is articulated[105] If the equal protection clause is intended only to protect blacks or former slaves, then the Fourteenth Amendment offers no basis for protection of women. Alternatively, if the concept of equality is stated more generally, the Court is obligated to scrutinize gender discrimination carefully. Conceptualism "demands an arbitrary choice among levels of abstraction."[106] This choice allows judges to find in any constitutional provision concepts so general that they permit any result.[107] Conceptualism, therefore, is completely indistinguishable from nonoriginalism except that under conceptualism judges must phrase their decision in terms of concepts and conceptions. Conceptualism permits the Court to use values neither stated nor intended in constitutional decision making.

This analysis is not a criticism of conceptualism as a method of interpretation. Rather, it is simply to say that conceptualism cannot claim to be an originalist theory because it provides for constitutional evolution by interpretation.

Even strict originalists at times attempt to use conceptualism to escape the problems of originalism. For example, one of the main difficulties originalists face is that *Brown v. Board of Education*—almost universally regarded as a desirable decision—cannot be justified under an originalist paradigm because the Framers of the equal protection clause did not intend to prevent segregated schooling.[108] Judge Robert Bork, usually a strict originalist, tries to get around this problem by invoking conceptualism. He defends *Brown* on the grounds that the "fourteenth amendment was intended to enforce a core idea of black equality against government discrimination."[109] But why for an originalist such as Judge Bork should the Framers' "core idea" be followed and not their specific intention?[110] And if only the core idea is authoritative, why cannot it be said that the core idea was the elimination of invidious government discrimination, an idea that permits what Bork deems illegitimate: judicial action protecting numerous groups such as women, aliens, and illegitimates? In fact, during the 1950s the Court's decision in *Brown* was attacked by originalists with all the vigor and force now directed to cases such as *Roe v. Wade*.[111]

In other words, originalists cannot rescue their paradigm by embracing conceptualism because by doing so they adopt a model that permits judges to come to results identical to nonoriginalism. Either originalism is wedded to a static Constitution—in which case, it is unacceptable—or it permits evolution by interpretation—in which case, in practice it is a form of nonoriginalism.

An alternative version of moderate originalism is for the interpreter to decide what the Framers would have done had they been confronted with modern circumstances. Lusky phrases this inquiry in its classical form: "What results would the drafters have intended had they been confronted with the problems and context of today's world?"[112] Tushnet labels this approach "transposition."[113]

Transposition is different from strict originalism because it does not limit the meaning of the Constitution to the specific intent of the Framers at the time of the document's drafting. Perry explains:

> The originalist project is not to speculate about what the ratifiers' current beliefs would have been had they survived to this day and then decide the case on the basis of those beliefs. Rather, the originalist project is to enforce those beliefs that were accorded authoritative status by the ratifiers, and therefore to sometimes refer to further beliefs of the sorts indicated.[114]

Transposition is different from conceptualism because it does not hold any part of the Constitution to be static; the entire Constitution is subject to change if the interpreter believes that the Framers would have made such a modification had they been alive to decide the modern case.

Transposition, like conceptualism, is completely indeterminate; there is no way to know what the Framers would have believed had they confronted modern problems.[115] A Court can come to any conclusion, imposing any values, and simply argue that because the result is just, that is what the Framers would have done. All nonoriginalist results can be justified. In fact, if the Framers are thought of as individuals believing in the same abstract values that we do, and if the Framers knew everything we know, then the transposed Framers are indistinguishable from the modern Court.[116] The Court can assume that everything it wants to do is exactly what the Framers would do if they were alive to see how society had changed. In other words, transposition allows the Court to phrase its opinions in terms of why the Framers would agree to the result.

Thus, both conceptualism and transposition, the primary forms of moderate originalism, are not forms of originalism but, rather, are completely open-ended and indistinguishable from nonoriginalism. Both allow the Constitution to evolve by interpretation.

A second major attempt to rescue originalism must be considered also. Some commentators, most notably Michael Perry and Stephen Carter, attempt to overcome the criticisms of originalism by limiting its applicability to certain parts of the Constitution.[117] Both Perry and Carter argue that originalism should be used only for the "political Constitution"—the parts of the Constitution dealing with the structure of government, separation of powers, and federalism.

Neither scholar justifies why the political Constitution should evolve only by amendment. For example, Carter presents three arguments as to why originalism is appropriate for the political Constitution. First, he says that "there may be no good reason not to try to discover the original understanding with respect to the provisions of our political Constitution."[118] This obviously is not an adequate defense of originalism. There must be some substantive theory, some normative explanation for why it is appropriate to interpret any part of the Constitution according to the Framers' intent.[119]

Similarly, Perry focuses his analysis on whether there is a justification for departing from originalism in the areas of separation of powers and federalism. But, as demonstrated at the beginning of this chapter, originalism should not be presumed to be appropriate until another contender is proved superior. In fact, given a long history of nonoriginalist interpretation, it is originalists who should bear the burden of proving the desirability of a change in interpretive methodology.

Second, Carter argues for originalism in applying the political Constitution because "with respect to these structural clauses, neither the moral problem of repugnant result nor the hermeneutical problem of unknowable history should prove insurmountable."[120] Even if this statement is correct, it still does not justify originalism. Even if the results are acceptable and determinate, that does not explain why this method of interpretation should be used, as opposed to others that also produce acceptable results and are workable.

Furthermore, Carter is wrong—originalism faces the identical problems when applied to the political Constitution as it does when applied in fundamental rights cases. As to the normative problems, Carter says that originalism is inappropriate in fundamental rights cases because it would lead to results that are regarded as "repugnant."[121] If repugnant results justify the rejection of originalism, then it also must be discarded for the political Constitution. Consider a simple example involving Article II, discussed earlier in this chapter. Because Article II refers to the president as "he," and the Framers intended to exclude women from politics, an originalist is compelled to declare unconstitutional the election of a woman as president or vice president.[122] This seems a paradigm example of what Carter terms the "moral problem of the repugnant result."

Nor is Carter correct when he asserts that the political Constitution poses no interpretive problems. In countless areas concerning the structure of government, the Constitution is silent or ambiguous. For example, when may the president exercise inherent authority, acting without express constitutional or statutory authority?[123] This question is critical in answering numerous questions, including whether the president can seize industries,[124] rescind treaties,[125] impound funds,[126] assert executive privilege,[127] or even wage war.[128] Similarly, with regard to the legislative power, the Constitution does not describe when Congress can delegate power or whether the exercise of delegated power can be subject to the legislative veto.[129]

Third, Carter argues that originalism is desirable because it is a "value-free" form of interpretation.[130] Carter writes:

> If judicial decisions aim self-consciously at keeping the structure of government close to the framers' conception, then with respect to the political Constitution, at least, the courts will be able to claim a relatively value-free rule of interpretation.[131]

According to Carter, originalism is desirable because it allows "adjudication under the political Constitution [to] be guided by rules of construction that will permit—or require—interpretations that are relatively value-free."[132]

But originalism is hardly value free. At the very least, the theory embodies a choice to follow the Framers' values—values that were racist and sexist. The Framers meant to exclude blacks and women from government office. Either we follow these values or we must reject originalism. No matter what, a value choice is made.

Moreover, as discussed in Chapter 3, the interpretive process is never value free. Frequently there will be conflicts about what the Framers intended because often the language of the Constitution and the records of the debates are ambiguous.[133] At the least, because conflicting positions were expressed at the Constitutional Convention and in the ratification debates, there is a major interpretive problem in deciding whose intent matters. Litigation develops precisely because there are conflicts over interpretation. Historians long have demonstrated that there is no such thing as value-free historical interpretation—a person's perceptions and conclusions are always affected by his or her beliefs.[134]

Furthermore, the process of applying the Framers' intent to modern circumstances requires inferences that can never be value free. Legal realists long ago demonstrated that formalism is impossible in deciding cases and the inevitable discretion ensures that values enter into the interpretive process.

In sum, Carter does not justify why originalism should be followed in deciding matters under the political Constitution. More fundamentally, it is specious to distinguish between the political Constitution and fundamental rights cases. The structure of government—separation of powers and federalism—is intended to best ensure protection of individual liberties. As explained in Chapter 2, the structure of government is delineated in the Constitution to prevent those in power from creating a dictatorship or changing the allocation of power to their advantage. There is no conceptual basis for distinguishing the political Constitution from the rest.

Furthermore, all the arguments presented in this chapter as to why the Constitution should evolve by interpretation apply with equal force to the political Constitution. In fact, in developing the arguments for a Constitution that evolves by interpretation, I intentionally provided examples dealing with the structure of government as well as fundamental rights and protecting minorities.

Originalism cannot be rescued. Any theory that allows evolution only by amendment is unacceptable. Any theory that allows the Court to decide cases based on modern values, permitting the Constitution to evolve by interpretation, is nonoriginalism.

5 Who Should Be the Authoritative Interpreter of the Constitution?

Once it is decided that the meaning of the Constitution should evolve by interpretation, the next question is, Who should interpret the Constitution? As indicated earlier, the correct answer is that all government officials and institutions are required to engage in constitutional interpretation. All elected officeholders take an oath to uphold the Constitution. Therefore, legislators—federal, state, and local—are obliged to consider the constitutionality of bills before ratifying them. The executive must consider constitutionality in deciding what laws to propose, which bills passed by the legislature to veto, and what executive policies to implement. The judiciary, at the very least, must consider the constitutionality of laws before applying them to decide cases and controversies. In short, the decision that society shall be governed by a Constitution necessitates that all branches and levels of government interpret the Constitution.

So the real question to be addressed is not who should interpret the Constitution but, more specifically, who should be the authoritative interpreter of the Constitution? When there is a disagreement over how the Constitution should be interpreted, who resolves the conflict? Who gets the final say in determining the meaning of a constitutional provision? (Final, that is, until the interpretation is overruled in a constitutional amendment or the interpreter changes its mind.) Disagreements over the meaning of the Constitution are inevitable. For example, Congress enacts a statute that it, implicitly or explicitly, declares to be constitutional. The judiciary, in considering the law, concludes that it is unconstitutional. Whose view triumphs? The president claims a right to keep certain documents secret because of executive privilege. The Court rules that executive privilege does not apply. Whose view triumphs? The president rescinds a treaty and asserts inherent constitutional authority to do so. The Senate believes that such recision without its advice and consent is unconstitutional. Whose view triumphs?

WHO IS THE AUTHORITATIVE INTERPRETER?

There are three possible answers to the question of who should be the authoritative interpreter of the Constitution. One approach is for no branch of government to be regarded as authoritative in constitutional interpretation. Each branch of government would have equal authority to determine the meaning of constitutional provisions, and conflicts would be resolved through political power and compromise. If Congress and the president believe that a law is constitutional, and they could implement it without assistance from the Court, they could disregard a judicial ruling of unconstitutionality. If the president believes a law to be unconstitutional, he or she could refuse to enforce it, notwithstanding declarations of its constitutionality from the legislature and judiciary.

This approach to constitutional interpretation finds support early in U.S. history from presidents such as Thomas Jefferson and Andrew Jackson. Jefferson wrote:

> But nothing in the Constitution has given . . . [the judges] a right to decide for the Executive, more than to the Executive to decide for them. Both magistracies are equally independent in the sphere of action assigned to them. The judges, believing the law constitutional, had a right to pass a sentence of fine and imprisonment; because that power was placed in their hands by the Constitution. But the Executive, believing the law to be unconstitutional, was bound to remit the execution of it; because that power is confided to him by the Constitution. That instrument meant that its coordinate branches should be checks on each other. But the opinion which gives to the judges the right to decide what laws are constitutional, and what not, not only for themselves in their own sphere of action, but for the Legislature and Executive also, would make the judiciary a despotic branch.[1]

Similarly, Andrew Jackson declared in vetoing a bill to recharter the Bank of the United States:

> The Congress, the Executive, and the Court must each for itself be guided by its own opinion of the Constitution. Each public officer who takes an oath to support the Constitution swears that he will support it as he understands it, and not as it is understood by others. It is as much the duty of the House of Representatives, of the Senate, and of the President to decide upon the constitutionality of any bill or resolution which may be presented to them for passage or approval as it is of the supreme judges when it may be brought before them for judicial decision. The opinion of the judges has no more authority over Congress than the opinion of Congress has over the judges, and on that point the President is independent of both. The authority of the Supreme Court must not, therefore, be permitted to control the Congress or the Executive when acting in their legislative capacities, but to have only such influence as the force of their reasoning may deserve.[2]

Under this first approach, there is no authoritative interpreter of the Constitution.

Support for this first approach is found not only in proclamations of long-dead presidents. Very recently, the Reagan administration articulated and advocated the view that each branch has equal authority to interpret the Constitution, and that the executive and legislature are not bound by the judiciary's rulings. Specifically, the president took this position in connection with his objection to the constitutionality of a provision in the Competition in Contracting Act (CICA).[3] Congress enacted the CICA in 1984 and in it gave the comptroller general the authority to freeze the awarding of government contracts under some circumstances.[4] The comptroller general is the highest ranking official in the General Accounting Office, a congressional agency.[5] The president signed the CICA but objected to the constitutionality of the provision giving the comptroller general the power to stay the award of public contracts.[6] The president, through an order issued by Budget Director David Stockman, commanded all executive agencies to disregard the unconstitutional provision of the statute.[7] The Justice Department explained the executive's position: "The President's duty to faithfully execute the law requires him not to observe a statute that is in conflict with the Constitution, the fundamental law of the land."[8]

On March 27, 1985, the United States District Court for the District of New Jersey upheld the constitutionality of the challenged provision of the law.[9] The Reagan administration, however, proclaimed that it was not obligated to follow the court's decision. Attorney General Edwin Meese declared that the executive, like the judiciary, has the duty to independently interpret the Constitution.

> Courts decide disputes between parties, not abstract questions of law. The President takes an oath to 'preserve, protect, and defend' the Constitution. This oath implies a duty to resist encroachments by the legislature upon his constitutional authority. Believing that the disputed provisions of the Competition in Contracting Act to be unconstitutional, the President has a duty not to execute them, especially because any other course would in all probability preclude obtaining a final judicial determination on the matter.[10]

Confronted with the executive's open defiance of a statute and a court decision upholding the law, the House Government Operations Committee voted a recommendation that "funds be withheld from the offices of the Attorney General and the director of the Office of Management and Budget until the Administration reverses its position."[11] The Reagan administration then announced that it would comply with the act, which subsequently was upheld as constitutional in a decision by the United States Court of Appeals for the Third Circuit.[12] The example is important because it reflects that even to this day there is support for the view that there is no authoritative interpreter of the Constitution and that each branch has equal right to decide constitutional questions.

In fact, in October 1986 Attorney General Edwin Meese gave a highly publicized speech in which he explicitly attacked the view that the judiciary is the ultimate arbiter of constitutional questions. Meese argued that each branch has equal authority to decide for itself the meaning of constitutional provisions. Meese remarked: "The Supreme Court, then, is not the only interpreter of the Constitution. Each of the three coordinate branches of government created and empowered by the Constitution—the executive and legislature no less than the judiciary—has a duty to interpret the Constitution in the performance of its official functions. In fact, every official takes an oath precisely to that effect."[13]

There is a second, distinct approach to the question of who is the authoritative interpreter of the Constitution: that for each part of the Constitution one branch of government is assigned the role of final arbiter of disputes, but it is not the same branch for all parts of the Constitution. Thus, each branch would be the authoritative interpreter for some constitutional provisions. Because the Constitution does not specify who should interpret the document, some institution would need to allocate interpretive authority among the branches of government.

Arguably, the second approach is the one that best describes the current system of constitutional interpretation. The judiciary has declared that cases arising under certain parts of the Constitution pose political questions and are matters to be decided by branches of government other than the courts. For example, the courts frequently have held that challenges to the president's conduct of foreign policy—such as whether the Vietnam War[14] or the current activities in Nicaragua[15] are unconstitutional—pose a political question not to be resolved by the judiciary. By declaring a matter to be a political question, the Court states that it is for the other branches of government to interpret the constitutional provisions in question and decide whether the Constitution is violated. The effect is the second approach: for each part of the Constitution, there is a final arbiter, but it is not the same branch for all constitutional provisions.

A third and final approach is to assign to one branch of government final authority for all constitutional interpretation. Although every governmental institution interprets the Constitution, one branch is assigned the role of umpire; its views resolve disputes and are final until reversed by constitutional amendment. Arguably, *Marbury v. Madison* endorses this approach. Chief Justice Marshall declared that "[i]t is emphatically the province and duty of the judicial department to say what the law is."[16] Similarly, in *United States v. Nixon*,[17] the Supreme Court held that it was the judiciary's duty to determine the meaning of the Constitution. In rejecting the president's claim that it was for the executive to determine the scope of executive privilege, Chief Justice Warren Burger, writing for the Court, stated:

> The President's counsel [reads] the Constitution as providing an absolute privilege of confidentiality for all Presidential communications. Many decisions of this Court, however, have unequivocally reaffirmed the holding of [*Marbury* v. *Madison*] that 'it is emphatically the province and duty of the judicial department to say what the law is.'[18]

Marbury v. Madison and *United States v. Nixon*, however, could be viewed as ambiguous and as not resolving the question of which of these three approaches is preferable. *Marbury* could be read narrowly as holding only that the Court is the final arbiter of the meaning of Article III of the Constitution, which defines the judicial power. The specific issue in *Marbury* was whether a section of the Judiciary Act of 1789 was inconsistent with Article III. Accordingly, *Marbury* could be interpreted, consistent with the second approach described above, as assigning to the judiciary only the responsibility for interpreting Article III. In fact, *Marbury* could even be seen as consistent with the first approach, that there is no final interpreter of the Constitution. By this view, *Marbury* simply holds that the judiciary may interpret the Constitution in deciding cases—it is one voice—and that it is not required to defer to legislative or executive interpretations. *Marbury*, according to this argument, says nothing about whether other branches of government are bound to follow the Court's interpretation. Chief Justice Marshall's declaration could be understood as emphatically declaring that the Courts do get a say. Under this approach, *Marbury v. Madison* says nothing about who is the authoritative interpreter of the Constitution.

Likewise, *United States v. Nixon* could be viewed as a limited ruling that the judiciary has the final say in cases raising the question of access to evidence necessary for criminal trials. The Court in *Nixon* emphasized the judiciary's special role in ensuring fair trials.

> The impediment that an absolute, unqualified privilege would place in the way of the primary constitutional duty of the Judicial Branch to do justice in criminal prosecutions would plainly conflict with the functions of the courts under Article III. . . . [T]o read the Article II powers of the President as providing an absolute privilege as against a subpoena essential to enforcement of criminal statutes on no more than a generalized claim of the public interest in confidentiality of non-military and non-diplomatic discussions would upset the constitutional balance of a 'workable government' and gravely impair the role of the courts under Article III.[19] The right to the production of all evidence at a criminal trial similarly has constitutional dimensions. [I]t is the manifest duty of the courts to vindicate [the Sixth and Fifth Amendment] guarantees and to accomplish that it is essential that all relevant and admissible evidence be produced.[20]

Thus, *United States v. Nixon* can be viewed as a narrow holding that the Court is the final arbiter in matters relating to the judiciary's powers under Article III.

Therefore, in determining who is the authoritative interpreter of the Constitution, it is necessary to choose among three approaches—that there is no final arbiter over cases presenting questions as to the Constitution's meaning; that each branch is the final arbiter for some constitutional provisions; and that one branch should be the final arbiter in all disputes over constitutional interpretation—each of which has some support. The next section of this chapter considers why the judiciary is better suited to engage in constitutional interpretation than Congress or the president. The final section of the chapter discusses why the judiciary should be the authoritative interpreter of all constitutional provisions—that is, why the third approach described above is preferable.

JUDICIAL INTERPRETATION

The federal courts, and especially the Supreme Court, are best suited to engage in constitutional interpretation for two separate, although interrelated, reasons. First, it is the institution most able to protect the Constitution's structure and values from majoritarian pressures. Second, the judiciary's decision-making method is preferable for constitutional interpretation and evolution.

Judiciary Protection from Majoritarian Pressures

Earlier, I argued that the Constitution exists to protect certain matters from majoritarian decision making. A society chooses to have a constitution, rather than just to be governed by statutes, in order to safeguard the structure of government and fundamental values from majority rule. In large part the decision to be governed by a constitution is animated by fear that a political majority could gain control of government and disenfranchise, and perhaps persecute, the minority. A constitution is unique primarily because of the difficulty of amending or altering it.

Accordingly, in deciding who should be the authoritative interpreter of the Constitution, a primary criterion should be determining which branch of government can best enforce the Constitution against the desires of political majorities. Under this criterion, the federal judiciary is the obvious choice. The judiciary is the institution most insulated from political pressures. Article III of the Constitution provides that federal court judges have life tenure, unless impeached, and that their salary may not be decreased during their terms of office. Unlike legislators or the president, federal judges never face reelection.

Furthermore, the method of federal judicial selection reinforces its antimajoritarian character. Unlike the House of Representatives, whose members are elected at the same time, or the Senate where one third of the members are chosen at each election, the Court's members are appointed one at a time, as vacancies arise. Therefore, generally, no single administration is able to appoint a majority of the Court or of the federal judiciary. The result is that the Court reflects many political views, not just that which is dominant at a particular time.

Certainly, it is not original or profound to observe that the judiciary's political insulation makes it well suited to uphold the Constitution. If anything is clear from the structure of the Constitution and the language of Article III, it is that the federal judiciary was given life tenure and salary protection precisely to ensure its independence. It, however, is worth elaborating why this insulation is so important in the process of constitutional evolution and interpretation.

First, the judiciary is the only institution obligated to hear the complaints of a single person. For the most part, the federal judiciary's jurisdiction is mandatory. Although the Supreme Court has discretion in choosing which cases to hear, with rare exceptions, a lower federal court must rule on every case properly filed with it.[21] Long ago, Chief Justice Marshall wrote, "[I]t is most true that this Court will not take jurisdiction if it should not but it is equally true that it must take jurisdiction if it should. . . . We have no more right to decline the exercise of jurisdiction which is given, than to usurp that which is not given.''[22]

In contrast, the legislature and the executive are under no duty to hear the complaints of a single person. An individual or small group complaining of an injustice to a legislator or the president could be ignored easily. If only a few constituents care about something, and if acting to help them would consume more time than it seems worth to get their votes in the future, they may be ignored. Moreover, if helping the few will hurt more constituents, the few are likely to be disregarded, no matter how just their cause. For example, prisoners are a constituency with relatively little political power. In many states, felons are permanently disenfranchised from voting, meaning that elected officials need worry little about meeting their demands.[23] Providing adequate resources for prisoners—sufficient money for their shelter, food, medical care, and training—requires expenditures of money unlikely to be popular with taxpayers. With no constituency to pressure for their humane treatment, the political process tends to ignore the rights and needs of prisoners.[24]

The courts, however, are obligated to rule on each person's properly filed complaint. It does not matter whether the litigant is rich or poor, powerful or powerless, incarcerated or not. The Constitution's purpose of protecting the minority from the tyranny of the majority is best fulfilled by an institution obligated to listen to the minority. Groups such as prisoners and mental patients are most likely to have their rights protected through an institution such as the judiciary that is required to address their complaints.[25] Similarly, the judiciary is much more likely than the legislature to listen to criminal defendants' claims that their rights were violated, or to poor individuals' objections that they are denied equal justice.

Second, the judiciary not only is most likely to listen to complaints, but it is also most likely to respond to them and apply the Constitution. The judiciary is supposed to decide each case on its own merits, subject only to the accepted norm that like cases should be treated alike.[26] Therefore, in every case where there is an allegation that the Constitution is being violated, the judiciary is obligated, if it has jurisdiction and if there is no way to decide the case on nonconstitutional grounds, to issue a constitutional ruling.[27] The legislature, by contrast, need not decide each matter before it on its own merits. Logrolling and voting trade-offs are accepted parts of the legislative process.[28] Although legislators are forbidden by their oath of office to enact laws that they believe to be unconstitutional, they are not required to provide a remedy every time someone complains that government is doing something unconstitutional. Only the judiciary is obligated to respond to unconstitutional practices—something that makes the courts an ideal forum for ensuring that the Constitution is upheld.

Third, the judiciary is most willing to enforce the Constitution when faced with strong pressures from political majorities. Even if the legislature and executive would listen to all claims and respond on the merits, they are still less likely to uphold the Constitution when faced with intense reactions from their constituents. The judiciary's insulation from politics makes it best suited to enforce the Constitution. It is this insulation that caused Alexis de Tocqueville to remark that "the power vested in the American courts of justice of pronouncing a statute unconstitutional forms one of the most powerful barriers that have been devised against the tyranny of political assemblies."[29]

The argument is not that legislators are likely to act in bad faith and disregard their oath to uphold the Constitution (although there may be cases where this does occur). Rather, the point is that constitutional interpretation inherently requires choices as to what the Constitution should mean. Constitutional interpretation requires decisions as to how the abstract values stated in the Constitution are best applied in specific situations. These choices are best made by an institution whose primary commitment is to the Constitution, not to gaining reelection. Owen Fiss observes that "[l]egislatures are not ideologically committed or institutionally suited to search for the meaning of constitutional values, but instead see their primary function in terms of registering the actual, current preferences of the people."[30] The judiciary, much more than the political branches of government, is to be trusted in deciding whether the Constitution should protect the speech activities of a politically unpopular group, such as the Nazi party. The judiciary, committed to upholding the First Amendment, and not faced with intense pressure from constituents, is in a better position to decide whether school prayer violates the Constitution. The judiciary, relatively insulated from intense lobbying, is better suited to deciding whether the right of privacy includes the right of a woman to decide whether to have an abortion.

The best institution for interpreting the Constitution is thus not the one that most reflects the current preferences of the majority. Rather, constitutional interpretation is best done by a politically insulated body. Harry Wellington explains:

> If society were to design an institution which had the job of finding society's set of moral principles and determining how they bear on concrete situations, that institution would be sharply different from one charged with proposing policies. The latter institution would be constructed with the understanding that it was to respond to the people's exercise of political power. . . . The former would be insulated from pressure. It would provide an environment conducive to rumination, reflection and analysis.[31]

Constitutional interpretation is a process of deciding what values are so fundamental that they should be safeguarded from political majorities. It makes little sense to allow the majoritarian process to decide what should be protected from itself. No matter what the appropriate process of identifying constitutional values—finding the natural law,[32] articulating the "deep consensus,"[33] applying traditions[34]—the judiciary's insulation and commitment to decisions based on the merits make it best suited for such interpretation. Alexander Bickel remarked that "courts have certain capacities for dealing with matters of principle that legislatures and the executive do not possess. Judges have, or should have, the leisure, the training, and the insulation to follow the ways of the scholar in pursuing the ends of government. This is crucial in sorting out the enduring values of a society.''[35] Constitutional interpretation requires an institution to serve as the nation's moral conscience; an institution responsible for identifying values so important that they should not be sacrificed and reminding the country when it is violating its own most cherished values. The Supreme Court frequently has defined its role in exactly these terms, as a moral conscience.[36]

Finally, the legislature is to be trusted least when the question is the constitutionality of a statute that it enacted. Constitutional values will not be protected from majority rule if the legislature can both enact laws and determine their constitutionality. Allowing review by another branch of government creates a check that otherwise would not exist. The executive veto provides something of a check; however, Congress can override a veto. Moreover, the president is electorally accountable and may reflect the same pressures as Congress. Thus, the judiciary is most detached and has the least involvement in the enactment of laws or the implementation of policies. The Court's only self-interest is in enhancing its long-term powers. Certainly, the judiciary's institutional self-interest justifies fear of its deciding cases to aggrandize its own powers. I would argue, however, that in resolving specific controversies it is better to trust an institution with only long-term interests than one with immediate interests in the outcome of the matter.

In sum, once it is decided that society should be governed by a constitution in order to make certain matters less amenable to majoritarian control, judicial review is a desirable mechanism for interpreting and enforcing the document.

The Judiciary's Decision-Making Methods

In addition to the conclusion that the courts are most able to protect the Constitution from majoritarian pressures, the methods of judicial decision making make it the best institution for constitutional interpretation. The judiciary is unique in that it is the only institution committed to arriving at decisions based entirely on arguments and reasoning.[37] Executive and legislative officials frequently offer no formal explanations for their decisions, and even when they provide statements, they usually do not purport to be comprehensive. The judicial method is a process of hearing arguments (written and oral) from the parties, reaching decisions based on the arguments, and justifying the results with a written opinion stating reasons for the decision. Although neither the Constitution nor any statute compels a court to write and publish opinions, publicly stated reasons for decision are embedded in the U.S. legal system.[38] In fact, it has long been recognized that the ''traditional means of protecting the public from judicial fiat . . . [are] that judges give reasons for their results.''[39]

The Court must write an opinion demonstrating that its decision is not arbitrary. The Court must explain both why the values it is protecting are worthy of constitutional status and how those values are embodied in legal principles.[40] Additionally, the Court must explain why its decision is consistent with prior holdings, is legitimately distinguishable from precedents, or justifies overruling conflicting cases.[41]

In contrast, the legislature and the executive need not follow any particular decision-making process. Neither Congress nor the president is required, either by law or by tradition, to state reasons for its decisions. Although Congress produces legislative histories and the president issues executive proclamations, only the judiciary is committed to reaching all decisions by logical reasoning from principles, rather than results based on political considerations. A legislature is allowed, even expected, to make arbitrary choices unsupported by a guiding principle. Even if all the Supreme Court's constitutional decisions are merely hunches or reflections of personal predilections,[42] the Court must still justify those conclusions in legally acceptable terms.[43] Moreover, only the judiciary is committed to following precedent in reaching its decisions.

For several reasons, constitutional interpretation is best done by an institution, such as the judiciary, committed to deciding issues based on arguments and reason. First, the judiciary's method helps ensure that the Constitution will serve as a constitutive document uniting the country. In announcing its decisions, the Court describes how it is applying the values of the Constitution. In deciding a case under the First Amendment, the judiciary explains why its result is consistent with society's commitment to freedom of speech. In ruling on a matter of presidential power, the Court explains why its holding preserves the principle of separation of powers. In other words, the judiciary is reinforcing the Constitution's underlying norms. The Court's opinion reminds the country of its most precious values; it ensures that the values are not forgotten in the press of making specific decisions.

Furthermore, the judicial opinion links the result in a particular case to the Constitution. In this way, it is shown that it is the Constitution that is governing. The Constitution remains at the center of society and performs its constitutive function. If results were reached without explanation of their relationship to the Constitution, it would be easier to assume that the Constitution was being ignored, and over time, the Constitution would seem progressively less important for society.

The application of general values to specific cases helps people to understand the central, abstract values, encouraging the internalization of these values and reinforcing that which unites a diverse country. Girardeau Spann writes that "[w]hen courts expound constitutional provisions, they restate society's fundamental values in concrete understandable terms, enabling individuals and institutions to incorporate these values into their conduct."[44]

In short, there is less reason for the people to believe that the legislature or the executive reached its decision based on consideration of the Constitution, rather than on political interests and expediencies. In viewing legislative and executive decisions, which generally are not justified with a written opinion, there is no way for the people to understand that constitutional values are governing. By contrast, the judiciary's commitment to decisions on the merits, and its statement of reasons for its decision, reminds the people that the Constitution—that which unites them—is governing.

Second, the judiciary's method increases the legitimacy of results in particular cases and therefore increases the likelihood that the Constitution will be complied with. The written opinion demonstrates that the result is not arbitrary or just the result of political compromise. The judicial decision shows that the ruling can be justified by analysis and argument.

At the very least, this helps the loser accept the result because he or she is shown that it is not capricious. John Dewey explained that a "rational statement which formulates grounds and exposes connecting or logical links . . . [is] an alternative to arbitrary [decisions] . . . accepted by the parties . . . only because of the authority of the [decision maker]".[45] People are more likely to respect a decision based on reasons than one that appears to be a purely arbitrary choice.

Furthermore, the very fact that the decision is explicitly linked to the Constitution increases the likelihood that it will be respected and complied with. Decisions that might otherwise be opposed, and thus threaten the stability of the government, gain support from the realization that the result is based on constitutional interpretation. People who disagree with the result, but support the Constitution and judicial review, face a situation labeled by social psychologists as *cognitive dissonance*.[46] There is a tension between their negative beliefs about the outcome of a case and their positive attitudes about the institution and its basis for decision. Some people might resolve this dissonance by changing their mind and accepting the Court's decision. At the least, their support for the government's structures and processes might lessen their opposition to the particular result.

Additionally, the judiciary's independence increases respect for its decisions. The strict standards of judicial ethics, ensuring that judges do not participate if they have any personal interest, encourage people to believe that the result does not reflect the self-interest of the decision maker. The political insulation of the judiciary, described above, helps people to accept that their loss was based on a consideration of principle, not on the fact that they were politically too powerless. If the legislature interpreted the Constitution and ruled against them, it would be much easier to attribute their loss to insufficient clout or political influence. Again, the effect of the judicial ruling is to increase the respect for the decision.

By defusing opposition to constitutional decisions, judicial opinions increase the likelihood that the decision will be complied with. In other words, society is more likely to accept and comply with the result that the Constitution is interpreted as requiring; there is a greater likelihood that the Constitution's protections will be implemented. In the long term, this reinforces the appearance that the Constitution is governing and helps the Constitution to remain at the center of society.

For example, if the legislature enacted a law protecting the right of a group to protest, its decision might be regarded as arbitrarily favoring demonstrators over the community, and it might be unclear whether the statute is based on constitutional interpretation. However, a judicial decision will state explicit reasons for the result and explain how the result is based on the First Amendment. This process increases the likelihood that the First Amendment will be complied with and reinforces freedom of speech as a fundamental value for society.

Thus, the very existence of an opinion, linking the result to the Constitution and issued from an independent judiciary, increases compliance with the Constitution. Moreover, the written opinion allows the Court to attempt to persuade those who would otherwise disagree. For example, the Court can appeal to a widely shared value and explain why the result follows from it. In interpreting the Constitution, the Court explains the implications of society's general values for particular cases. In the desegregation cases, for instance, the Court declared that given society's commitment to equality, racial separation was unacceptable. In *Brown v. Board of Education* the Court appealed to the widely shared belief that quality education is essential and argued that it could never be achieved in segregated schools.[47] In the abortion cases, the Court explained why accepted notions of privacy and personal autonomy require allowing women to choose whether to have abortions.[48]

History shows that judicial decisions do have persuasive effect. Popular opinion polls show a substantial increase in public support for desegregation and legalized abortions after the Supreme Court's decisions.[49] The overall result is to increase compliance with the Constitution and reinforce the importance of the Constitution for the society.

Third, the judiciary's method is preferable for constitutional interpretation because it exposes errors and facilitates the correction of mistakes. The competing arguments of the parties help to ensure that all relevant factors are considered by the courts.[50] Furthermore, the process of writing an opinion requires the Court to think through its decision and be able to justify the results. Errors in reasoning can be revealed to a court as it tries to explain its decision. Imagine two types of decision making. In one the decider only declares the result with no explanation. In the other the decider must explain the basis for the result. Virtually everyone would agree that under the latter approach decision makers would be more careful in reaching their results, and their increased thoughtfulness likely would prevent errors.

Furthermore, the process of articulating reasons for a decision facilitates criticism, which helps to correct mistakes. If just the result is announced, there is nothing to criticize except the outcome. Without an explanation for a decision, it is impossible to argue with someone's reasoning or to expose errors in their premises. Judicial opinions that explicitly state their premises and their logic allow commentators and future litigants to argue that errors were made or to point to inconsistencies in the reasoning of various decisions. As a result, mistakes can be identified and corrected. There are numerous cases in which the Supreme Court has reversed itself and overruled precedents.[51] It is likely that in many of these instances the reversals reflected the exposure of errors in the earlier decisions. For example, when the Court reversed its restrictive interpretations of the commerce clause, it did so by directly attacking the reasoning of the earlier cases and pointing out the errors in the earlier holdings.[52]

Additionally, the statement of reasons in an opinion facilitates constitutional evolution because the justification helps future courts to identify when the earlier decision is out-of-date. In other words, if the reasons are known, it is possible to identify when the reasons are no longer applicable. *Betts v. Brady* was overruled by *Gideon v. Wainwright* when it became clear that the reasoning in the former case, especially its view of federalism, was inconsistent with other decisions and anachronistic.[53] When the reasons are stated, inconsistencies become apparent and can be remedied. In short, the judicial process of written reasoned elaboration is best for interpretation because it aids in the identification and correction of mistakes.

Fourth, the judiciary's written opinions announce constitutional standards, permitting government to know what it must do to act constitutionally. Government officials can shape their actions because they know in advance what is, and is not, permissible. The Constitution's mandates can be enforced much more effectively when its requirements are clearly articulated.

For example, in *Roe v. Wade* the Court instructed the legislature as to what type of regulation of abortions is permissible in each trimester of pregnancy.[54] Some have criticized the Court's opinion in *Roe*, arguing that it was poor opinion drafting for the judiciary to issue a decision that so closely resembled a statute. But the alternative to the Court's approach would have been to declare the statutes before it unconstitutional without spelling out what types of regulations would be deemed permissible. Subsequently, legislatures would try different types of statutes, and through a series of decisions, ultimately the Court's trimester distinctions would emerge. By describing the appropriate standards at the outset, the Court was able to provide clear guidance to legislatures, increasing the likelihood that constitutional laws would be enacted.

Similarly, in *Miranda v. Arizona*[55] the Court told police officers exactly what they needed to do in order to prevent coerced confessions. In *Brandenburg v. Ohio*[56] the Court announced the circumstances under which a person can be punished for advocating illegality. In *Miller v. California*[57] the Court described what materials may be deemed obscene and censored. In *Lemon v. Kurtzman*[58] the Court announced a three-part test for determining whether a government action is an unconstitutional establishment of religion.

The examples are endless. Although the standards in these cases can be criticized, what is important is the very existence of the criteria announced in the decisions. The standards provide notice to government officials as to when and how they may act. The standards give the Constitution concrete meaning. Without written opinions, it would be much harder for officials to decide what they could and could not do. As a result, unconstitutional activity would be much more frequent.

In addition, the requirement that standards be articulated helps the judiciary to identify instances where an approach cannot work precisely because standards cannot be formulated. Recently, the Court announced that it was overruling its decision in *National League of Cities v. Usery* because it could not formulate a workable test for determining what congressional activities infringe state sovereignty.[59] In *National League of Cities* the Court spoke of the Tenth Amendment's reserving to the states a zone of activities ''traditionally'' left to the states and ''integral'' to the states' existence.[60] Nine years later, after numerous decisions construing the meaning of this test, the Court concluded that it could not devise a principle for determining what are traditional or integral state activities.[61] The Court overruled *National League of Cities*, reflecting how written opinions aid in the identification of errors in constitutional reasoning and the improvement in constitutional doctrine.

Fifth, judicial opinions facilitate stare decisis, respect and adherence to precedent in decision making. Michael Moore explains the values of stare decisis:

> Equality, in its guise as formal justice, is served by a court treating like cases alike. Liberty is advanced by the enhanced predictability such consistent interpretation makes possible. To the extent that people do rely on court precedent, substantive fairness is served as well by attaching some weight to past decisions. Finally, efficiency may be furthered by some doctrine of precedent operating; for the doctrine of precedent forecloses some issues from being reargued and redecided, encourages settlements, and generally allows more focused litigation.[62]

At the very least, the judiciary is best suited for constitutional interpretation because it is the only branch of government that follows precedent in reaching decisions. Moreover, written opinions help future courts know when a decision is controlling and when it is distinguishable. By articulating the facts that are central to reaching a decision, it is possible to know which future cases are alike, and should be treated alike, and which are different.[63]

Because of precedents, constitutional interpretation is not just a series of random decisions based on intuitions in particular cases.[64] Instead, constitutional provisions are given meaning that grows increasingly detailed over time. The precedents provide a justification for future decisions, which allow courts to explain their results as nonarbitrary, increasing compliance to, and the legitimacy of, the decisions.

Sixth and finally, the judiciary's method facilitates the moral reasoning that should be a part of constitutional decision making. As explained previously, constitutional interpretation involves deciding what values are sufficiently important that they should be protected from political majorities. Those who believe that there is a moral reality—an objectively true set of moral precepts—would say that the Court should identify those values that are true and protect them from political pressures.[65] Michael Perry, who identifies himself as a moral realist, provides a persuasive argument that the Court can serve as a moral prophet, helping society evolve toward moral truths. Perry writes that the ''politically insulated judiciary is more likely when the human rights issue is a deeply controversial one, to move us in the direction of a right answer . . . than is the political process left to its own devices which tend to resolve issues by reflective, mechanical reference to established moral conventions.''[66] Perry argues that judicial review has ''functioned, on balance, as an instrument of deepening moral insight and of moral growth.''[67]

From the perspective of the moral realist, judicial decisions provide a dialogue—with commentators, other branches of government, subsequent litigants, and future courts. This dialogue helps identify errors, for the reasons described above, and therefore helps society toward finding moral truths. Because of its insulation, the Court can serve as a moral leader.

Many who deny the existence of a moral reality believe that values arise from shared premises. Under this view the judicial process provides a way of identifying shared values and reasoning from them. In other words the ''Court's task is to ascertain the weight of the principle in conventional morality and to convert the moral principle into a legal one by connecting it with the body of constitutional law.''[68]

Some believe that the Supreme Court should determine the values deserving constitutional protection by looking to U.S. traditions,[69] whereas others argue that the Court should identify ''deeply embedded cultural values.''[70] Regardless of the specific approach, the Court is best suited to identify values worthy of constitutional protection. Because of its insulation from politics, the judiciary is most able to determine what tradition requires and to articulate the content of the deep consensus. The Court can show society the conclusions that follow from its values.

In any event, from both of these perspectives the appropriate moral standards are best identified through a process of rational exploration and decision. The judicial process most ensures rationality because of its requirement for argument and elaboration. Furthermore, ''the Court's decisions . . . stimulate better ultimate choices, because of their tendency to require the polity to think again about whether it really does wish to pursue the policies rejected by the Court.''[71]

In sum, the judiciary's method make it best suited for constitutional interpretation. Additionally, the courts are preferable to the executive and the legislature for constitutional interpretation because they are the most insulated from political pressures.

WHY THE JUDICIARY SHOULD BE THE FINAL ARBITER

For the most part, government operates without a need for constitutional interpretation. Many provisions of the Constitution are sufficiently clear and specific to provide adequate instructions for the conduct of government. For example, there is usually no dispute as to how federal government officials are elected, the length of their terms of office, or the procedures they are to follow in enacting laws.[72] There are, however, many constitutional provisions that are ambiguous and lack the degree of specificity found in sections of the Constitution dealing with the selection process. Because of constitutional provisions that are not completely clear, constitutional conflicts do arise—controversies posing questions as to the proper meaning of specific constitutional provisions and questions about how to resolve conflicts among various sections of the document. The question posed at the beginning of this chapter is, How should these conflicts be resolved? Put another way, who should be the authoritative interpreter of the Constitution?

The worst approach is if no branch of government is authoritative, with all constitutional questions resolved by political power and compromise. Under this approach, the executive and legislature would be under no obligation to follow judicial interpretations of the Constitution. Each branch could interpret the Constitution for itself, without regard to the others' views. As such, the legislature and executive could institute a policy of persecuting minorities and simply ignore judicial declarations invalidating their policy. The judiciary's functions as an antimajoritarian check would be lost if the politically accountable branches could disregard virtually all judicial rulings.

Furthermore, the Constitution would not have an articulated meaning. There would be a series of Court decisions, some followed, some not. The ultimate results would simply reflect the respective powers of the various branches and not the Constitution's mandates. The benefits of the judiciary's method of decision making would be lost, as the other branches would be authoritative for many constitutional decisions.

Constitutional crises would be commonplace if no branch of government were the authoritative interpreter of the Constitution. For example, what would happen if the judiciary declared an executive practice unconstitutional and enjoined it, but the executive steadfastly maintained it was constitutional and ignored the injunction? The example is not farfetched—if no branch were regarded as authoritative in constitutional interpretation, what would have happened after *United States v. Nixon* when the judiciary and the president disagreed over the proper scope of executive privilege?[73] One possibility is that Congress could try to impeach the president for ignoring a judicial order. This option is obviously extreme, highly disruptive of government, and unlikely to be used except in rare circumstances. Alternatively, the Court could hold the president in contempt and impose judicial sanctions on the chief executive. It is unclear whether it is constitutional to impose such sanctions on a sitting president.[74] Furthermore, because it is unlikely that the Court will implement its own punishment for contempt (having the Court marshal arrest the president and hold him or her in jail), the judiciary needs to depend either on the executive to act against the president or on impeachment. Any of these options would provoke major constitutional crises.

To develop the meaning of the Constitution in an orderly, coherent manner and ensure that its mandates are observed, society needs an authoritative interpreter of the Constitution. The previous section described why the Supreme Court, and the federal judiciary, is best suited to serve in this role. Now I want to argue that the Court should be the authoritative interpreter of the meaning of *all* constitutional provisions.

Currently, there are many parts of the Constitution that the Court refuses to interpret. For these provisions, the political branches are the authoritative interpreters. For example, in a series of decisions the Supreme Court has said that certain constitutional challenges only state a "generalized grievance" and therefore no plaintiff has standing to sue. In *United States v. Richardson*,[75] the plaintiff claimed that statutes providing for the secrecy of the Central Intelligence Agency budget violated the Constitution's requirement for a regular statement and account of all government expenditures. The Court refused to rule on whether the challenged statute violated the Constitution. The Court held that the plaintiff's case only presented a "generalized grievance," and hence the plaintiff lacked standing to sue. The Court concluded that because the plaintiff could not show that his personal rights were violated, but instead only could claim injury as a citizen and taxpayer, the Court should not rule. The Court held that ultimately the statements and accounts clause was a part of the Constitution to be enforced not by the judiciary but rather by the political process.

> It can be argued that if respondent is not permitted to litigate this issue, no one can do so. In a very real sense, the absence of any particular individual or class to litigate these claims gives support to the argument that the subject matter is committed to the surveillance of Congress, and ultimately to the political process.[76]

Similarly, in *Schlesinger v. Reservists Committee to Stop the War*, the plaintiffs sued to enjoin members of Congress from serving in the military reserves.[77] Article I, section 6, of the Constitution prevents a senator or representative from holding civil offices. Again, the Court refused to rule on the plaintiffs' claim of unconstitutionality, holding that the matter posed a generalized grievance; that is, plaintiffs could only allege injuries as citizens and taxpayers. The Court concluded that ultimately it was for the political process to enforce this constitutional provision.

> Respondents seek to have the Judicial Branch to compel the Executive Branch to act in conformity with the Incompatibility Clause, an interest shared by all citizens. . . . [The] claimed nonobservance [with the Constitution] adversely affect[s] only the generalized interests of all citizens in constitutional governance and that is an abstract injury. . . . Our system of government leaves many crucial decisions to the political process. The assumption that if respondents have no standing to sue, no one would have standing, is not a reason to find standing.[78]

Likewise, a few years later in *Valley Forge Christian College v. Americans United for Church and State*,[79] the Court refused to rule on a claim that the federal government violated the First Amendment's prohibition against government establishment of religion. The government was alleged to have given over $500,000 worth of surplus property to a religious school. Despite the claim that a key provision of the Bill of Rights was violated, the Court held that taxpayers did not have sufficient injury to sue in federal court. Because it is difficult to imagine anyone's having a more specific injury than these taxpayers, the Court could never rule on the constitutionality of the executive's action. Justice Rehnquist, writing for the majority, stated:

> The complaint in this case shared a common deficiency with those in *Schlesinger* and *Richardson*. Although they claim that the Constitution has been violated, they claim nothing else. . . . We simply cannot see that respondents have alleged an injury of any kind, economic or otherwise, sufficient to confer standing.[80]

The effect of decisions such as *Richardson*, *Schlesinger*, and *Valley Forge* is to assign to the political branches the responsibility for interpreting and enforcing certain constitutional provisions. Although the plaintiffs claim that the government is blatantly violating the explicit words of the Constitution, the Court concluded that the matter was for the political process and not the judiciary to decide.[81]

These decisions leaving constitutional interpretation to other branches of government cannot be understood as conclusions required by the text of Article III, which limits the judiciary to resolving "cases and controversies." Article III limits the judiciary to cases and controversies, but there is nothing that says that cases such as these do not fit within that phrase.[82] The *cases* before the Court and the *controversies* over the meaning of specific constitutional provisions are sufficient to meet the textual requirements of Article III. Moreover, the Court in subsequent decisions has explicitly stated that the bar against federal courts hearing generalized grievances does *not* arise from the Constitution but rather is entirely prudential, reflecting what the Court deems to be prudent judicial policy.[83]

In addition to these standing rules, the political question doctrine allocates interpretation of some constitutional provisions to the electorally accountable branches of government. By declaring certain subject matter to pose a political question, the Court states that it will not rule on claims of unconstitutionality. The political branches are given the ultimate say as to the meaning of those provisions. In other words the political question doctrine is invoked by the courts to avoid ruling on a matter when it deems the resolution of the controversy to be committed to another branch of government.[84] Historically, the political question doctrine can be traced to Chief Justice John Marshall's opinion in *Marbury v. Madison*.

> By the Constitution of the United States, the President is invested with certain important political powers, in the exercise of which he is to use his own discretion, and is accountable only to his country in his political character and to his own conscience. [A]nd whatever opinion may be entertained of the manner in which the discretion may be used, there still

exists, and can exist, no power to control that discretion. The subjects are political. . . . [B]eing entrusted to the executive, the decision of the executive is conclusive. . . . Questions, in their nature political, or which are, by the constitution and laws, submitted to the executive, can never be made in this court.[85]

For example, the Supreme Court has held repeatedly that constitutional challenges to the conduct of foreign policy pose a political question.[86] In *Goldwater v. Carter*,[87] the Court refused to rule on the constitutionality of President Carter's rescission of the Taiwan treaty. Although it was claimed that the president's unilateral rescission violated the Constitution and usurped the Senate's powers, the Court, in a plurality opinion, concluded that the case "presented a nonjusticiable political dispute that should be left for resolution by the Executive and Legislative branches of government."[88] Similarly, most cases challenging the constitutionality of the Vietnam War were dismissed on political question grounds.[89]

In addition, the Court has held that cases arising under Article IV, section 4's requirement that "[t]he United States shall guarantee to every State in this Union a Republican form of Government" pose a political question.[90] Again, this means that even claims of blatant violations will not be reviewed by the judiciary but instead will be left to the political process. The Court also ruled that questions related to the legality of constitutional amendments are to be left entirely to the political process.[91]

The net effect of these justiciability doctrines is that numerous constitutional provisions are interpreted and enforced only through the political process. This result is inconsistent with the most fundamental purpose of the Constitution: safeguarding matters from majority rule. Each part of the Constitution exists to protect something from easy change by political majorities. The statements and accounts clause, the incompatibility clause, the establishment clause, and the sections of the Constitution pertaining to foreign policy decision-making create certain requirements for the operation of government. These requirements are placed in the Constitution because they are deemed so important that government should not be able to ignore them or to alter them easily.

However, by assigning interpretation of these clauses to the political branches, their antimajoritarian function is undermined. The political branches are given exclusive authority to determine if there has been a constitutional violation. The legislature and executive can completely disregard a constitutional provision, which they arguably did in *Richardson*, *Schlesinger*, and *Valley Forge*. Moreover, the political branches that are accused of violating the Constitution are allowed to judge the constitutionality of their own behavior. No check exists. Nor is there the reasoned elaboration of the meaning of these constitutional provisions, something only the judiciary provides.

In dismissing cases because they present a generalized grievance or a political question, the Court repeatedly states that resolution of the specific constitutional controversy is left ultimately to the political process. This is undesirable because the whole point of placing something in a constitution is to insulate it from the political process. In essence, some constitutional provisions are made meaningless.

The inappropriateness of allocating constitutional decision making to the political branches can be demonstrated by considering a recent proposal by Jesse Choper that all questions of separation of powers be deemed political questions and therefore not reviewable by the courts.[92] Choper contends that the courts should declare that litigation contesting the constitutionality of presidential actions is nonjusticiable.

> The federal judiciary should not decide constitutional questions concerning the respective powers of Congress and the president vis-à-vis one another; rather, the ultimate constitutional issues of whether executive action (or inaction) violates the prerogatives of Congress . . . should be held to be non-justiciable, their final resolution to be remitted to the interplay of the national political process.[93]

Choper's approach would leave all questions of separation of powers to resolution by the political branches.

Such an approach is inconsistent with a Constitution committed to protecting separation of powers. The Constitution creates the structure of government, in part, to prevent those in power from increasing their authority. Yet Choper's approach would allow the president to be given almost unlimited authority, usurping virtually all power allocated to Congress in the Constitution, so long as Congress agrees. For example, under Choper's approach, the Court could not declare unconstitutional the president's seizure of steel mills[94] or the president's impoundment of congressionally appropriated funds.[95] Unless Congress acted to stop the president, the executive could completely disregard the Constitution's allocation of powers to Congress.

Thus, Choper's approach sanctions an almost total transfer of legislative power to the executive so long as Congress does not object. Repeated congressional inaction would result in a tremendous shift of power to the White House. Such a growth in executive authority could threaten the entire system of checks and balances. As Justice Felix Frankfurter noted: "The accretion of dangerous power does not come in a day. It does come, however slowly, from the generative force of unchecked disregard of the restrictions that fence in even the most disinterested assertion of authority."[96]

Moreover, Choper's approach assumes that Congress has the authority to restrain unconstitutional presidential actions. If the president acts unconstitutionally, say by seizing an industry or impounding funds, what can Congress do? Congress could pass a statute directing the president to cease the unconstitutional activity. However, the president could veto the law. This means that Congress could stop the president only if two thirds of both houses of Congress were willing to act. Political realities, including support for a president from his or her own political party, might make such an override of a veto unlikely.

History shows that Congress is generally unwilling to restrain the president.[97] "[C]ongressional review of executive policy-making is sporadic, and the executive frequently makes policy without Congress' either taking responsibility for it or repudiating it. The result is a system sharply skewed towards executive policy-making."[98] Paul Gewirtz explains many reasons why Congress may not act even though a majority of its members disagree with the president:

> [W]hen Congress is faced with an executive policy that is in place and functioning, Congress often acquiesces in the executive's action for reasons which have nothing to do with the majority's preferences on the policy issues involved. . . . In such a situation, Congress may not want to be viewed as disruptive; or Congresspersons may not want to embarrass the President; or Congress may want to score political points by attacking the executive's action rather than accepting political responsibility for some action itself; or Congresspersons may be busy running for reelection or tending to constituents' individual problems; or Congress may be lazy and prefer another recess.[99]

In short, Choper's approach permits separation of powers to be rendered nonexistent. The Constitution's function of preventing the accumulation of power in one branch of government would be undermined. I believe that the judiciary should resolve claims that the President is acting in excess of the Constitution's grant of power to the executive and unconstitutionally usurping legislative power. Judicial review exists to protect the Constitution—including the provisions defining the structure of government—from majority rule. To ensure that the Constitution is protected from majoritarian pressures, the judiciary should be the authoritative interpreter of all provisions. The judiciary should abandon the justiciability doctrines, such as the generalized grievance standing requirement and the political question doctrine, which allocate interpretation of certain parts of the Constitution to the political branches. The courts should be the authoritative arbiter of the entire Constitution.

Several objections might be made to this conclusion. First, it might be argued that my approach is inconsistent with 200 years of judicial declarations that certain subjects pose a political question. Although I could respond by dismissing this objection as normatively irrelevant, I contend that it is Choper's approach that misconstrues the historical meaning of the political question doctrine when he claims that it should prevent the courts from deciding whether the president has usurped another branch's powers. The political question doctrine, as set forth in *Marbury v. Madison*, provides that the courts should not review an official's performance of duties in which he or she has discretion.[100] Only the exercise of lawful discretion should be unreviewable. Claims that an official is acting without constitutional authority or violating a constitutional provision are not political questions.

Phrased differently, in each case involving a separation of powers issue, the question is whether the official has the power to act and, if so, whether the act is discretionary or mandated by some external authority. The inquiries of whether the official has the authority to act or an obligation to act in a particular manner are not political questions. Only if the act is discretionary is the official's conduct an unreviewable political question. As the Court declared in *Baker v. Carr*:

> Deciding whether a matter has in any measure been committed by the Constitution to another branch of government, of whether the action of that branch exceeds whatever authority has been committed, is itself a delicate exercise in constitutional interpretation, *and is a responsibility* of this Court as ultimate interpreter of the Constitution.[101]

Thus, the political question doctrine simply precludes review of the exercise of discretionary power; it does not prevent a court from determining whether the executive's conduct is an unconstitutional usurpation of judicial or legislative power. Justice William Brennan explained that the political question "doctrine does not pertain when a court is faced with the *antecedent* question whether a political branch has been constitutionally delegated as the repository of political decision-making power. The issue of decision-making authority must be resolved as a matter of constitutional law, not political discretion; accordingly it falls within the competence of the courts."[102]

In other words, the president has discretion in choosing whom to appoint to office or whether to veto a bill. These decisions are obviously not judicially reviewable. These matters are what should be deemed political questions. The political question doctrine does not, and should not, require the judiciary to ignore claims that the president is violating the Constitution.

Second, it can be argued that the political question doctrine and allocation of constitutional decision making to the legislature or executive is desirable because other branches of government have special expertise for some subject matters. For example, it is argued that the president has special expertise in the area of foreign policy.[103] However, this only justifies deference to the executive's foreign policy choices and careful consideration of the president's expert opinions. There is no reason why the president's expertise requires complete abdication and total deference when there are allegations of unconstitutional actions.

Moreover, in most instances, the political question doctrine is invoked in situations where expertise is completely irrelevant. The question of whether the Vietnam War was unconstitutional because the president was waging war without a congressional declaration does not turn on foreign policy expertise. Rather, it poses a fairly standard constitutional question concerning the meaning of two abstract provisions: the president's power as commander in chief and the congressional power to declare war. Similarly, expertise does not justify judicial abdication in the generalized grievance cases where the Court defers to the political process. The question of whether it is unconstitutional for members of Congress to serve in the army reserves, the issue in the *Schlesinger* case, turns on an interpretation of a constitutional provision, not factual information possessed by an expert. The *Valley Forge* case required an interpretation of the establishment clause of the First Amendment—something at which the Court is most expert.

Third, it can be argued that there are some instances where the stakes are too high and the basis for judicial decisions are too unclear to permit court involvement. An example of this would be impeachment. If a president were impeached, should the Court review the case to determine if there were a "high crime or misdemeanor" or whether the proper procedures specified in Article I were followed? The argument is that the Court would exacerbate, not solve, a constitutional crisis if it declared unconstitutional the impeachment of a president. It is a nightmare to imagine a situation where the House impeached a president and the Senate voted for conviction, but the Court ruled that the president should remain in office. Thus, to avoid this possibility, it could be argued that the judiciary should deem itself to lack authority to review all impeachment cases.

Yet, I would argue that this is an argument for great caution and judicial deference, not for total noninvolvement no matter what the circumstances. What if a president were impeached for an act which was completely lawful and within his constitutional powers? Although perhaps unlikely, probability of occurrence is not the relevant test because it also is unlikely that the Court would declare an impeachment unconstitutional in the absence of compelling circumstances. Also, it must not be forgotten that Andrew Johnson was impeached and almost removed from office for exercising the Chief Executive's prerogative to remove Cabinet officers. Or what if the Senate declared a president to be convicted by less than a two-thirds vote, for example, on the basis of a committee's determination?

In such circumstances, judicial review is essential. It is primarily necessary to uphold the Constitution. The provisions dealing with impeachment become meaningless if the legislature can impeach by whatever procedures or standards it desires. Judicial involvement is also necessary to uphold the separation of powers. If the legislature could disregard the Constitution and impeach whenever it chooses, there is a danger of a great shift in power towards the legislature and a threat to the structure of government.

Again, to say that there is a judicial role does not speak to the substantive standards of review that the Court should use. Especially in situations like impeachment, great judicial deference on the merits is appropriate. But there is an enormous difference between automatically denying review in every case and, in contrast, hearing the case with a strong presumption in favor of the legislature's action.

Fourth, my conclusion that the Court should be the authoritative arbiter of all constitutional meaning can be challenged by arguing that the Court's self-interest should disqualify it from ruling on certain matters. Specifically, because constitutional amendments are the only way to overturn a Supreme Court decision, the judiciary, according to this argument, should not become involved in evaluating the constitutionality of the ratification process.[104] Justice Powell, for example, spoke of the dangers of having the Court "oversee the very constitutional process used to reverse [its] decisions."[105] Thus, in *Coleman v. Miller* a plurality of the justices declared that Congress has "sole and complete control over the amendment process, subject to no judicial review."[106]

Frankly, I find this the most persuasive case for the political question doctrine and judicial abdication, leaving Article V of the Constitution entirely to the political branches for enforcement. However, what if the political branches declare something to be a constitutional amendment even though it has not been ratified by the requisite three quarters of the states? Is the judiciary required to enforce the amendment as law even though it was improperly adopted? Consider a hypothetical situation. Congress, strongly desiring a particular constitutional change, coerces the states into ratifying the amendment, for example, by telling them that they will receive no federal monies until they approved the amendment. Furthermore, in this hypothetical situation, some of the states that originally ratified the amendment rescind their ratification. Nonetheless, Congress declares the amendment to be part of the Constitution. Should the Court simply defer to the congressional declaration? If so, a crucial aspect of constitutionalism—protection of the document from majority will—is lost. The very safeguards that the document provides, the difficulty of change, are rendered impotent if the political process is allowed to disregard Article V.

Nor is my hypothetical case fanciful. It is exactly what happened in adopting the Fourteenth Amendment. Congress, in the Reconstruction Act, stated that rebel states could not be readmitted to the Union unless they ratified the amendment.[107] Some of the ratifying states rescinded their ratification but nonetheless were counted toward the necessary three quarters of the states.

Perhaps above all else, if the Constitution is to serve as an antimajoritarian document, it is essential that Article V, which specifies the amendment process, be observed. It is the difficulty of amendment that makes the Constitution a powerful check on majority rule. Therefore, judicial review is necessary to ensure that the political process does not disregard the restrictions of Article V. Certainly, the Court should be extremely deferential when there are proposed amendments to overturn earlier judicial decisions. The Court must be careful not to use the power of interpretation to frustrate one of the only mechanisms existing to check the judiciary. But such deference should not be total abdication, which allows the violation of Article V.[108]

Finally, it might be argued that judicial restraint, such as that described by Choper, is necessary to protect the Court's legitimacy and credibility. Choper argues that the judiciary should not become involved in separation of powers or federalism issues so as to reserve its institutional influence for individual rights cases.[109] Choper's position follows the views of those, such as Alexander Bickel and Felix Frankfurter, who contend that the courts must preserve their institutional credibility by avoiding decisions that will draw the ire of the other branches of government.[110] They argue that owing to the judiciary's limited power to implement its decisions the courts must depend on voluntary compliance by the legislature and executive.[111] The amount of compliance that the courts can expect depends on the courts' credibility in the eyes of those whose behavior the courts seek to regulate. Accordingly, the courts must preserve their legitimacy by avoiding involvements in controversies that will risk the courts' political capital.[112]

I wish to postpone a lengthy consideration of the issue of judicial credibility until the final chapter, where I analyze the objection that my conclusions would undermine the legitimacy of the Court. At this point, I simply want to point out the assumptions that Choper's argument makes. Choper apparently assumes that judicial decisions in separation of powers cases lessen the Court's credibility and legitimacy. Yet there is absolutely no evidence supporting this conclusion. To the contrary, the Court's ruling in cases such as *Youngstown Sheet and Tube v. Sawyer*[113] and *United States v. Nixon*[114] likely enhanced the Court's credibility. The decisions were highly respected and viewed as necessary checks on the president[115].

In fact, although judicial review is often criticized as being countermajoritarian, the courts actually perform a "promajoritarian" function when they act to control unconstitutional presidential acts.[116] The courts, by preserving congressional powers, help to ensure rule by the majority. Thus, judicial review of the presidency is at least as likely to enhance as it is to diminish the credibility of the courts.

Additionally, Choper assumes that the degree of lessened credibility will translate into disregard for judicial decisions. Although Choper offers examples where the judiciary was ignored,[117] there is no evidence that the decreased credibility from separation of powers or federalism rulings will be sufficient to cause increased disregard of Court decrees. In short, Choper offers no evidence that the Court's credibility is so fragile that a few unpopular separation of powers decisions will undermine its authority. Nor is there any evidence that the Court's separation of powers decisions undermine its institutional legitimacy more than its decisions in other areas.

Finally, Choper assumes that maintaining credibility is more important than upholding separation of powers or federalism. He must be assuming either that separation of powers is relatively unimportant or that the long-term benefits of Court rulings in other areas outweighs the need for judicial protection of the structure of government. Neither of these assumptions is supported.

This discussion has attempted to establish that the judiciary should be the authoritative interpreter of all constitutional provisions. For the Constitution to serve its function as a restraint on political majorities, there is a need for Court enforcement of its strictures. Furthermore, judicial elaboration is the best means for constitutional interpretation. It is undesirable to allocate constitutional decision making to other branches of government through the political question doctrine and the generalized grievance standing rule. The Constitution is best upheld if one branch, the judiciary, is the authoritative interpreter.

6 What Limits Exist on the Interpretive Process?

THE QUEST FOR DETERMINACY

Once it is decided that the Constitution should evolve by interpretation and that the judiciary should be the authoritative interpreter, a concern arises that there is a need to constrain judicial discretion in constitutional decision making. What limits exist on the judiciary as it gives meaning and effect to specific constitutional provisions? The obsession of modern constitutional law scholarship has been to try to devise constraints on the interpretive process.[1] The goal has been to articulate a model of judicial decision making that informs the courts how to rule in particular cases and prevents courts from deciding issues based solely on the values of the individual judges. The search has been for "sources of decisions external to the decider's own or 'subjective' standards of value."[2]

Conservative critics argue that decisions based on the personal values of the judges are illegitimate in a democracy committed to majority rule.[3] Judge Robert Bork, for example, writes that "a Court which makes rather than implements value choices cannot be squared with a democratic society. . . . We are driven to the conclusion that a legitimate Court must be controlled by principles exterior to the will of the Justices."[4] Conservatives objected to the activism of the Warren Court by claiming that the Court was imposing its own political preferences.

At the same time, critics from the Left, such as Mark Tushnet, argue that liberalism "requires adjudication without regard to the values held by the adjudicators."[5] They argue that the liberal premise of government under law cannot co-exist with a judiciary that imposes the personal views of its members. Tushnet argues that the inherent inability to prevent judges from imposing their own values is an important illustration of the contradictions inherent in liberalism.[6]

In response to the critics from the Right and the Left, constitutional scholars have tried mightily to devise a method of judicial review that constrains the judiciary and prevents judges from deciding cases based on their personal ideologies. They have searched for a method that provides determinacy, that directs the Court how to rule in particular cases. Their goal is a model that allows no judicial discretion, for discretion permits the introduction of the judges' ideologies. As Larry Simon explains:

> During much of this century . . . the task of explaining the function of constitutional law came to be conflated with a search for a way of constraining the Justices. . . . For this reason, many judges, lawyers, and scholars have yearned for 'objectivity' in constitutional judgement.[7]

In this context, *determinacy* refers to a method of constitutional decision making that allows justices to decide cases without regard to their own values. A model is determinate if any two judges using it would come to identical results. Judicial discretion is the antithesis of determinacy. The cry for objectivity is a demand for determinacy—a search for a way in which justices can determine constitutional rules based on "principles" external to their views.

In fact, constitutional theorists have developed a number of theories of judicial review, each designed to avoid judges deciding cases based on their personal values. To a large extent, each theory was developed because the prior theories failed to provide determinacy. Literalism is the view that all constitutional interpretation must be based solely on the constitutional text.[8] Under this approach, no extraconstitutional materials are relevant. Instead, the Court's task is "to lay the Article of the Constitution which is involved beside the statute which is challenged and to decide whether the latter squares with the former."[9] Justice Hugo Black, for example, argued that judicial decisions are illegitimate if based on anything other than the text of the Constitution.[10]

Originalism is a theory that "accords binding authority to the text of the Constitution or the intention of its adopters."[11] Unlike literalism, originalism permits the Court to look beyond the language of the Constitution but limits it to ascertaining the meaning that the Framers intended.[12] Under this approach, "[t]he whole aim of construction, as applied to a provision of the Constitution . . . is . . . to ascertain and give effect to the intent of its framers and the people who adopted it."[13] In other words, the meaning of the Constitution is static until amended; the only relevant sources of constitutional interpretation are the language of a provision and its preratification history.

Conceptualism requires the Court to determine the underlying purpose of a constitutional provision and to apply this purpose in developing modern governing principles.[14] Unlike originalism, conceptualism does not require that the Court follow the Framers' specific intentions. Instead, the justices are asked to identify the underlying "concept" of a provision and to use it in formulating modern "conceptions" to guide decision making.[15] Each constitutional provision has a core meaning that is static, which the courts apply to modern circumstances.[16]

Cultural values theories require the Court to use basic social values not expressed in the constitutional text as the basis for constitutional decision making.[17] Some culture value theorists argue that the Court should find cultural values in U.S. traditions;[18] others argue that they should be found in moral consensus[19] or in the natural law.[20] Although the source of the values is quite different under these theories, the common characteristic of these approaches is that the Court interprets constitutional provisions on the basis of values not necessarily expressed in the test of the Framer's interpretation.

Finally, process-based modernism permits the Court to decide cases based on contemporary values but limits such discretion to improving the process of government by ensuring fair representation or adjudication.[21] Under this theory, the Court must use the originalism paradigm except for matters that relate to the fair process of government. In this area, the Court may act on norms not mentioned in the Constitution or intended by the Framers.[22] This theory has been advanced most prominently by John Hart Ely and was discussed previously in chapter 1.[23] There are other process-based theories in addition to Ely's, though his is undoubtedly the most prominent.

Each of these approaches is offered as a way to constrain judicial discretion. Each, it is argued, provides an alternative to judges deciding cases based on their personal ideologies. As Ely explains: "[F]ew come right out and argue for the judge's own values as a source of constitutional judgment. Instead the search purports to be objective and value neutral; the reference is to something 'out there' waiting to be discovered."[24] The quest is for determinacy: a model of judicial review that unequivocally informs the Court when to become involved, what values to protect, and what result to reach.

Each of these approaches might be thought of as an alternative to a model termed *open-ended modernism*—an approach that permits the Court to give meaning to all constitutional provisions on the basis of contemporary values that the justices regard as worthy of constitutional protection. Under open-ended modernism, the Constitution is viewed as outlining basic concerns—separation of powers, freedom of speech, protection of criminal defendants—and the Court in each generation is entrusted to give content and meaning to them in their application to contemporary situations.

The core characteristic of open-ended modernism is its explicit premise that justices have, and should have, discretion in deciding constitutional cases, and that their decisions are inevitably based on their personal values. Open-ended modernism is not inconsistent with the use of many of the above methodologies, except to the extent that the alternatives are predicated on the belief that they significantly constrain judicial decision making. For example, an open-ended modernist could decide to identify the concept behind constitutional provisions and decide particular cases on the basis of contemporary conceptions. An open-ended modernist could choose what values are worthy of constitutional protection on the basis of natural law theories, or on the basis of tradition, or on the basis of deeply embedded cultural values, or on the basis of process values.

But the open-ended modernist would recognize that whatever the endeavor, decision making inescapably involves personal value choices by the individual judge.

THE IMPOSSIBILITY OF DETERMINACY

The search for determinacy is inherently futile. No model of constitutional decision making can provide both constitutional evolution by interpretation and determinate results. Constitutional interpretation is an inherently open-ended process, with judges accorded great discretion in determining what values are so important that they should be constitutionalized and therefore immunized from majority pressures. Although there are different degrees of indeterminacy, all methods of constitutional interpretation are nonobjective in the sense that all require choices that inevitably are influenced by the justices' values. The constant search for a model that yields constitutional principles without regard to the identity of the justices is misguided.

Ronald Dworkin explains what it means to say that a judge has discretion in this sense:

> An official's discretion means not that he is free to decide without recourse to standards of sense and fairness, but only that his decision is not controlled by a standard furnished by the particular authority we have in mind when we raise the question of discretion.[25]

In other words, all would agree that a court's discretion is limited in some ways. The judge should not rule based on what is best for his or her own financial interests or his or her affection or dislike for particular litigants.[26] However, apart from these constraints, discretion exists and there is not a method of decision making that allows decisions without judges making choices—choices that inherently will be influenced by the judge's own ideology.

Judicial decision making would be discretionless only if two things existed. First, there would need to be absolutely clear premises, constitutional rules, that permitted the decision maker no discretion in determining the meaning of the premises. For each case, there would need to be just one premise (a choice of more than one premise would create discretion), and that premise would have to be completely unambiguous (since ambiguity requires choices in meaning). Second, there would need to be a reasoning process that allows results to be determined entirely by deduction from the premises. Unless courts could apply the premises to particular cases in a syllogistic fashion, judges would have discretion in determining the outcome. In other words, determinacy exists only if there is a clear rule that can be applied deductively to determine the result in a specific case. This method of decision making has long been termed *formalism*.[27]

At least since the time of the legal realists at the beginning of this century, formalism has been regarded, almost universally, as impossible. First, the constitutional premises from which results are deduced are rarely clear. No model of constitutional decision making can eliminate the need for courts to make choices as to what a constitutional provision means. For example, the inherent vagueness and ambiguity of language require courts to make choices in deciding the meaning of a provision.[28] As Chief Justice Marshall noted early in U.S. constitutional history, ''Such is the character of human language that no word conveys to the mind, in all situations, one single definite idea; and nothing is more common than to use words in a figurative sense.''[29]

The choice to have a constitution written in abstract, general language—something that allows it to serve as a constitutive document—ensures that choices must be made in giving specific content to individual provisions. This indeterminacy is especially apparent in phrases like ''due process of law,'' ''freedom of speech,'' ''equal protection,'' ''cruel and unusual punishment,'' and ''privileges and immunities of citizens.'' Because these terms have no determinate meaning, a literal reading of the Constitution cannot guide the Court in construing them. Inevitably, the judiciary must make choices as to what meaning to give these terms.

Even the constitutional language that is more specific is indeterminate. Article I of the Constitution grants Congress the power ''[t]o make all laws which shall be necessary and proper for carrying into Execution . . . [its] powers.''[30] Does ''necessary'' mean ''indispensable''—that Congress may take only those actions essential to implementing its powers? Or does ''necessary'' mean that Congress can take any action that can be viewed rationally as implementing its powers?[31] Similarly, what government actions constitute a ''taking of property''? What actions of state governments constitute an ''impairment of the obligation of contracts''? What is an ''unreasonable search and seizure''?

These examples and countless similar ones illustrate that the general nature of the Constitution's language requires choices as to meaning. H. L. A. Hart argues that the inherent limitations and defects of language ensure that rules will be drafted in ''open-textured'' language that makes interpretation inevitable.[32] Hart argues that the open texture of language necessitates judicial discretion.

> The open texture of law means that there are areas of conduct where much must be left to be developed by courts or officials striking a balance, in the light of circumstances, between competing interests which may vary in weight from case to case.[33]

Even the most specific language in the Constitution does not eliminate judicial discretion. For instance, Perry distinguishes value judgments that go beyond the Constitution from those that go against the Constitution.[34] According to Perry, the latter, termed ''contra-constitutional judgments,'' are deemed impermissible. The assumption is that some things are specified by the language of the document and that the Court cannot ignore or overrule that which is specified.

However, even the most specific language in the Constitution might be modified through interpretation. For example, perhaps the least ambiguous constitutional provisions are those that specify the required age for election to the House of Representatives, the Senate, and the presidency. Yet it is not inconceivable that the Court could decide that these age restrictions are altered by the equal protection guarantees of the Fifth Amendment, with the amendment modifying the text of the document.[35] Or the Court could conclude that the ages specified were meant to refer to a percentage of the human life span, which has changed since the Constitution was written. The latter possibility is not as implausible as it sounds. Recently, an Illinois appellate court held that a statute applying to those under the age of 13 could apply to a retarded boy of 16 because what the statute really referred to (though never specified) was mental age.[36]

I am not suggesting that all language is equally ambiguous or that courts do not have to justify ignoring seemingly clear wording. The greater the apparent clarity, the more important the reasons need to be to justify disregarding the text. Nor do I contend that the federal courts are likely in the foreseeable future to invalidate the age provisions contained in the federal Constitution. Rather, I am arguing that all constitutional provisions, even seemingly unambiguous ones, might present questions of interpretation. This makes a clear distinction between extraconstitutional and contraconstitutional interpretation impossible. Language, even in its most precise form, cannot eliminate all discretion or foreclose the possibility of interpretation.

Nor can the indeterminacy of language be overcome by resort to the intention of the Constitution's Framers. At the very least, reliance on the Framers' intent to determine constitutional values would mean that the Constitution has a static meaning, fixed to what the drafters intended. Chapters 3 and 4 demonstrated why such an approach is undesirable and why it is preferable to have the Constitution evolve by interpretation—which prevents reliance on the Framers' intent to eliminate judicial discretion.

Moreover, as argued in Chapter 3, embracing originalism would neither eliminate judicial discretion nor provide determinacy in constitutional decision making. Numerous people were involved in the drafting and ratification of each part of the Constitution. Choices must be made as to whose views count as intent.[37] Even if the relevant group could be identified, those regarded as Framers undoubtedly had a number of different and perhaps conflicting reasons for adopting a particular constitutional provision. Social choice theorists prove that it is impossible to determine a group's preferences based on the preferences of individual members of a group.[38] Choices must be made as to which views count as intent. Additionally, historiographers argue that any reading of historical records is inherently subjective, with the values of the interpreter affecting the conclusions reached. Thus, originalism does not eliminate judicial discretion nor provide determinacy in determining the premises for constitutional decision making.

Nor do any of the other models of judicial review end discretion or permit determinacy. Conceptualism is indeterminate because the Court can state the concept behind any constitutional provision at many different levels of generality.[39] As described in Chapter 4, the concept behind the equal protection clause might be to protect former slaves; or it might be to protect blacks; or it might be to protect all racial minorities; or it might be to protect all "insular" political minorities; or it might be to require that all government classifications be justified by a legitimate government purpose.[40] The result in specific cases will depend on the level of generality at which the concept is articulated. For example, whether the equal protection clause applies to gender discrimination turns entirely on the choice of the concept behind the provision. As Paul Brest observed, the "fact is that all adjudication requires making choices among the levels of generality on which to articulate principles and all such choices are inherently non-neutral."[41] Thus, conceptualism does not eliminate discretion or provide determinacy because it "demands an arbitrary choice among levels of abstraction."[42]

Recognizing the failure of these approaches, some theorists have abandoned constitutional interpretation based on the Framers' intent. Instead, they try to provide an external source for judicial decision making by arguing that the Court should look to "deeply embedded cultural values" in interpreting the Constitution.[43] They propose various sources for determining such values, including natural law, tradition, and consensus.[44] However, all these sources of decision making are indeterminate, permitting judges to justify reaching virtually any result. Although I agree that the Court's function is to articulate fundamental values and protect them from majority rule, these theories provide no constraint on judicial decision making. Cultural values can be identified to support almost every conclusion. Judges acting in completely good faith can support almost any conclusion by invoking some aspect of U.S. culture and traditions. In fact, in practice, cultural values theories are indistinguishable from "open-ended modernism," although the cultural values theories do describe the rhetoric the Court should use in justifying its results.

Natural law, for example, is not composed of specific, judicially discoverable principles. To the contrary, people can claim that any idea is part of the natural order. As Ely explains, "[N]atural law has been summoned in support of all manner of causes in this country—some worthy, others nefarious—and often on both sides of the same issue."[45] Ely offers an excellent example: the Supreme Court's decision in *Bradwell v. Illinois* where the Court declared: "The paramount destiny and mission of women are to fulfill the noble and benign offices of wife and mother. This is the law of the creator."[46] Asking judges to follow natural law gives them license to decide the values they believe should be protected.

Nor is the requirement that the Court look to tradition a constraint on judicial decision making. U.S. history is so diverse that almost any value can be found in some tradition. As Garry Wills notes, "Running men out of town on a rail is at least as much an American tradition as declaring unalienable rights."[47] Discrimination against blacks and women is far more a U.S. tradition than is egalitarianism. Permitting decisions based on tradition allows the Court to justify its arbitrary choices simply by invoking a historical practice as support.

Finally, those who argue that the Court should look to social consensus in deciding what values to protect do not mean that the Court should identify constitutional values based on the Gallup Poll. As Ely explains, "[I]t makes no sense to employ the value judgments of the majority as the vehicle for protecting minorities from the value judgments of the majority."[48] Instead, consensus theorists refer to a deep, underlying consensus to basic values that transcends current viewpoints. Margaret Jane Radin observes that what is really the source of values is a "notion of [a] deep or coherent consensus."[49] Likewise, Harry Wellington rejects simple consensus in the form of the majority's current preferences and instead says courts must be "reasonably confident that they draw on conventional morality and screen out contemporary bias, passion, and prejudice."[50] In short, what consensus really means in the context of constitutional decision making is that deeply embedded in our society there is a long-term, underlying consensus that courts should look to as a source of rights.

The process of identifying this deep consensus is inherently indeterminate. There is no formula that a court can use to ascertain what the deep consensus is. Undoubtedly, a person "can convince one's self that some invocable consensus supports almost any position a civilized person might want to see supported."[51] I am not arguing that courts should refrain from trying to ascertain the deep consensus or from protecting cultural values. Rather, my claim is just that such an approach does not avoid the need for judges to use their own values in deciding constitutional principles.

Finally, process-based modernism, too, fails to provide courts with a discretion-free way of determining premises for constitutional decision making. Process-based modernism allows the courts to use contemporary norms in deciding cases, but only in creating a fair process of government—that is, what is fair adjudication and representation. As discussed in Chapter 1, this theory is indeterminate, first, because it provides no basis for judicial decisions under the substantive provisions of the Constitution.[52] What standards *should* the Court use in deciding what is a "cruel and unusual punishment," or what is a "taking" of property, or what constitutes the "establishment" of religion? All such decisions require judicial choices. Second, the judiciary has discretion in deciding what is a fair process. There are no preexisting criteria that lead to determinate results in deciding what is a fair electoral process or what rights criminal suspects should possess.

The point of this discussion is to establish that there is no way to eliminate judicial discretion in determining the premises for constitutional decision making. No matter what model is adopted, judicial choices, undoubtedly influenced by the judges' ideology, are inevitable. I am not arguing that all theories necessarily allow judges the same degree of discretion. One theory might be indeterminate because it allows a choice among several alternatives, whereas another might allow selection among a great many more choices. Instead, the claim is a more limited one: the goal of judicial decisions based totally on sources extrinsic to the judges' own values is unattainable.

Furthermore, the primary difference in the discretion allowed is between the originalist theories and the nonoriginalist ones. Requiring judges to defend their conclusions based on the text or the Framers' intent does confine judges more than allowing them to reach any result that can be justified by invoking tradition or consensus. If, however, originalist theories are rejected for the reasons discussed in earlier chapters, I contend there is relatively little difference among the nonoriginalist theories in the degree of discretion accorded to the Court. Whether judges choose the concepts and the conceptions, or determine the deep consensus, or identify traditions, they are engaging in a process which is very heavily dependent on their own values and beliefs about what is so important as to be worthy of constitutional protection. Because concepts, natural law premises, deeply embedded values, and traditions all can be stated at very high degrees of abstraction, conscientious judges could use them interchangeably to reach the same results. For example, consider the Court's discretion under each of these theories in determining whether there is a right to privacy. The concept behind the Fourth Amendment can be said to be privacy. Privacy can be viewed as an integral part of America's traditions. Certainly, privacy could be regarded to be a value that is part of the deep consensus of our culture. I cannot identify any difference in the discretion allowed, the range of choices permitted, under these nonoriginalist theories.

The choice among these theories is ultimately a decision based on considerations such as one's philosophical beliefs (is there a belief in a natural law or the existence of a deep consensus?) and rhetorical choices (will a court articulating its decision on considerations of social traditions or underlying concepts be more likely to gain acceptance of its decisions?) My point is that it is wrong to choose among the nonoriginalist theories based on a desire to constrain judicial decision making.

Furthermore, even if the premises, the Constitution's requirements, were clear, inevitably judges would still have discretion in applying the premises to decide specific controversies. Discretion is eliminated only if the premises can be applied deductively to yield conclusions. However, legal reasoning is rarely syllogistic. Generally, legal reasoning is described as being analogical, reasoning by example from one case to the next. Edward Levi provides a classic description of legal reasoning:

> The basic pattern of legal reasoning is reasoning by example. It is reasoning from case to case. It is a three-step process . . . in which a proposition descriptive of the first case is made into a rule of law and then applied to a next similar situation. The steps are these: similarity is seen between cases; next the rule of law inherent to the first case is announced; then the rule of law is made applicable to the second case.[53]

This inductive method is inherently discretionary. Courts must make choices in deciding whether cases are similar or dissimilar. Under the Fourteenth Amendment, is discrimination against women or aliens or the handicapped to be treated the same or differently from discrimination against blacks? Is the need for government-provided counsel the same in misdemeanor cases as in felonies, or is there a relevant difference? Deciding whether a precedent is controlling or distinguishable inevitably requires the Court to make a choice that cannot be arrived at deductively.

Additionally, the process of articulating the principle that the former case establishes is inherently discretionary. Every first-year law student quickly learns that the holding of any case can be stated at many different levels of abstraction and generality. The reasoning process described by Levi ensures judicial choices.

Furthermore, much of constitutional decision making is resolving conflicts between constitutional values, a process that is much more likely to involve balancing than deduction. For instance, many constitutional law cases involve tensions between constitutionally protected liberty and constitutionally guaranteed equality. May the state prevent a group such as the Jaycees[54] or a private school[55] from discriminating? There is a tension between the group members' right to freedom of association and the individual's right to equal protection. Often constitutional law involves conflicts between constitutionally protected liberties. For example, what may courts do to prevent prejudicial pretrial publicity and ensure fair trials?[56] Restrictions on the press threaten First Amendment values; the absence of controls on pretrial publicity threatens the defendant's Sixth Amendment right to a fair trial. Some parts of the Constitution are written in language that ensures value conflicts. For example, any time the government acts with the purpose of facilitating religious worship, arguably it is establishing a religion.[57] On the other hand, the government's failure to accommodate religion (for example, by not providing chaplains for prisoners or soldiers), arguably denies free exercise of religion.

Choosing between competing constitutional values is inherently discretionary. No reasoning process exists to ensure determinate results. A choice must be made and the process of choosing inevitably permits the judge's ideology to influence the outcome. Likewise, because no constitutional rights are treated as absolute, a potential issue in every case is whether there is a sufficiently compelling rationale to justify infringement of the right. Deductive reasoning cannot disclose what interests are important enough to outweigh constitutional values.

Thus, the search for determinacy that has obsessed constitutional scholarship is misguided. No model of judicial review can eliminate discretion in the identification of constitutional values and their application in particular cases. The existence of discretion ensures that the judges' values will influence the outcome. Value-free decision making is an impossible quest. John Nowak explains that there is "no demonstrably correct set of legal principles which will dictate the resolution of constitutional issues apart from the political philosophy and the exercise of political power by the justices."[58] Similarly, Perry concludes, "Inevitably each justice will deal with human rights problems in terms of particular political-moral criteria that are, in the justices' view, authoritative. I do not see how it could be otherwise. . . . [T]he ultimate source of decisional norms is the judge's own values."[59]

Again, establishing that all theories are indeterminate only demonstrates that under each, justices have discretion to make choices that inescapably will be influenced by their own values. But showing that all judicial review is indeterminate does not prove that every approach accords judges the same amount of discretion. I readily admit that one of the differences between originalism and non—originalism is in the degree of discretion allowed. In fact, in choosing among the theories one could conclude that the "basic question from the standpoint of American constitutionalism is how much discretionary power the people are willing to consign to the judges."[60]

Earlier, in Chapter 4, I detailed reasons why the degree of discretion permitted under originalism is inadequate to achieve the underlying purposes of the Constitution. Here my point is that originalists cannot defend their paradigm by arguing that it produces determinate results or eliminates discretion. If the search for determinacy and objectivity were not so prominent in much of the constitutional law literature, I would fear that this discussion would be dismissed as merely attacking a straw man. Yet, it is precisely because nonoriginalist theories are so frequently criticized as allowing judges to make decisions based on their personal values that it is important to note that all theories of decision making are susceptible to this criticism. No theory can claim the ability to provide value-neutral adjudication.

To this point, I have only demonstrated that it is futile to search for determinacy and misguided to criticize any particular theory because it allows the individual judge's values to influence decision making. The ideology of the judges determines results under all approaches. The next question to be addressed is whether judicial discretion is something to be minimized to the greatest extent possible, such as under originalism, or whether expanding the judicial discretion of nonoriginalism is desirable. Phrased in other words, thus far in this chapter, I have established only the descriptive proposition that judicial discretion is inevitable once it is decided that the judiciary should interpret the Constitution. This conclusion, of course, has no normative force. I would argue further, in response to the critics from both the Right and the Left, that judicial discretion is desirable in constitutional decision making.

THE DESIRABILITY OF DISCRETION

How much discretion should be accorded the judiciary in constitutional interpretation? A truly honest answer would be that it depends on the identity of the justices. When there are justices I like (whose values I agree with), I want them to have a great deal of discretion. But if the justices' beliefs are contrary to mine, I want to restrain them. This simple observation explains much of modern constitutional scholarship. It is no coincidence that conservatives who dislike the results of Supreme Court decisions desegregating the schools, protecting access to contraceptives and abortion, limiting state support for religion, upholding the rights of criminal defendants, and the like, now argue for the theories of judicial review entailing the least discretion. Nor is it surprising that during the 1930s, when the Supreme Court struck down countless progressive laws, it was the liberals who espoused originalism. The degree of discretion a person wants the judiciary to have really comes down to whether one believes that it will lead to more good or more bad results.

Ultimately, then, choosing the appropriate degree of discretion is a matter of defending a view of what is a "good" or "bad" result and making a prediction about what kinds of people will likely be appointed to the bench and how they will behave in office. The more one believes that the future justices will advance the good, the more discretion a person is willing to accord the Court. But the more it seems that the Court's future members will retard social progress or cause bad results for society, the more one wants to limit the judiciary's ability to cause harm.

Such a discussion about what is a good or a bad result requires exposition of a moral or political theory. I, however, certainly am not prepared to present a well-developed account of what is "the good" or "the just," an account that would probably occupy several volumes in itself. But I contend that even without a full exposition of a political theory, the conclusions established in the earlier chapters justify the belief that judicial discretion, on balance, will lead to good results for society.

Specifically, Chapter 2 established that the existence of a constitution reflects society's commitment to protecting fundamental values and the rights of political and social minorities from majority rule. Chapters 3 and 4 described why achieving these objectives requires a constitution that evolves by judicial interpretation. Protecting minorities and safeguarding basic rights from current threats necessitates that the interpretive process be open-ended. As Chapter 4 established, a constitution that evolves only by amendment—according the judiciary relatively little discretion—is inferior to a process of evolution by interpretation. Reducing judicial discretion keeps the Court from protecting crucial values and minority groups. Thus, as discussed in Chapter 4, constitutional decision making requires choices as to what modern values are so important that they are worthy of constitutional protection.

Furthermore, Chapter 2 described the social benefits of having a constitution written sufficiently abstractly that almost everyone agrees to the values it contains. Such a document serves important symbolic and unifying functions. However, the very fact that the document is abstract means that the interpretation process will be open-ended, as judges decide what specific content to give to general provisions. Discretion is inherent, and an originalist methodology is precluded under such a constitution because the text and the Framers' intent are usually too ambiguous to guide interpretation.

In other words, if the conclusions from the earlier chapters are accepted, the desirability of discretion follows. Judges in interpreting the Constitution should identify and articulate those crucial values deserving protection from majoritarian decision making. The conclusion is that society is better off having an institution insulated from the political process, such as the judiciary, determine what values are worthy of constitutional protection. Society is better off because the Court had discretion to compel desegregation of the South, to apply the Bill of Rights to the states, and to protect the right of privacy, to mention just a few examples. There is a risk that discretion will be used for bad ends and produce undesirable results. The specter of Lochnerism haunts all defenses of judicial discretion. But, as I argue later in this chapter, the judicial method of decision making and historical experience convince me that on balance society is better off having an institution like the Court expound and interpret the meaning of the Constitution. Contrary to those who claim that is is a criticism of the judiciary to reveal its discretion, I contend that society benefits from the judiciary's ability to identify and protect minorities and basic rights.

What makes a legislator different from a judge is not that only the former makes value choices.[61] Obviously, both must do so. A court is different from a legislature because the judiciary is insulated from electoral politics and the legislature is not. Also, a court is different because its primary role is to enforce and uphold the Constitution, not to please constituents or to seek reelection. A court, moreover, is different in its method, its process of deciding based on arguments with elaboration of reasons justifying the result. It is precisely these differences that make the judiciary the proper institution for constitutional interpretation.

The conclusion that judges make value choices is hardly new or profound. The legal realists pointed this out decades ago. Why, then, is there so much aversion to this conclusion and so much effort devoted to developing models to try to eliminate judicial discretion? Perhaps there is a psychological need for certainty, a need to believe that there are determinate answers to be found.[62] Perhaps it is that open acceptance of broad judicial discretion does create tension with important social values and even with the underlying rationale for having the Constitution. Even though majority rule is not the sole component of a correct definition of American democracy, it is an important aspect. Broad judicial discretion, albeit advancing the Constitution's underlying values, is in tension with a desire for majoritarian decision making. Moreover, if a primary purpose of the Constitution is "pre-commitment" to basic values, how much is there really a pre-commitment to anything if the Justices have broad discretion to determine the meaning of the Constitution?

These objections cannot be dismissed lightly or brushed aside. As to the concern for majority rule, the answer must be found in the justifications for having a Constitution: it is desirable for society to exempt some deeply cared about matters from majoritarian control. Some values, such as separation of powers, equality and individual rights, are deemed more important than majority rule. As argued above, to protect these values adequately requires a Constitution that evolves by interpretation and that necessitates substantial judicial discretion.

Even more troubling is the argument that the existence of judicial discretion undermines the purposes of a Constitution. The Constitution's goal of protecting basic values from majority rule is lost if the Court can follow the wishes of the majority in its decision making and abandon minorities and individual liberties. More generally, if a Constitution represents society's tying its hand to prevent future harm (as argued in Chapter 2), are those binds very meaningful if the Court can cut them at will? A paradox seems to emerge: for the Constitution to achieve its purpose the Court must have substantial discretion; but if the Court has substantial discretion can the Constitution achieve its basic purpose of serving as a precommitment and constraint for society?

I do not have an easy answer. There is an inherent tension between wanting to prevent change to preserve basic values, and wanting to allow change to permit progress. Yet, I believe that the Constitution and the judiciary with substantial discretion to interpret it offers the best mediation of this tension. The Constitution embodies society's commitment to fundamental values. If the legislature could overrule those values at will, there would be little preservation of the precommitment. Alternatively, as argued in Chapter 3 and 4, if there was no opportunity for evolution by interpretation, technological and moral progress would make the Constitution outdated and a failure at protecting its basic values.

Judicial interpretation offers a compromise between the two undesirable possibilities. There is evolution by interpretation, yet there also is a check on the majority in its ability to disregard the Constitution. As argued in Chapter 5, the judiciary's methods of decision making make it especially well-suited to the task of articulating and applying the Constitution. The commitment to basic values is preserved and enhanced by the judiciary's ability to give them contemporary meaning and, at the same time, there is some insulation from majoritarian pressure. Certainly, at any given point in time, this balance might not work. The Court, itself, might fall prey to social pressures or it might fail to adapt sufficiently to changed circumstances. Yet, my argument is that over the long term, the best way to mediate the fundamental tension between commitment and change is through a Constitution and a judiciary whose role is to preserve, protect, and advance the Constitution's values.

Yet another reason for the quest for limits on the interpretive process reflects a fear of judicial tyranny. U.S. government is premised on a distrust of those in power.[63] The structure of government embodied in the Constitution reflects a belief in the need to limit and check power. The search for limits on the judiciary is thus part of the desire to constrain all who hold positions of authority. If a model of decision making exists that allows no discretion, then there is no need to fear judicial decisions. In contrast, a judiciary that possesses great discretion and is not easily checked by any other institution creates fear of tyrannical rule.

This objection cannot be dismissed lightly; defending the existence of expansive judicial discretion requires that fear of judicial power be addressed directly. At the outset, it is necessary to clarify what *judicial tyranny* means. After all, *tyranny* is a loaded word, carrying extremely negative connotations. Does *judicial tyranny* mean that the Court will become a despotic dictator, running the country by fiat? This seems unlikely because the Court cannot act directly and can only rule on those cases before it. Obviously, the Court cannot arrest people, confiscate property, or declare war. As Alexander Bickel remarked, "[H]uge areas of governmental action remain wholly outside the Court's reach."[64] Moreover, if the Court orders Congress or the president to act tyrannically, each can ignore the order. "Government by judiciary" is an obvious exaggeration and misnomer.[65]

Judicial tyranny can be understood only as a fear that the Court will frustrate the will of the majority by striking down socially desirable legislation on the basis of misguided constitutional interpretations. This is a legitimate fear, but it is the specific concern over misguided judicial activism that must be analyzed, not some vague notion of *tyranny*. Of course, it is difficult to even speak of errors or mistakes unless there are some criteria to separate good decisions from bad ones. For the purposes of this discussion, *errors* or *mistakes* simply refers to judicial opinions widely regarded by the interpretive community to be wrong, or to judgments that come to be regarded by history as manifestly incorrect. Although I recognize that this definition begs crucial questions about what is a good decision, I am simply using it to have some sense of what *errors* and *mistakes* might mean in the context of judicial decisions.

In considering the concern about judicial tyranny, it should be recognized that the Court is not tyrannical merely because it acts in an antimajoritarian fashion, for judicial review is supposed to be antimajoritarian. Rather, the concern is that the Court will strike down socially important legislation based on misguided interpretations—mistakes that cannot be corrected easily because of the difficulty of overruling constitutional decisions through the amendment process. In fact, this fear seems to be the underlying motive for almost all contemporary constitutional theory. The desire to devise a model that limits judicial discretion is inspired by the perceived need to constrain the Court and avoid another Lochner era.[66] For fifty years, from 1887 until 1937, the Court struck down progressive state and federal legislation designed to protect consumers and workers. Most modern commentators view the Court's zealous protection of laizzez-faire capitalism during the Lochner era as a mistake.[67] Thus, scholars are searching for a theory that will permit judicial review without the risk of Lochnerism.

It cannot be overemphasized that the fear of Lochnerism is the driving force behind modern constitutional theory and especially the search for limits on the interpretive process. Ely, for example, stated that it is "most imperative for liberals to distinguish *Lochner v. New York*" from decisions such as *Griswold v. Connecticut* and *Roe v. Wade*.[68] Likewise, Monaghan remarked that "[i]f you conclude . . . that you can't distinguish *Lochner* from *Roe*, that might tell you something about the legitimacy of noninterpretive modes of reasoning about the Constitution."[69]

Initially, it must be recognized that although judicial errors are possible, so are legislative and executive ones.[70] Fiss notes that "[h]istory is as filled with legislative and executive mistakes as it is filled with judicial ones."[71] Also, errors—even blatant disregard of the Constitution—by state and local governments have occurred throughout U.S. history.[72] Few would deny that political officials have frequently violated rights, discriminated, and acted unconstitutionally. One feature of U.S. government that makes the Constitution particularly necessary is federalism, the decentralization of power to state and local governments and the need to ensure that these nonfederal officials stay within the Constitution's limits.

The crucial question becomes, Which risk of errors is more acceptable? Is society better off limiting judicial review and trusting the majority to restrain itself and to not violate fundamental rights or discriminate against minorities not explicitly protected in the text? Or should society grant the power of judicial review and trust the Court not to err by unjustly overruling desirable social policies? Given that any institution can make mistakes, the issue is what institution's errors pose less risk. Tribe explains the choice:

> The price we pay is that, for various periods of time, an enlightened consensus may be blocked by judicial adherence to constitutional views we will later come to regret. But the price of the alternative course is that, for other periods, the enlightened consensus that judges may help to catalyze in the name of the Constitution might be blocked by more self-interested or self-serving majorities.[73]

In other words, the danger of judicial review is court obstruction of social progress; the price of not having relatively broad judicial discretion is that political majorities are able to violate basic values and discriminate against groups deserving of protection. If Lochnerism is the cost of judicial discretion, then the benefits are reflected in decisions such as those striking down the Jim Crow laws that segregated the South, reapportioning legislatures, and ensuring defendants of counsel in criminal cases. Ultimately, are the values of judicial discretion worth the risks?

In examining this balance, it is important to recognize that if the Court is denied discretion in order to prevent mistakes, it also is denied discretion to make good decisions.[74] For example, without judicial discretion, without a constitution that evolves by interpretation, the Court would have been unable to outlaw school segregation[75] or to protect the right of privacy.[76] Are critics of judicial activism saying that the values of desegregation and privacy are unimportant? Or are they saying that the legislatures would have protected these rights adequately without Court action?[77] Neither of these assumptions seems plausible. The argument must be that the risk of errors is so great that it outweighs the benefits of discretion. This claim has not been proved or even argued for by opponents of judicial activism. They have been content to attach labels such as "undemocratic" and cry for "objectivity" and raise the ghost of Lochnerism. They have avoided any attempt at on-balance analysis of the relative benefits and costs of open-ended judicial review.

Furthermore, in evaluating the risk of judicial errors, it must be recognized that the danger is inherent to allowing judicial review. Ironically, the most frequently criticized decisions in U.S. history justified their conclusions with an explicit reliance on an originalist methodology. For example, the Court in *Dred Scott v.*

Sandford—widely regarded as one of the most tragic court decisions in U.S. history—explicitly premised its decision on an originalist methodology.[78] Lochnerism could be justified under originalism (the Framers' intent to limit government and protect contracts), conceptualism (the concept of freedom of contract), or the cultural values theories (natural law or the tradition against regulation). Simply put, the risk of errors is inherent to judicial review; errors are possible under any approach to constitutional interpretation.

Originalists must claim that the lessened degree of judicial discretion under their theory reduces the possibility of errors. This, however, is a conclusion that must be justified, not merely asserted. Originalists cannot argue that historically most errors would have been avoided with an originalist approach because the most frequently identified serious mistakes, especially the *Dred Scott* decision and Lochnerism, were originalist, at least in the justifications offered by the Court. Furthermore, many of the most highly respected decisions—rulings such as *Marbury v. Madison*, *Brown v. Board of Education*, *Baker v. Carr*—were openly nonoriginalist in their approach.

Nor is there any analytic reason to believe that originalism risks fewer errors just because it entails less discretion. Under originalism, the judiciary lacks discretion to escape outdated principles and policies. As explained earlier, an honest application of originalism would make the election of a woman as president or vice president unconstitutional because the Framers intended only for men to serve in those offices and the text of Article II refers to the chief executive as "he."[79] Moreover, discretion can be used for good or evil; the lessened degree of discretion under originalism reduces the possibility of good decisions. If originalists want to argue that their methodology risks fewer errors, they must explain why that is so, accounting for the bad decisions that result from blind obedience to the Framers' intent, and then demonstrate that the reduced errors outweigh the benefits that only nonoriginalism provides. To my knowledge, originalists have not begun to meet this burden. Ultimately, the question is whether the risks of judicial errors outweigh the benefits of having expansive judicial discretion.

In order to answer this inquiry it is necessary to consider how likely it is that there will be serious long-term errors. Several factors reduce the possibility of mistakes. I am not contending that these factors eliminate judicial discretion or provide determinacy in decision making. Rather, I am claiming only that these factors influence decision making and lessen the likelihood of errors.

First, there are sociological influences that decrease the chance that the Court will protect values that are not worthy of constitutional status. As members of society, the judges share common understandings and values. Although the meaning of language is indeterminate, there certainly are shared understandings. For example, no matter what the equal protection clause means, no one would think that it says anything about whether the United States should sell arms abroad. Similarly, the shared understandings of the equal protection clause make it unthinkable that the Court would read it as only permitting white Anglo-Saxon protestants to vote in national elections. The Sixth Amendment's right to a fair trial would not be understood as saying anything about what medical services should be reimbursed under the Medicaid program.

Additionally, the judges are unlikely to select values foreign to society. The members of the judiciary are generally drawn from prominent social positions. If anything, they tend to be elites and therefore have upper-middle-class values.[80] The risk is that elitist judges, insensitive to the needs of most U.S. citizens, will rule in favor of the wealthy and powerful and against those most needing judicial assistance. Although this is a substantial danger, the courts still are likely to be superior to the legislature in protecting society's poorest and least powerful members. Legislatures are beholden to those with power, money, and influence. The judiciary rules on the claims of all, and its relative insulation often makes it more responsible than the politically accountable branches of government. This is not to deny that the judicial process is used by the rich and powerful to preserve their status and situation. It is to say that the least powerful in society nonetheless are better off with a judiciary where they have the possibility of being heard and receiving protection.

Although judges reflect society's values and are therefore unlikely to depart from them and cause major errors, that does not mean that judges always reflect the majority's values. To the contrary, it is desirable that the judiciary overrules current preferences in upholding fundamental rights. Nor do I contend that the shared meanings provide a substantial check on judicial discretion. Rather, my contention is merely that basic sociology decreases the chance that the Court will go off on a frolic and protect inappropriate values. Even the Lochner Court's protection of laissez-faire capitalism was understandable and widely supported at the end of the nineteenth century.[81]

Second, political limits also reduce the chance and effect of errors. For example, the interactions of the Court with the other branches of government lessen the need to fear judicial decision making. The Court must often depend on the other branches of government to enforce its decisions. As Alexander Hamilton noted in his famous *Federalist No. 78*: "The judiciary . . . may truly be said to have neither FORCE nor WILL, but merely judgment; and must ultimately depend upon the aid of the executive arm even for the efficacy of its judgments."[82] Thus, the Court must always be mindful of the fact that its decisions can be ignored. Choper offers examples of presidential nullification of judicial decisions.

> The presidential response may range from Abraham Lincoln's outright refusal to obey Chief Justice Taney's order in *Ex Parte Merryman* to Franklin Roosevelt's plan to openly defy the full bench if it ruled adversely in the *Gold Clause Cases* . . . to Andrew Jackson's alleged edict that he would leave John Marshall to enforce his own decision in the *Cherokee Indian Cases* to Dwight Eisenhower's seeming ambivalence following the *School Desegregation Cases*.[83]

The need to hand down decisions that will be obeyed serves as an outer boundary on judicial discretion. Moreover, if the Court's decisions were clearly erroneous and dangerous, they could be disregarded.

Again, the claim is not that such disregard is frequent. If it were, the Court could not perform its antimajoritarian function. Instead, I would argue that political influences lessen the chance of dangerous errors.

Furthermore, the possibility that the Court will be seriously out of touch with society is reduced by the appointment of new justices to the bench. Presidents obviously appoint Supreme Court justices with an eye toward how they will exercise discretion. The ability of a president to appoint, on the average, two justices means that the "policy views dominant on the Court are never for long out of line with the policy views dominant among the lawmaking majorities of the United States. Consequently, it would be most unrealistic to suppose that the Court would, for more than a few years, at most, stand against any alternative sought by a lawmaking majority."[84] The appointment power is not a majoritarian *control* of the judiciary; rather, it is just an influence that reduces the likelihood of Court invalidation of policies regarded by society as vital.

Third, the role of the judges helps to lessen the possibility of errors. A *role* is the set of norms that defines the proper behavior for each person in a particular position or situation. Social psychologists and organizational theorists have developed the concept of the role to account for how the definition of a person's tasks influences the way that person performs.[85] Experimental literature has consistently identified a positive relationship between role expectations and behavior.[86]

Above all, the Supreme Court's role is to uphold the Constitution of the United States. Therefore, errors that might be caused by external influences—lobbying, pressures, corruption—are substantially reduced. The fact that the Court is making a good-faith attempt to focus solely on what the Constitution should mean lessens the possibility of mistakes.

Moreover, part of the judiciary's role requires that it decide cases solely on the merits and that it issue written opinions justifying the result. The previous chapter discussed why the opinion-writing function is so important and why it helps to prevent errors and facilitates the correction of mistakes.[87] Robert Bennett explains that the "tradition of justification in the form of judicial opinion is a primary mechanism of constraint, exposing judicial decisions to the discipline of reason and judicial reasoning to the judgment of the world."[88]

Furthermore, adherence to stare decisis is an accepted part of the judicial role, and therefore courts attempt to come to decisions that are consistent with prior holdings, legitimately distinguishable from precedents, or that justify overruling conflicting cases. Although precedents are often disregarded and overruled in constitutional law, the general acceptance of stare decisis lessens the chance of mistakes because "precedents can and do have the effect of disciplining judicial reasoning."[89] It is not that precedents yield determinate results, just that they, too, influence decisions and reduce the risk of errors.

Fourth, the ability to amend the Constitution to overrule judicial decisions provides protection against Court tyranny. If a Court decision were truly out of touch with society, the Constitution could be amended. On four occasions, constitutional amendments have reversed Supreme Court decisions. The Eleventh

Amendment overturned *Chisholm v. Georgia*[90] and made states immune to suits in federal court. The Fourteenth Amendment overturned, in part, the Court's decision in *Dred Scott v. Sandford*[91] and said that slaves are persons and all persons are citizens of the United States. The Sixteenth Amendment overturned the holding in *Pollock v. Farmers' Loan & Trust Co.*,[92] permitting Congress to enact a personal income tax. Most recently, the Twenty-sixth Amendment overturned *Oregon v. Mitchell*[93] and gave 18- to 21-year-olds the right to vote in federal elections.

The claim, of course, is not that amendments provide a significant check on the judiciary. The difficult process required for amendment makes them quite unlikely. But they are possible and have been used when the Court's decisions have been widely viewed as erroneous. They, too, provide some protection against judicial mistakes.

I have repeatedly emphasized the limited point that I am trying to make in identifying these influences on the judicial process. Frequently, opponents of activist judicial review analyze these factors and point out that they do not eliminate judicial discretion or provide means by which the political branches oversee judicial action.[94] I agree completely with this and contend only that these factors influence choices; courts still possess tremendous discretion. Judicial discretion is essential, and inevitable, if the Court is to perform its task of adapting the Constitution to changing circumstances. Nonetheless, I contend that these influences combine to decrease the likelihood of serious, repeated judicial errors. Dworkin observes:

> [Although] we run a risk that judges may make wrong decisions . . . [w]e must not exaggerate the danger. Truly unpopular decisions will be eroded because public compliance will be grudging . . . and because old judges will retire or die and be replaced by new judges because they agree with a President who has been elected by the people.[95]

Of course, all these pressures can limit the Court's ability to do good as well as reduce the likelihood of harm. It is a difficult balance between wanting the Court to have sufficient discretion to produce good results in protecting minorities and individual liberties but not so much discretion to be without any check or limit. Ultimately, especially as argued in the next chapter, I believe that the constraints described above lessen the "down-side risk" of judicial review but that its potential remains high as an instrument for positive social change as reflected in the decisions of the last quarter century.

Phrased differently, I might be accused of undermining my earlier points by recognizing that there are limits on the Court's discretion. If there are these limits, how can it be known whether there is sufficient discretion remaining to permit the Court to achieve the underlying purposes of the Constitution? Although there is no way to definitively answer this question, it must be remembered that the limits exist only in the broadest sense as outer boundary constraints and within that boundary the judiciary still possesses great discretion to achieve all of the purposes described in earlier chapters. My point is that it is not a binary choice between complete constraints and no limits. Although boundary limits only minimally constrain discretion, these should not be ignored in evaluating the likely risks of judicial decision making.

Thus, the conclusion is that the risks of errors with expansive judicial discretion are less than usually claimed. In part, this is because of the above analysis describing the factors that reduce the chance of error. In part, too, it is because the mistakes that do occur seem less dangerous than unchecked legislative or executive errors. One type of judicial error is a failure to uphold the Constitution and declare unconstitutional executive and legislative actions that should be invalidated. For example, many would criticize the Court's decision in *Korematsu v. United States*[96] because it did not declare unconstitutional the evacuation and internment of Japanese Americans during World War II.[97] Likewise, many criticize the judicial restraint of the Burger Court and its failure to declare unconstitutional injustices such as inequalities in the provision of public education.[98] However, this type of mistake does not justify eliminating judicial review because the Court's decision is adding minimal additional evil.[99] Certainly, there is some harm to judicial approval of deprivation of rights, but the government's actions themselves are the same as if there were no judicial review.

A second type of error occurs when the judiciary invalidates socially necessary legislation that it should sustain. This is the criticism of the Court's decision in *Dred Scott v. Sandford*,[100] where the Court declared unconstitutional the Missouri Compromise, and of the Lochner Court's invalidation of progressive legislation. In such instances, the judiciary effectively prevents the government from acting. Although the absence of needed government intervention can be seriously harmful, in general I believe that the absence of action is less risky than unrestrained action. That is, without judicial review, there would be little protection against tyranny by the majority or the disregard of constitutional provisions. The harms of such despotic rule are more to be feared than the overzealous judicial invalidation of legislation.

Having demonstrated that the risks of expansive discretion are less than usually thought, what remains is to show its benefits. I believe that the earlier chapters did exactly this. Previously, I established that only a constitution that evolves by interpretation can adequately protect minorities and safeguard fundamental rights. A judiciary insulated from the political process is uniquely suited to articulate society's deepest values and apply them to protect interests and groups most in need of assistance. The powerful in society can succeed in the legislature, but the powerless and unpopular need judicial protection. The Warren Court's legacy is a lesson of the benefits that can result from judicial discretion. No other institution but the Court would have desegregated the South. No other institution but the Court would have reapportioned state legislatures. No other institution but the Court would have had the courage to uphold the right to reproductive autonomy. Majority rule is a cornerstone of U.S. government, but there is a need to curb its excesses. Court review is the best means yet devised, and broad judicial discretion is essential if the Court is to fulfill its mission.

At the very least, this chapter demonstrated that it is misguided to search for a model of judicial review that eliminates discretion. Further, expansive judicial discretion is desirable. There is no proof that originalism, which limits discretion, risks fewer errors or will produce better decisions. Additionally, expansive judicial discretion—inevitable under a Constitution that evolves by judicial interpretation—can provide benefits justifying the risk of errors that it entails.

7 Is Open-Ended Modernism a Desirable Method of Constitutional Interpretation?

Thus far, several conclusions have been established: that society should be governed by a constitution, that the meaning of the Constitution should evolve, that such evolution should occur by interpretation and not only by amendment, that the judiciary is the preferable interpreter, and that the process of interpretation is inherently open-ended and indeterminate. In other words, it is desirable for society to have an institution, such as the judiciary, that is accorded great discretion in imparting specific, modern content to constitutional provisions. The Supreme Court's role in interpreting the general language of the Constitution is to identify those values so important that they should be protected from majority rule. I term this approach to constitutional interpretation *open-ended modernism*.

I choose the label *open-ended modernism* advisedly. Two concepts are contained within it. One is that current concerns and conceptions should provide the specific meaning of the Constitution's open-textured clauses. The Constitution identifies enduring values—freedom of speech, privacy, equality. In applying them to contemporary problems and situations, the Court should not be limited to the understandings of men who lived one or two centuries ago. Hence, the model of review that I espouse must be termed *modernistic*. Modernistic does not imply that the Court is precluded from considering traditions or even the Framers' intent. Rather, it means that the Court is not bound by these considerations. In deciding whether the right to privacy protects private consensual homosexual activity, the result should not be dictated by the sexual mores of the Framers. As argued throughout this book, the proper method of constitutional decision making is one that allows evolution by interpretation, a process that inevitably is heavily influenced by modern conditions and values. The judicial role is to articulate the meaning of basic values in the contemporary context and to protect these values from unjustified infringement.

At the same time, I am not presenting a single normative or political theory to guide the Court in deciding cases before it. I studiously have avoided defending a particular moral or political theory. In part, this choice has been strategic. I hope to persuade people having many different beliefs of my argument about the judiciary and constitutional interpretation. Also, as I confessed in the Preface, I do not have a well-developed theory of justice to present. Thus, I see the appropriate model of constitutional decision making as open-ended in the sense that it is capable of being used to implement a variety of moral and political theories that will provide the specific content of the Constitution's provisions.

Although the term *open-ended modernism* seems heretical, this description of the judicial role should not be surprising because it is exactly the approach that has been followed throughout U.S. history. The Court has always interpreted the Constitution in an open-ended manner to meet the current society's needs. Throughout U.S. history, "the justices have employed their own beliefs and values as the foundation of constitutional rulings."[1] These values and beliefs are expressed in opinions that justify the results using acceptable forms of reasoning and argument. For example, during the pre–Civil War period, when there was a widespread belief in the existence of a natural law,[2] the judiciary's role was to discover this law and apply it to decide specific cases. The Court was implementing the ideology of the justices, although cloaking its decisions in the rhetoric of the natural law so as to give the "impression that, rather than creating law, it was discovering or revealing pre-existing law."[3]

For example, in *Calder v. Bull*, in 1790, the Court spoke of its ability to invalidate state and federal legislation if they violated "vital principles," even if those principles were not expressly stated in the Constitution.[4] Justice Samuel Chase stated:

> There are certain vital principles in our free Republican governments, which will determine and over-rule an apparent and flagrant abuse of legislative power. . . . An ACT of the legislature (for I cannot call it a law) contrary to the great first principles of the social compact, cannot be considered a rightful exercise of legislative authority . . . A law that punished a citizen for an innocent act; a law that makes a man a Judge in his own cause; or a law that takes property from A and gives it to B. It is against all reason and justice for a people to entrust a Legislature with such powers and, therefore, it cannot be presumed that they have done it.[5]

Similarly, in *Fletcher v. Peck*, in 1810, the Supreme Court invalidated a Georgia effort to revoke a land grant, concluding that the result could be justified "either by general principles which are common to our free institutions, or by the particular provisions of the Constitution of the United States."[6] The Court justified its conclusions by reference to "general principles which are common to free institutions," "natural law," and "certain great principles of justice whose authority is universally acknowledged."[7]

Toward the end of the pre–Civil War period, the Court invoked natural law principles in the infamous case of *Dred Scott v. Sandford* to explain why Congress could not bar slavery from the territories and consequently why the Missouri Compromise was unconstitutional.[8] In ruling that slaves were the property of their owners and not citizens protected by the Constitution, the Court's interpretation of the Constitution helped precipitate the Civil War.[9]

As explained in the previous chapter, the natural law obviously has no determinate content. In these and other cases, the Court was engaging in an open-ended process to give specific natural law meanings to abstract constitutional provisions. Shaman explains that "[b]y resort to this artifice, the Court was able to constitutionalize the personal convictions held by the justices. Behind the facade of predetermination, the premodern Court constitutionalized personal values and beliefs held by the justices."[10]

Although after the Civil War belief in the existence of a natural law faded,[11] the Court continued to interpret the Constitution to protect then-modern values. During the period from 1887 until 1937—often referred to as the Lochner era—the Court invalidated literally hundreds of federal and state statutes based on its constitutional interpretations. For example, it interpreted the Tenth Amendment as reserving a zone of power exclusively for the states[12]—a view that previously had been rejected by the Court in Justice Marshall's famous opinion in *Gibbons v. Ogden*.[13] To protect this zone of state regulatory authority, from the late nineteenth century until 1937 the Supreme Court narrowly interpreted the commerce clause and invalidated numerous attempts by Congress to enact national regulations.[14]

For instance, the Court held that the term *commerce* only referred to the final stage of business and hence Congress could not use its commerce powers to regulate other aspects of business such as mining, manufacturing, or production.[15] The reach of the commerce clause was narrowed further by the Court's repeated holding that Congress could regulate only those aspects of business that had a "direct" effect on interstate commerce.[16] Moreover, the Court held that Congress could not use its power to prohibit commerce between the states as a means of controlling intrastate production.[17]

The Court was obligated neither by the language of the document nor the intent of its Framers to so drastically limit Congress's power under the commerce clause. In fact, there was compelling evidence that many of the Framers intended the commerce clause to grant Congress broad, plenary regulatory authority.[18] In *Gibbons v. Ogden*, in 1824, the Court had endorsed such an expansive view of Congress's authority. Justices, strongly opposed to government regulation and committed to laissez-faire capitalism, effectuated their beliefs by narrowly interpreting the commerce clause.

Also during this time period, the Court interpreted the "liberty" protected by the due process clause as safeguarding numerous values that were not explicitly protected in the Constitution's text. For example, in 1897, in *Allgeyer v. Louisiana*, the Court declared:

> The liberty mentioned in that amendment means not only the right of the citizen to be free from the mere physical restraint of his person, as by incarceration, but the term is designed to embrace the right of the citizen to be free in the enjoyment of all his faculties; to be free

to use them in all lawful ways; to live and work where he will; to earn his livelihood by any lawful calling; to pursue any livelihood or avocation, and for that purpose to enter into all contracts which may be proper, necessary and essential to his carrying out to a successful conclusion the purposes above mentioned.[19]

Similarly, in *Meyer v. Nebraska*, in 1923, the Court stated that the liberty of the due process clause protected "the right of the individual to contract, to engage in any of the common occupations of life, to acquire useful knowledge, to marry, to establish a home and bring up children, to worship God according to the dictates of his own conscience, and generally to enjoy those privileges long recognized at common law as essential to the orderly pursuit of happiness by free men."[20]

In *Meyer* the Court invalidated a state law that prohibited the teaching of German in the public schools because the Court deemed such a restriction to interfere with the liberty of parents to control the upbringing of their children.[21] Similarly, in *Pierce v. Society of Sisters* the Court declared that an Oregon statute prohibiting parochial education unconstitutionally interfered with the "liberty of parents and guardians to direct the upbringing and education of children under their control."[22] Nothing in the Constitution's text or history specifies protection of family autonomy. The Court used its discretion to interpret the abstract term *liberty* to protect something it deemed extremely important.

Most notably during this period, the Court interpreted the liberty of the due process clause as protecting freedom of individuals to enter into contracts and held that states could limit this freedom only if the restriction was necessary to achieve an important public health, safety, or moral purpose.[23] The Court implemented its commitment to laissez-faire capitalism by striking down almost 200 state and local laws that attempted to protect workers and consumers.[24] Again, the decisions were not based on explicit textual or historical support. Rather, the Court applied its own modern values in deciding the content of a constitutional provision.

After 1937 the Court abandoned the earlier restrictive interpretations of the commerce clause[25] and the protection of economic liberties through the due process clause.[26] These choices reflected a shift in social values; the Court exercised its discretion to reflect changing conceptions about the proper role of government. Since 1937, economic liberties and the protection of property have been deemphasized; the focus has been on safeguarding political freedoms and "insular minorities."[27]

It is hardly controversial to point out that virtually every major decision in the last 50 years, and especially since the Warren Court began in 1954, reflects a nonoriginalist methodology. The ambiguous language of the equal protection clause did not compel the Court to end school segregation and invalidate Jim Crow laws. The right to a fair trail embodied in the Sixth Amendment does not necessarily mean that the government has the obligation to provide free counsel to indigents; in fact, an earlier case explicitly held that no such requirement exists.[28] The Constitution does not necessitate the exclusion of evidence obtained in violation of the Fourth, Fifth, and Sixth amendments.[29] Prayers in public schools and financial aid to parochial schools are not explicitly forbidden by the First Amendment.[30] The right to travel is nowhere mentioned in the Constitution.[31] Nothing in the document or its history prevents a state from prohibiting the use of contraceptives or forbidding abortions.[32] In fact, the Constitution's text does not even state that the Bill of Rights must apply to the states.[33]

In each of these cases, the Court made a value choice. The decisions reflected the Court's judgment about what the Constitution should mean. The results were not the product of reasoning from a static, unchanging document; they were the result of open-ended interpretation. Frequently, the Court has admitted openly that its decisions reflect not determinate solutions to constitutional issues but, rather, judicial choices as to what the Constitution should mean.[34]

In other words, since the earliest days of U.S. history, open-ended modernism has been the model that best describes constitutional decision making. The Court has always used contemporary morality to determine the appropriate constitutional norms. Predictions of doom—that society could not accept a government where judges had discretion to choose constitutional values[35]—are disproved by history. The Court has survived and thrived while doing exactly what critics say will make it unviable. My conclusions are not radical calls for reformation of the U.S. political system; they are descriptions of 200 years of practice.

Thus, properly focused, the debate over constitutional interpretation is really about the question of whether open-ended modernism should continue. This book has attempted to provide a normative defense of the desirability of such an approach. In concluding, it is worth considering possible objections to my position. Several possible objections have already been answered in previous chapters. For example, Chapter 1 explained why it is misguided to criticize judicial decision making as being antimajoritarian. Chapters 3 and 4 discussed why there is nothing inherent to a constitution that requires that its meaning be fixed to that which its drafters intended. Chapter 6 responded to the argument that open-ended Court review risks judicial tyranny.

I can identify three other objections that might be offered against open-ended modernism. The first and probably most frequent, and perhaps most important, objection is that the candid public admission that the Court was following open-ended modernism would cost the judiciary its institutional legitimacy. Political theorists point out that compliance with an institution's decrees is dependent on the body's legitimacy.[36] Max Weber, who began the discussion of legitimacy among social scientists in the 1890s, wrote that "where authority is accepted as legitimate, [behavior of those being ruled] is influenced in such a way that they obey commands as if they were self-evident, natural, and identical with their own convictions."[37] In other words, "legitimacy produces a reservoir of support guaranteeing the cooperation of members of the polity even in the case of quite unpleasant policies."[38]

The judiciary's legitimacy is especially important because courts lack authority to enforce their own rulings. As such, it is argued that other branches of government will comply with the Court only if it maintains its credibility.[39] Without this credibility, judicial decisions will be disobeyed and the Court will become an ineffective institution. For this reason, constitutional experts such as Felix Frankfurter, Alexander Bickel, and most recently, Jesse Choper have argued that the Court's approach to constitutional interpretation must consciously strive to protect the judiciary's institutional legitimacy.[40]

Critics of open-ended modernism argue that the Court's credibility depends on people believing that the Court is merely applying the Constitution in a determinate, discretion-free manner to decide particular cases. Daniel Conkle recently stated that open-ended judicial decision making in human rights cases "would undermine . . . the fragile legitimacy that attaches to Supreme Court pronouncements of constitutional law; shorn of that legitimacy the Court's constitutional decisions would face all but certain popular repudiation and the Court's powerful voice would fall to a whisper."[41] Similarly, Richard Saphire remarked that a "candid confession of the policymaking nature of noninterpretive review may not only undermine its ability to protect human rights . . . but may also adversely affect its ability to perform an interpretive function."[42] In essence, it is argued that even though the Court has always followed open-ended modernism, the people do not really know this. If the deception were to end, if the people were to realize that the emperor really has no clothes, the Court's legitimacy would crumble.

First, the claims about the fragility of judicial legitimacy are mere assertions, unsupported by any empirical or theoretical support. Legitimacy is an empirical notion, requiring measurement of the degree of support for the Court's decisions and the extent of disobedience that corresponds to various levels of support. As such, arguments about legitimacy require an analysis of which types of decisions, and popular beliefs about those decisions, produce what degree of respect or disrespect for the Court. Yet those who use the concept offer no empirical support for their conclusions that particular theories of judicial discretion will undermine the Court's legitimacy. Nor do they support their conclusion with the voluminous writings from political scientists concerning the factors that account for an institution's legitimacy. In the current literature about judicial credibility, there is nothing but an assertion that the Court's legitimacy is fragile and that it would be undermined by a realization that the judiciary followed open-ended modernism.[43] At the very least, discussions about legitimacy should wait until empirical work is done of the sources of judicial legitimacy and the factors that might undermine it. For decades, critics of judicial activism have been making legitimacy arguments that are completely unsupported assertions.

Second, the argument about legitimacy assumes that the people believe that judicial decisions are entirely formalistic, with the Court reasoning from clear constitutional premises to determinate conclusions. Although this, too, is an empirical question about public attitudes, I find it difficult to accept that the people seriously believe that the text of the Constitution protects a woman's right to an abortion or prohibits prayers in public schools. I believe that the public understands that "judicial decisions are not babies brought by constitutional storks."[44] At some point in their lives, they have studied the Constitution and realize that it is written in general language that does not provide determinate answers to constitutional controversies. Popular press coverage of decisions such as *Brown v. Board of Education* and *Roe v. Wade* remind people that it is the Court making the decision—not the Constitution being mechanically applied to desegregate the schools or protect a right to abortions.

Third, I believe that history demonstrates that judicial legitimacy is not fragile. Throughout this century, the Court has handed down controversial rulings not supported by the text of the document or the intent of the Framers. Yet the Court has retained its legitimacy and its rulings have not been disregarded. Judge John Gibbons remarked that the "historical record suggests that far from being the fragile popular institution that scholars like Professor Choper . . . and Alexander Bickel have perceived it to be, judicial review is in fact quite robust."[45]

In fact, even at the times of the most intense criticism of the Supreme Court, the institution has retained its credibility. For example, opposition to the Court was probably at its height in the mid–1930s. In the midst of a depression, the Court was striking down statutes thought to be necessary for an economic recovery.[46] In an attempt to change the Court's ideology, President Franklin D. Roosevelt proposed to change the membership of the Court by increasing its size—often referred to as "Court packing."[47] Roosevelt's proposal received little support. The Senate Judiciary Committee rejected the proposal and strongly reaffirmed the need for an independent judiciary.

> Let us now set a salutary precedent that will never be violated. Let us, the Seventy-fifth Congress, declare that we would rather have an independent judiciary, a fearless Court, that will dare to announce its honest opinions in what it believes to be defense of liberties of the people, than a Court that, out of fear or sense of obligation to the appointing power or factional passion, approves any measure we may enact.[48]

This is a telling quotation and a powerful example because if anything should have undermined the Court's legitimacy, it was an unpopular Court striking down popular laws enacted by a popular administration in a time of crisis. Yet even then the Court and the Constitution retained their credibility and legitimacy.

Nor did the activism of the Warren Court lessen the judiciary's credibility. Certainly, its decisions desegregating schools and ending prayers in public schools were controversial and engendered intense opposition. But opinion polls show that in a time of general distrust of government the Court has suffered the least erosion of public confidence of any branch of government.[49] There is no indication that the Warren Court's activism has jeopardized the Court's legitimacy or that disregard of judicial decisions is imminent. Ely remarked that

> [T]he possibility of judicial emasculation by way of popular reaction against constitutional review by the courts has not in fact materialized in more than a century and a half of American experience. The warnings probably reached their peak during the Warren years;

they were not notably heeded; yet nothing resembling destruction materialized. In fact, the Court's power continued to grow and probably never has been greater than it has been over the past two decades.[50]

Why *has* the Court maintained its legitimacy even when issuing highly controversial rulings? Social science theories of legitimacy offer some explanation. Max Weber wrote that there are three major bases for an institution's legitimacy: tradition, rationality, and affective ties.[51] That which historically has existed tends to be accepted as legitimate.[52] Therefore, 200 years of judicial review grants the Court enormous credibility. Additionally, that which is rational is likely to be regarded as legitimate. The judiciary's method of giving detailed reasons for its conclusions thus helps to ensure its credibility. Finally, that which is charismatic, things to which people have strong affective ties, are accorded legitimacy. It has long been demonstrated that people feel great loyalty to the Constitution.[53] Therefore, Court decisions deciding constitutional claims also are likely to be regarded as legitimate.

In part, too, the Court's legitimacy is based on the public's desire to be governed by a constitution and society's recognition that there needs to be an institution to resolve disputes for which there is no ''right'' answer. Certainly everyone recognizes that conflicts arise in deciding what a provision means or how it should be applied in particular situations. The judiciary is accepted as a useful institution to resolve controversies, even when people disagree with the Court's ruling.

Finally, arguments about judicial legitimacy wrongly assume that the Court's credibility is related to its theory of decision making. In fact, few besides academics pay close attention to the theoretical underpinnings of decisions. Instead, the Court's legitimacy is attributable largely to public acceptance of the results of particular decisions and the methods used to reach those results. If the results in a large number of cases are unacceptable over a long period of time, the Court's legitimacy may suffer regardless of the theory of judicial review. Conversely, if the results in most cases are acceptable to most people, the Court's credibility will be enhanced.[54] I believe, for example, that the Supreme Court's desegregation decisions, although highly controversial at the time and fiercely opposed, have increased the Court's credibility. By ending laws that explicitly discriminated against blacks, the Court performed a vital social function and enhanced its legitimacy.

Additionally, the Court's credibility seems to rest upon the public perception of the Court as free from political pressure, bound by the convention of reaching rational decisions that are justified in opinions, and capable of protecting people from arbitrary government. Social scientists have established that an institution receives legitimacy by following accepted procedures.[55] Thus, the courts gain legitimacy from the judicial method, from the scrupulous avoidance of personal interests, and from the commitment to reaching decisions on the merits. Additionally, the Court enhances its credibility by writing persuasive opinions that justify its conclusions.[56] Judicial opinions, as explained in Chapter 5, demonstrate that the decision is not arbitrary and can persuade opinion leaders for matters concerning the legal system—scholars and lawyers—as to the appropriateness of the results.

In fact, a strong case can be made that it is the originalists' attack on the Court that runs the greatest risk of undermining the Court's credibility and legitimacy. Conservatives in the Reagan administration and in academia repeatedly state publicly how the Court's decisions lack constitutional authority and are in excess of the judicial role. If anything might undermine the Court's credibility, it would be these attacks. I am not, of course, advocating censorship of the conservative critics. I just wish to observe that the judiciary's credibility is the product of many factors, including the actions of the critics. It is paradoxical for the critics to claim judicial credibility as a primary justification for their approach to judicial review when it is their criticism that potentially threatens the Court's credibility.

In other words, so long as the Court's results and methods are accepted, the judiciary will retain its legitimacy, even if the people realize (if they do not already know) that the Court is following open-ended modernism. It is easy to assert that almost anything can undermine the Court's credibility. The reality is that even a frank admission of the judicial method is unlikely to diminish the institution's legitimacy.

A second major objection to open-ended modernism is that it renders the Constitution unnecessary and constitutional law meaningless. If judges can give a provision almost any meaning, why have a constitution at all?[57] If interpretation is truly open-ended, does the document serve any purpose? It would be argued that the choice to be governed by a document is a commitment to be ruled by something specific, so that constitutional law must search for a way to give determinate meaning to constitutional provisions.

In large part, this argument is answered by analysis presented earlier. Society benefits from having a constitutive document written in general language. The abstract language in the document serves as a vessel that the Court fills with modern meanings. The process of interpretation does not render the abstract language meaningless. To the contrary, the document is valuable because it states the fundamental values that unite society—liberty, equality, freedom of speech. The Court's determination of the specific content of these values reinforces their importance and increases their internalization by members of society. To say that there is great discretion in filling the vessel does not establish that the vessel, the Constitution, is unimportant or nonexistent. In other words, the fact that an abstract document gains specific meaning from interpretation does not render the document unnecessary. The Constitution is a vehicle for the protection of fundamental values from majoritarian pressures and a symbol that unites the country.

But, it might be argued, if constitutional law is a matter of judges choosing values, is it not all arbitrary? Is it even possible to discuss constitutional law if doctrines just reflect ideological choices of the justices? What is constitutional law about under open-ended modernism? Surely, it is not about what the Framers intended, because their intent is not determinative under a document that evolves by interpretation. Nor, for the reasons discussed earlier in this chapter, is it about how to construct a methodology of judicial review that will preserve the Court's legitimacy.

I suggest that discussions about the Constitution—both by courts and commentators—should focus on three questions: What values are worthy of constitutional status? How should those values be applied in particular situations? and Has the Court's result been adequately justified? Certainly, these are difficult questions about which there will be tremendous disagreement, but they are questions of enormous importance for society.

Inescapably, constitutional law requires normative analysis about what values should be protected from majoritarian decision making. Because the Constitution states values at a high level of abstraction (e.g., equality, liberty), and because there are no definitive sources for determining specific meanings, choosing values inevitably is an inquiry into political and moral theory. There probably is no more crucial or enlightening question than asking what we as a nation should care about most deeply and what is so vital that it should be constitutionalized.

Certainly, academic literature can play an essential role by advocating and discussing the importance of various interests. In fact, much of the literature about constitutional interpretation is valuable, not because of its discussion of how to reconcile judicial review with majority rule but because of its exploration of the values that the Court should protect. Jesse Choper demonstrates that the Court's mission should be to protect individual liberties.[58] John Hart Ely establishes that participational values must be safeguarded by the Court in a democratic society.[59] Michael Perry demonstrates that the Court must act to protect institutionalized persons who are usually ignored by the political process.[60]

The judiciary should be asked, through a process of argument and reflection, to identify values so fundamental as to merit constitutional protection. The political branches of government and critics can respond to the Court's rulings so that, in essence, a dialogue about values develops. This process puts consititutional law at the center of society—exactly where a constitutive document should be.

Perhaps the aversion to this view of constitutional law reflects a feeling that because all value choices are subjective, it is useless to discuss values and impossible to reason about them. In a society where there is general acceptance of moral skepticism and little apparent belief that there is a natural law, discussion of values might appear futile. After all, for a moral skeptic it is impossible ever to prove absolutely that a value is true or that one value is preferable to another.

However, even accepting the premise of value relativism, discussions about values are possible and indeed essential. It is possible to identify common, shared values and reason from them. If quality education is an accepted value, and studies prove that separate schools deny quality education to blacks, then it can be argued that it is necessary to desegregate schools. If fair trials are valued, and if counsel is believed to be essential to a fair trial, and if society believes the poor are entitled to equal justice, then it is possible to argue for government-provided counsel for indigent defendants. In other words, for a skeptic, moral reasoning consists of identifying shared values, common premises, and reasoning from them. The fact that the premises cannot be proved to be true does not render the process unimportant or nonexistent.

Society benefits from open discussions about values. Values are what we as a society care about. To ignore them because of the difficulty of discourse is to risk undermining that which is regarded as most important. The inability to ever resolve the dialogue, the fact that it is inherently open-ended, is what makes it essential that the discussion occur. If correct values were easily identifiable, constitutional decision making would be an easy, noncontroversial process. But given value conflicts and disagreements over how to resolve them, dialogue is essential to identify shared values and provide rational decision making. Above all, therefore, constitutional law is a discourse about what values should be protected.

Additionally, constitutional law is a discussion about how the values should be applied in particular cases. As explained previously, conflicts among constitutional values are inevitable. Society desires many objectives that often conflict. There is a tension between liberty and equality, between the interests of the individual and the community. No matter what—with or without judicial action—choices are made between the conflicting values. For example, how should the tension be resolved between protecting an individual's reputation and the adverse effects of the libel law on the First Amendment? Or, how should the community's right to define its morality be weighed against an individual's right to view obscenity? Without judicial action, these questions are decided in the political process. Constitutional law provides an alternative process for decisions, one emphasizing reflection and careful choice.

Thus, constitutional law is not just about what values are worthy of protection; it is also about how to implement those values, especially when there is a conflict with other important norms. Constitutional law exists to substitute rational choices for political fiat. Commentators inform the process by pointing to inconsistencies in the reasoning process and exposing errors in the balancing of competing interests. The open criticism of judicial decisions allows other branches of government, scholars, and future litigants both to persuade the Court that it erred in earlier balancings and to influence subsequent decisions.

Finally, constitutional law is a discussion of judicial opinions, a consideration of whether the Court has adequately justified the results in particular cases. Has the Court sufficiently defended its premises, correctly reasoned from them, accurately stated precedent, properly reconciled its decision with earlier holdings? These are the questions asked about decisions in every field; they are the focus of virtually every class in law school. It is hardly surprising that they are also the subject matter of constitutional law.

Thus, constitutional law is about values. It is the vehicle society has chosen to protect that which it deems to be most important. I believe that brushing aside futile inquiries as to the Framers' intent, and recognizing that constitutional law is about moral choices, will focus attention on, and increase dialogue about values. Conflicting views about values do not disappear just because they are ignored. Open discussion is society's best hope.

Again, I openly recognize what was discussed in Chapter 6: that defining constitutional law in this way does create a tension with one of the basic purposes of a Constitution, precommitment to and preservation of basic values. The more open-ended constitutional law is, the more it can be doubted whether there is any assurance of protection of the Constitution's values. There is a tension between wanting commitment to protect fundamental values and desiring change to permit progress. Yet, as argued in Chapter 6, the Constitution and judicial review offer the best mediation of this tension. A court, whose role is defined as protecting and applying the Constitution's values, offers more protection than would exist without judicial review; and a judiciary with authority to interpret the Constitution enables its underlying purposes to be served much more than if there were no opportunity for evolution by interpretation.

A final objection to my position is that this is the wrong time for someone with my liberal values to be arguing in favor of judicial activism. With a majority of the Supreme Court's justices being over 75 years of age, and with a conservative president, there is the prospect for an extremely conservative Court for the foreseeable future. According to this argument, liberals should be arguing for judicial restraint or devising theories that will yield the progressive holdings of the Warren Court but not the reactionary rulings of a Reagan or Rehnquist Court.

I do not minimize the damage the Burger Court has done to constitutional rights I value. Nor do I underestimate the possible harms of a Reagan Court, which could last well into the twenty-first century. However, I believe that it is futile to search for a model that produces liberal but not conservative interpretations. There is no theory that ensures that in the future the Court will behave like the Warren Court and not the Lochner Court. The judiciary chooses certain values to protect, and these values depend on the identity of the justices. Nor do I deny that judges tend to be appointed from elite backgrounds and historically the Court has been quite conservative.

Thus, the question in deciding whether there should be constitutional judicial review is whether the benefits of a Warren Court, discounted by its future improbability, are worth the costs of a Lochner, a Burger, or a Reagan Court. For a conservative, obviously, the examples are reversed: Are the harms to their values from a Warren Court worth the benefits they see from a future Reagan Court? The conclusions I have established throughout this book explain why it is impossible to gain the benefits of judicial discretion without accepting the costs. Discretion can produce good or bad decisions; it is wishful thinking to believe that there is a model that ensures that an indeterminate process will always produce a certain result.

I see two possible ways to argue that, on balance, judicial review is desirable. One is to focus on the examples and argue from history. I believe that the benefits from the the Warren Court were enormous and illustrate the need for a politically insulated institution to identify and protect fundamental values. Desegregation of the South and the movement toward racial equality would have been much slower and more difficult without judicial action. The South would not have voluntarily eliminated its Jim Crow laws, and Congress during the 1950s was not about to act to protect southern blacks. Equal justice, still more an illusion than a reality, was immeasurably advanced by decisions like *Gideon v. Wainwright*, which ensured counsel for indigent defendants.[61] It is almost unthinkable that the federal government should be able to discriminate on the basis of race or gender because there is no express constitutional provision compelling the national government to provide equal protection. The reapportionment of state legislatures would not have occurred without judicial action, and the Court's enforcement of a "one person/one vote" rule has made state legislatures much more responsive and effective in dealing with urban problems.[62] The Warren Court demonstrated how large the benefits of constitutional review can be in its protection of blacks, its commitment to equal justice for the poor, its safeguarding of the rights of criminal defendants, and its protection of rights such as privacy, travel, and speech.

I realize that my examples and the conclusions drawn from them can be challenged. There were only a relative handful of decisions protecting individual liberties before the Warren Court. I am hopeful that history will prove that the Warren Court is not an aberration, that the future will again show that the judiciary is the best institution for protecting fundamental values. I believe that the enormous benefits of the Warren Court will make it a model for future Courts and help ensure that the Court will be a progressive force for liberty and equality in society. Furthermore, if misleading methodological criticisms of judicial activism are removed, perhaps it will be even more likely that the Court will reach its potential as a voice for social equality and individual rights.

Yet I have no way of proving this. It is difficult to know how to add up the benefits of all past "good" decisions and weight them against the costs of all past "bad" decisions. Therefore, I suggest that the best way to determine the proper method of constitutional decision making is not to try and add up the examples but rather to structure an inquiry about government that will focus discussion on the purposes of the Constitution and the best way to accomplish them. The focus should be on basic normative questions: Should society be governed by a constitution? Should the Constitution evolve or remain static? Should evolution be by interpretation or by amendment only? Who should be the authoritative interpreter of the Constitution? and What limits should exist in the interpretive process?

This book has begun to provide my answers to these questions and to describe why, on balance, it is desirable for society to be governed by a constitution that evolves by open-ended judicial interpretation.

Notes

I find it distracting in reading a book to have to shift back and forth between the text and the notes. Therefore, to minimize such distractions, I tried to avoid textual notes and generally tried to reduce the number of notes. Nonetheless, given the rich literature on this subject, the notes are still plentiful. My compromise has been to write the text so that it can be understood without reference to the notes but to make the notes as complete as possible for those interested in my references.

PREFACE

1. For examples of attacks by Attorney General Edwin Meese and Assistant Attorney General William Bradford Reynolds against the current Supreme Court and especially Justice William Brennan's approach to constitutional interpretation, *see Reynolds Accuses Justice of Misinterpreting Fourteenth Amendment; Rights Enforcer Assails Brennan's View of Constitution*, Los Angeles Times, Sept. 14, 1986, at 4, col. 1; *Meese Attacks Judicial Activism; Intensifies Criticisms of Decisions Based on Social Theories*, Los Angeles Times, Nov. 16, 1985, at 4, col. 1. Justice Brennan publicly, in speeches, responded, attacking the critics and defending his vision of the Constitution. *See, Justice Brennan Calls Criticism of Court Disguised Arrogance*, Los Angeles Times, Oct. 13, 1985, at 5, col. 1.

2. In the last several years, a number of prominent books have been written on constitutional interpretation and judicial review, including J. Agresto, *The Supreme Court and Constitutional Democracy* (1985); P. Bobbitt, *Constitutional Fate* (1980); J. Ely, *Democracy and Distrust: A Theory of Judicial Review* (1980); A. Miller, *Toward Increased Judicial Activism* (1982); M. Perry, *The Constitution, the Courts, and Human Rights* (1982). Additionally, there have been several symposiums devoted to constitutional interpretation and judicial review. *See, e.g., Constitutional Adjudication and Democratic Theory*, 56 N.Y.U. L. Rev. 259 (1981); *Interpretation Symposium*, 58 S. Cal. L. Rev. 1

(1985); *Judicial Review and the Constitution—The Text and Beyond*, 8 U. Dayton L. Rev. 443 (1983); *Judicial Review versus Democracy*, 42 Ohio St. L. Rev. 1 (1981).

3. Bowers v. Hardwick, 106 S.Ct. 2841 (1986) (upholding a Georgia statute that prohibited oral-genital and anal-genital contacts, even in private between consenting adults).

4. *Id.*, at 2846 ("The Court is most vulnerable and comes nearest to illegitimacy when it deals with judge-made constitutional law having little or no cognizable roots in the language or design of the Constitution. . . . There should be, therefore, great resistance to expand the substantive reach of those clauses, particularly if it requires redefining the category of rights deemed to be fundamental").

5. *See* discussion in Chapter 1, infra, text accompanying notes 14–29 (describing focus of current debate as centering on reconciling judicial review with majority rule).

6. *See* discussion in Chapter 6, text accompanying notes 1–24 (describing search for objective, discretion-free, constitutional interpretation).

7. The terminology of the debate has varied somewhat. The terms *originalism* and *interpretivism* have been used interchangeably, as have the words *nonoriginalism* and *noninterpretivism*. Throughout this book, I will use *originalism* and *nonoriginalism* to refer to the two basic paradigms. In part, this is because all forms of decision making claim to be interpretation and also because the term *originalism* reflects its essential premise—decision making based on the Framers' original intentions.

Thomas Grey is credited with originating the distinction in these terms. Grey, *Do We Have an Unwritten Constitution?* 27 Stan. L. Rev. 703 (1975). The debate over judicial review has continued in these terms. *See, e.g.*, J. Ely, *supra* note 2, 1–14; M. Perry, *supra* note 2, at 1; Saphire, *Judicial Review in the Name of the Constitution*, 8 U. Dayton L. Rev. 745–746 (1983).

As Ely observes, the distinction between originalism and nonoriginalism parallels the more general distinction between positivism and natural law; originalism is similar to positivism, and natural law is one type of nonoriginalism. J. Ely, *supra* note 2, at 1 (emphasis omitted).

CHAPTER 1

1. As Dean Choper points out, "Reconciling judicial review with American representative democracy has been the subject of powerful debate since the earliest days of the Republic." J. Choper, *Judicial Review and the National Political Process* 4 (1980). *See, e.g.*, L. Goldberg and E. Levinson, *Lawless Judges* (1935); Black, *The Supreme Court and Democracy*, 50 Yale L. J. 188 (1961); Commager, *Judicial Review and Democracy*, 19 Va. Q. Rev. 417 (1943); McClesky, *Judicial Review in a Democracy: A Dissenting Opinion*, 3 Hous. L. Rev. 354 (1966); Rostow, *The Democratic Character of Judicial Review*, 66 Harv. L. Rev. 193 (1952); Thayer, *The Origin and Scope of the American Doctrine of Constitutional Law*, 7 Harv. L. Rev. 129 (1893); Wright, *The Role of the Supreme Court in a Democratic Society*, 54 Cornell L. Rev. 1 (1968).

I should clarify at the outset that my focus in this book is only on interpretation of the United States Constitution. Although state constitutions are similar in many respects, they usually differ so greatly from the United States Constitution that interpretation of state constitutions would be a separate inquiry. *See, e.g.*, L. Tribe, *Constitutional Choices* 26, 289 n.43 (1985) (greater detail of state constitutions means they engender less respect); J.

Corsi, *An Introduction to Judicial Politics* 104–114 (1984) (under state constitutions, most state judges are directly accountable to the electorate).

2. Although there is a general agreement that the debate over the legitimacy of judicial review has intensified, there is no consensus over why it is occurring now. Some see it as a response to the activism of the Warren Court. *See, e.g.*, Benedict, *To Secure These Rights: Rights, Democracy, and Judicial Review in Anglo-American Constitutional Heritage*, 42 Ohio St. L. J. 69, 69 (1981). Other commentators link the controversy over judicial review to specific decisions, most notably Roe v. Wade, 410 U.S. 113 (1973). *See, e.g.*, Meeks, *Foreward*, 42 Ohio St. L. J. 1, 2 (1981). Still others see the current debate as the continuation of a controversy that has been under way for years. *See, e.g.*, Berns, *Judicial Review and the Rights and Laws of Nature*, 1982 Sup. Ct. Rev. 49.

3. R. Berger, *Government by Judiciary: The Transformation of the Fourteenth Amendment* (1977); Bork, *Neutral Principles and Some First Amendment Problems*, 47 Ind. L. J. 1 (1971); Rehnquist, *The Notion of a Living Constitution*, 54 Texas L. Rev. 693 (1976).

4. *See* R. Berger, *supra* note 3, at 410 (arguing that "[r]espect for the limits on [judicial] power are the essence of a democratic society"); Bork, *supra* note 3, at 6 (noting that "a court that makes rather than implements value choices cannot be squared with the propositions of a democratic society"); Rehnquist, *supra* note 3, at 695–696 (noting that "the ideal of judicial review has basically antidemocratic and antimajoritarian facets that must be justified in this nation"); *see also* Grano, *Judicial Review and a Written Constitution in a Democratic Society*, 28 Wayne L. Rev. 1, 7 (1981); Posner, *The DeFunis Case and the Constitutionality of Preferential Treatment of Racial Minorities*, 1974 Sup. Ct. Rev. 1, 28.

5. J. Ely, *Democracy and Distrust: A Theory of Judicial Review* vii (1980) (claiming that his theory "is consistent with . . . the underlying democratic assumptions of our system"); M. Perry, *The Constitution, The Courts, and Human Rights* 10 (1982) (task is to accept the principle of electorally accountable policymaking and to defend judicial review as consistent with it.); Choper, *supra* note 1; Choper, *The Supreme Court and the Political Branches: Democratic Theory and Practice*, 122 U. Pa. L. Rev. 810, 815 (1974) ("[T]he procedure of judicial review is in conflict with the fundamental principle of democracy—majority rule under conditions of political freedom").

6. *See, e.g.*, *Constitutional Adjudication and Democratic Theory*, 56 N.Y.U. L. Rev. 259 (1981); *Interpretation Symposium*, 58 S. Cal. L. Rev. 1 (1985); *Judicial Review and the Constitution—The Text and Beyond*, 8 U. Dayton L. Rev. 443 (1983); *Judicial Review versus Democracy*, 42 Ohio St. L. Rev. 1 (1981).

7. *See* Grey, *Do We Have an Unwritten Constitution?* 27 Stan. L. Rev. 703 (1975) (describing distinction between these two models of constitutional interpretation). *See also* J. Ely, *supra* note 5, 1–14; M. Perry, *supra* note 5, at 1; Saphire, *Judicial Review in the Name of the Constitution*, 8 U. Dayton L. Rev. 745–746 (1983) (articulating issue in terms of a choice between originalism [interpretivism] and nonoriginalism [noninterpretivism]).

8. *See* Bork, *supra* note 3, at 8–9 (claiming that the constitutional protection of privacy cannot be justified under an originalist approach). For notable decisions protecting privacy, *see* Roe v. Wade, 410 U.S. 113 (1973); Doe v. Bolton, 410 U.S. 179 (1973); Griswold v. Connecticut, 381 U.S. 479 (1965).

9. M. Perry, *supra* note 5, at 2.

10. *See* Trimble v. Gordon, 430 U.S. 762, 777–786 (1977) (Rehnquist, J., dissenting)

(arguing that the Fourteenth Amendment was intended only to protect racial minorities). For notable decisions that use the Fourteenth Amendment to prevent gender discrimination, *see* Mississippi Univ. for Women v. Hogan, 458 U.S. 718 (1982); Craig v. Boren, 429 U.S. 190 (1976); Reed v. Reed, 404 U.S. 71 (1971).

11. *See* Kurland, *The Irrelevance of the Constitution: The First Amendment's Freedom of Speech and Freedom of Press Clauses*, 29 Drake L. Rev. 1, 12 (1979) (virtually all recent First Amendment decisions go beyond the Framers' intent).

12. *See* Fairman, *Does the Fourteenth Amendment Incorporate the Bill of Rights?: The Original Understanding*, 2 Stan. L. Rev. 5 (1949) (arguing that the Framers of the Fourteenth Amendment did not intend to apply the Bill of Rights to the states).

13. Even most nonoriginalists tend to agree that few recent Supreme Court cases protecting individual liberties can be justified under an originalist approach. *See, e.g.*, J. Choper, *supra* note 1, at 137; M. Perry, *supra* note 5, at 2.

14. M. Perry, *supra* note 5, at 9.

15. The very title of Ely's book, *Democracy and Distrust*, reflects his goal of trying to reconcile judicial review with democratic theory. See also J. Ely, *supra* note 5, at 5 (observing that representative democracy always has been accepted as a core aspect of the American system of government).

16. *Id.*, at 7.

17. Attanasio, *Everyman's Constitutional Law: A Theory of the Power of Judicial Review*, 72 Georgetown L. J. 1665, 1666 n. 4 (1984).

18. Richard Saphire observed that "most theorists accept, as a general proposition, that in our democracy the development and implementation of public policy is entrusted to institutions and individuals who are accountable to the electorate." Saphire, *Making Noninterpretivism Respectable: Michael J. Perry's Contributions to Constitutional Theory*, 81 Mich. L. Rev. 781, 783 n.6 (1983).

19. M. Perry, *supra* note 5, at 4 (quoting J. Pennock, *Democratic Political Theory* 7 [1979]).

20. For example, sometimes in the literature *majority rule* refers to a requirement that decisions be made by the majority, sometimes it refers to a requirement that decisions be made by officials who are electorally accountable, and sometimes it refers to a requirement that decisions be subject to control by electorally accountable officials. Each of these definitions requires a great deal of elaboration. For instance, under the latter definition, what degree of control is sufficient to meet the requirements of majority rule? The key point is that there are countless different ways of defining *democracy* and *majority rule*, and the definition chosen must be explained and justified. *See* M. Edleman, *Democratic Theories and the Constitution* 5, 7 (1984) ("[T]here is considerable disagreement about what democracy means and implies," and there is no one correct definition).

For excellent discussions of the meaning of the term *democracy* in the political science literature, *see, e.g.*, H. Ball, *Courts and Politics* (1980); E. Edelman, *supra* note 20; H. Mayo, *An Introduction to Democratic Theory* (1960); W. Nelson, *On Justifying Democracy* (1980); A. Ross, *Why Democracy?* (1952); C. Ryn, *Democracy and the Ethical Life* (1977).

21. *See, e.g.*, A. Bickel, *The Least Dangerous Branch* 16–17 (1962); Mace, *The Antidemocratic Character of Judicial Review*, 60 Calif. L. Rev. 1140, 1145 (1972); Richards, *Sexual Autonomy and the Constitutional Right to Privacy: A Case Study in Human Rights and the Unwritten Constitution*, 30 Hastings L. J. 957, 958 (1979).

22. A Bickel, *supra* note 21, at 16–20.

23. Brest, *The Fundamental Rights Controversy: The Essential Contradictions of Normative Constitutional Scholarship*, 90 Yale L. J. 1063 (1981) ("[t]he controversy over the legitimacy of judicial review in a democratic polity . . . [is] the historic obsession of constitutional law scholarship"); Attanasio, *supra* note 17, at 1669 ("American lawyers have been obsessed by arguments over the validity of the Supreme Court's counter-majoritarian power").

24. Berger, *Ely's Theory of Judicial Review*, 42 Ohio St. L. J. 87, 87 (1981).

25. Bork, *supra* note 3, at 6. Justice Rehnquist expresses similar sentiments: "How can government by the elected representatives of the people coexist with the power of the federal judiciary, whose members are constitutionally insulated from responsiveness to the popular will, to declare invalid laws duly enacted by the popular branches of government?" Furman v. Georgia, 408 U.S. 238, 466 (1972) (Rehnquist, J., dissenting).

26. Conkle, *The Legitimacy of Judicial Review in Individual Rights Cases: Michael Perry's Constitutional Theory and Beyond*, 69 Minn. L. Rev. 587, 619 (1985).

27. M. Perry, *supra* note 5, at 10.

28. J. Ely, *supra* note 5, at 75–104.

29. M. Perry, *supra* note 5, at 126–138.

30. *Id.*, at 9, 10.

31. M. Edelman, *supra* note 20, at 5, 7.

32. 319 U.S. 624, 638 (1943).

33. Webster's Third New International Dictionary 600 (1966).

34. *See, e.g.*, W. Nelson, *On Justifying Democracy 94–129 (1980); H. Mayo, supra* note 20, at 218–241; A. Rossa, supra note 20, at 96–108; C. Ryn. *supra* note 20, at 16–65.

35. H. Arendt, *On Revolution* 143 (1977 ed.).

36. 1 M. Farrand, *The Records of the Federal Convention of 1787* 48 (1937 ed.).

37. Richards, *Interpretation and Historiography*, 56 S. Cal. L. Rev. 489, 511 (1985) (quoting *The Federalist No. 10* [J. Madison]); M. Edelman, *supra* note 20, at 15.

38. R. Dahl, *A Preface to Democratic Theory* 35 (1956).

39. Choper, *supra* note 5, at 810, 821 (senators representing 15 percent of the population can thwart the will of senators representing 85 percent of the people).

40. Marbury v. Madison, 5 U.S. (1 Cranch) 137 (1803).

41. *See, e.g.*, Harper v. Board of Elections, 383 U.S. 663, 669 (1966); United States v. Classic, 313 U.S. 299, 315–316 (1941); Home Building and Loan Assn. v. Blaisdell, 290 U.S. 398 (1934); Weems v. United States, 217 U.S. 349, 373 (1910); Cohens v. Va., 19 U.S. (6 Wheat.) 264, 387 (1821); Fletcher v. Peck, 10 U.S. (6 Cranch) 87 (1810); Calder v. Bull, 3 U.S. (3 Dall.) 386 (1798) (decisions containing open recognition of their nonoriginalist methodology).

42. *See, e.g.*, J. Choper, *supra* note 1, at 29–46. In fact, as Brilmayer points out, even a legislature that applies the Constitution acts in a countermajoritarian fashion: "Where there is a written constitution, some measure of countermajoritarianism is positively desirable. And in seeking to limit judicial contradiction of majority will, proponents of judicial restraint are relying upon an irrelevant fact, namely, the fact that federal judges do not run for office. This fact is irrelevant because if legislatures seriously fulfill their responsibilities to consider whether their activities are constitutional, they also risk behaving in a countermajoritarian fashion." Brilmayer, *The Jurisprudence of Article III: Perspectives on the "Cases or Controversies" Requirement*, 93 Harv. L. Rev. 297, 304 (1979).

43. There are attempts by some political theorists to defend procedural definitions of

democracy. *See, e.g.*, B. Barry, *Is Democracy Special?* in *Philosophy, Politics and Society* (Fifth Series) 155, (P. Laslett & J. Fishkin eds. 1979) ("I follow . . . those who insist that 'democracy' is to be understood in procedural terms. That is to say, I reject the notion that one should build into democracy any constraints on the substantive outcomes produced, such as substantive equality, respect for human rights, concern for the general welfare, personal liberty or the rule of law"). However, in the debate over constitutional interpretation, complete majoritarian decision making has been assumed to be desirable, not established as normatively or descriptively correct.

44. H. Mayo, *supra* note 20, at 218–241.

45. *Id.*, at 228–230, 237–241.

46. *See, e.g.*, A. Ross, *supra* note 20, at 96–108; C. Ryn, *supra* note 20, at 160–65.

47. A. Bickel, *supra* note 21, at 18 (labeling judicial review a "deviant institution in American government"); *see also* H. Commager, *Majority Rule and Minority Rights* 56 (1943) (describing judicial review as a "drag . . . upon democracy").

48. R. Dahl, *supra* note 38, at 34–62 (democracy does not require majority rule for all purposes); *Commentary*, 56 N.Y.U. L. Rev. 525, 536 (1981) ("There is nothing in the Constitution that elevates principles of majoritarianism above other rights-bearing principles with which that document is laced").

49. *See, e.g.*, R. Harris, *The Quest for Equality: The Constitution, Congress, and the Supreme Court* (1960); H. L. A. Hart, *The Concept of Law* (1961); *but see* Westen, *The Empty Idea of Equality*, 95 Harv. L. Rev. 537 (1982).

50. *See, e.g.*, R. Dworkin, *Taking Rights Seriously* (1977).

51. *See, e.g.*, L. Fisher, *The President and Congress* (1972); R. Neustadt, *Presidential Power* (1960); E. Corwin, *The President Office and Power* (rth ed. 1957).

52. If the definition of democracy includes substantive values, such as freedom of speech and equality, then judicial review enhances democracy by protecting these values.

53. By this view, the overall goal is "good government," and democracy (defined as majority rule) is one characteristic of good government; equality, rights, separation of powers are others.

54. *See* discussion accompanying notes 14–27, *supra*.

55. It might be argued that if democracy is defined as including substantive values then we would lack a vocabulary for discussing conflicts between democracy and these other values. This is not a problem, however, because the discussion would focus on the conflict between aspects of democracy, such as the frequently identified conflict between majority rule and minority rights.

56. M. Perry, *supra* note 5, at 93.

57. *Id.*, at 98–99, 101–114.

58. *Id.*, at 126. The Constitution provides that the Supreme Court "shall have appellate jurisdiction, both as to law and fact, with such exceptions and under such regulations as the Congress shall make." U.S. Const. art. III, §2. The Constitution also provides for congressional discretion to "ordain and establish" lower federal courts. *Id.*, at §1. Apparently, "the decision with respect to the inferior federal courts . . . of defining their jurisdiction . . . was left to the discretion of Congress." Palmore v. United States, 411 U.S. 389, 401 (1973). *But see* Martin v. Hunter's Lessee, 14 U.S. (1 Wheat.) 304, 331 (1816) (Justice Story's view that "the whole judicial power of the United States should be, at all times, vested in either original or appellate form, in some [federal] courts").

59. M. Perry, *supra* note 5, at 138. Charles Black advances a similar theory: that activist judicial review is consistent with democratic theory because of congressional

power to limit the jurisdiction of federal courts. C. Black, *Decision According to Law* 17–19, 37–39 (1981).

60. Kay, *Limiting Federal Court Jurisdiction: The Unforeseen Impact on Courts and Congress*, 65 Judicature 185, 187 (1981) ("Removal of court jurisdiction over specific subject matter does not repair any damage. The simple fact is that withdrawing the Supreme Court's jurisdiction over school prayer does not return prayer to the schools. Withdrawing court jurisdiction over abortion does not outlaw abortion").

61. *See, e.g.*, S. 158, 97th Cong., 1st Sess. (1981); H. R. 3225, 97th Cong, 1st Sess. (1981) (bills restricting federal court jurisdiction over abortion cases).

62. *See, e.g.*, S. 481, 97th Cong., 1st Sess. (1981); H. R. 327, 97th Cong., 1st Sess. (1981) (bills restricting federal court jurisdiction over cases that involve voluntary school prayers).

63. *See* Cooper v. Aaron, 358 U.S. 1, 18 (1958) (Supreme Court decisions state "the supreme law of the land" and state officials are obligated to follow them); Grano, *supra* note 4, at 42 ("If state officials behave lawfully—if they adhere to their oath to support the Constitution—they will still be bound by the Court's decisions, which would remain the law of the land").

64. *See* Kay, *supra* note 60, at 187; Wechsler, *The Courts and the Constitution*, 65 Colum. L. Rev. 1001, 1006–1007 (1965) ("[t]he jurisdictional withdrawal might work to freeze the very doctrines that had prompted its enactment").

65. *See* Kay, *supra* note 60, at 188 ("The end result of [the] . . . proposals is that constitutional protections become illusory. . . . The protections of the Constitution will only be what 51 percent of the House and 51 percent of the Senate say they are").

66. M. Perry, *supra* note 5, at 130–131. Although Perry argues that there is a difference between restricting jurisdiction and reversing decisions—*id.*, at 136—the *effect* of each is the same. Majority rule is achieved only if laws are enacted that violate the Supreme Court's interpretation of the Constitution. In fact, Congress enacts restrictions on jurisdiction with the goal of changing the substantive law. *See* Alexander, *Painting without the Numbers: Noninterpretive Judicial Review*, 8 U. Dayton L. Rev. 447, 456–457 (1983) ("There is very little difference between legislative overrules of judicial decisions and legislative withdrawals of jurisdiction").

67. As Sager observes: "If Congress enacts a selective jurisdictional restriction for cases that concern state conduct, it will be issuing an open, unambiguous invitation to state and local officials to engage in the conduct that the Supreme Court has explicitly held unconstitutional. . . . If, for example, Congress were to enact legislation insulating 'voluntary' school prayers from federal judicial scrutiny, there would inevitably be an epidemic of school prayer programs." Sager, *Foreward: Constitutional Limitations on Congress' Authority to Regulate the Jurisdiction of the Federal Courts*, 95 Harv. L. Rev. 17, 69 (1981).

68. *See* Tribe, *Jurisdictional Gerrymandering: Zoning Disfavored Rights Out of Federal Court*, 16 Harv. Civ. Rights-Civ. Lib. L. Rev. 129, 129–30 (1981) (goal of jurisdictional restrictions is the "de facto reversal, by means far less burdensome than those required of a constitutional amendment, of several highly controversial Supreme Court rulings dealing with such matters as abortion, school prayer, and busing").

69. *See* Ratner, *Congressional Power over the Appellate Jurisdiction of the Supreme Court*, 109 U. Pa. L. Rev. 157, 158 (1960) (noting that with a jurisdiction-limiting statute,

Congress "can all but destroy the coordinate judicial branch and upset the delicately posed constitutional system of checks and balances").

70. 5 U.S. (1 Cranch) 137 (1803).

71. On numerous occasions, the Supreme Court has declared that the central purpose of judicial review is to ensure that the states uniformly follow federal law, including the Constitution. *See, e.g.*, Dodge v. Woosley, 59 U.S. (How.) 331, 335 (1855); Cohens v. Virginia, 19 U.S. (6 Wheat.) 264, 386–387 (1821). As the Supreme Court declared: "Thirteen independent courts . . . of final jurisdiction over the same causes, arising upon the same laws, is a hydra in government, from which nothing but contradiction and confusion can proceed." Cohens v. Virginia, 19 U.S., at 415–416 (quoting *The Federalist No. 80* [A. Hamilton]).

72. M. Perry, *supra* note 5, at 130–134. Subsequently, Perry has written that if Congress has the power to restrict federal court jurisdiction, this power will extend to precluding review of originalist as well as nonoriginalist decisions. Perry, *The Authority of Text, Tradition, and Reason: A Theory of Constitutional Interpretation*, 58 S. Cal. L. Rev. 551, 580n. 89 (1985).

73. M. Perry, *supra* note 5, at 2 (Almost all modern constitutional decisions are non-originalist).

74. Perry admits this in a subsequent article, admitting that the power to restrict jurisdiction applies in both originalist and nonoriginalist cases. Perry, *supra* note 72, at 580n. 89.

75. *See* Alexander, *supra* note 66, at 453; Lupu, *Constitutional Theory and the Search for the Workable Premise*, 8 U. Dayton L. Rev. 579, 609 (1983).

76. Sager, *supra* note 67, at 39; *see also* Burt, *Constitutional Law and the Teaching of the Parables*, 93 Yale L. J. 455, 484–485n. 93 (1984) ("Perry finds himself caught in a contradiction between his conception of moral leadership for judges and the apparently superior authoritative claims of majoritarian institutions"); Wellington, *History and Morals in Constitutional Adjudication* (Book Review), 97 Harv. L. Rev. 326, 328 (1983) ("But what kind of dialogue is it when one participant can silence the other by cutting out his tongue when offended by his words?").

77. *See* M. Perry, *supra* note 5, at 134. Arguably, Congress has never completely restricted federal court review because even in *Ex Parte* McCardle, 74 U.S. (7 Wall.) 506 (1869), the primary example of congressional power under the exceptions clause, the plaintiff had other avenues of access to the federal courts. M. Redish, *Federal Jurisdiction: Tensions in the Allocation of Judicial Power* 18 (1980).

78. In 1981, for example, 18 proposals were introduced in Congress to restrict federal court jurisdiction. *See* Tribe, *supra* note 68, at 129. "In the fifteen years between 1953 and 1968, over sixty bills were introduced in Congress to eliminate the jurisdiction of the federal courts over a variety of specific subjects; none of these became law." P. Bator, P. Mishkin, D. Shapiro & H. Wechsler, *Hart and Wechsler's the Federal Courts and the Federal System* 360 (2d ed. 1973).

79. Tushnet, *Legal Realism, Structural Review, and Prophecy*, 8 Dayton L. Rev. 809, 813 (1983).

80. *See, e.g.*, M. Redish, *supra* note 77; Eisenberg, *Congressional Authority to Restrict Lower Federal Court Jurisdiction*, 83 Yale L. J. 498 (1974); Hart, *The Power of Congress to Limit the Jurisdiction of the Federal Courts: An Exercise in Dialectic*, 66 Harv. L. Rev. 1362 (1953); Ratner, *supra* note 69; Sager, *supra* note 67.

81. J. Ely, *supra* note 5, at 87.

82. *See id.*, at 75.

83. *Id.*, at 87. Ely argues that the Court should protect participational values because those are the ones which the Constitution is preeminently concerned with. Their protection reinforces democracy, and the Court has special expertise as to questions of process. *Id.*, at 75 n.*. Ely argues that this theory is the underlying concept expressed in the famous footnote in United States v. Carolene Prods. Co., 304 U.S. 144, 152–153n.4 (1938). *See* J. Ely, *supra* note 5, at 75–77.

84. J. Ely, *supra* note 5, at 88. Tribe explains why Ely's theory is so appealing: "It is easy to see why the courts would be attracted to this way of describing the content and role of constitutional law. Such an account permits courts to perceive and portray themselves as servants of democracy even as they strike down the actions of supposedly democratic governments." Tribe, *The Puzzling Persistence of Process-Based Constitutional Theories*, 89 Yale L. J. 1063, 1063 (1980).

85. J. Ely, *supra* note 5, at 87–88.

86. As Tribe points out: "Religious freedom, antislavery, private property: much of our constitutional history can be written by reference to just these social institutions and substantive values. That the Constitution has long addressed such matters, and often with beneficial effect, ought to surprise no one. What is puzzling is that anyone can say, in the face of this reality, that the Constitution is or should be predominately concerned with *process* and not *substance*." Tribe, *supra* note 84, at 1067 (emphasis in original).

87. Ely argues that the right to travel would be upheld under a process model because a person should have the ability to leave an incompatible majority. J. Ely, *supra* note 5, at 179.

88. *See, e.g.*, Shapiro v. Thompson, 394 U.S. 618, 630 (1969) ("[W]e have no occasion to ascribe the source of this right [to travel.]"); United States v. Guest, 383 U.S. 745, 758 (1966) ("that right finds no explicit mention in the Constitution").

89. Roe v. Wade, 410 U.S. 113 (1973) (striking down Texas statute forbidding abortion as violating Fourteenth Amendment).

90. J. Ely, *supra* note 5, at 247n. 52; Ely, *The Wages of Crying Wolf: A Comment on Roe v. Wade*, 82 Yale L. J. 920 (1973).

91. According to Ely, the Constitution is based on the "quite sensible assumption that an effective majority will not inordinately threaten its own rights, and . . . [seeks] to assure that such a majority will not systematically treat others less well than it treats itself." J. Ely, *supra* note 5, at 100–101.

92. This argument and its flaws are outlined in Chemerinsky, *Rationalizing the Abortion Debate: Legal Rhetoric and the Abortion Controversy*, 31 Buffalo L. Rev. 107, 117–122, 138–139 (1982).

93. Cox, *Book Review*, 94 Harv. L. Rev. 700, 710–711 (1981); Dworkin, *The Forum of Principle*, 56 N.Y.U. L. Rev. 469, 515–516 (1981) (arguing that Ely's theory could be used to justify creating a right to legalized abortions). Frank Michelman argues that Ely's theory can justify judicial action guaranteeing all citizens a right to basic entitlements, an action likely to be regarded as the height of judicial activism. Michelman, *Welfare Rights in a Constitutional Democracy*, 1979 Wash. U. L. Q. 659, 674–680.

94. J. Ely, *supra* note 5, at 73–104.

95. *See* Tribe, *supra* note 84, at 1069–1070.

96. *See, e.g.*, Abbate v. Mundt, 403 U.S. 182 (1971) (sustaining deviations from mathematical equality by a range of up to 11.9 percent); Reynolds v. Sims, 377 U.S. 533, 579–580 (1964) (describing instances in which deviations from one person/one vote are

permissible); Lucas v. Colorado Gen. Assembly, 377 U.S. 713 (1964) (holding that approval in a popular referendum cannot sustain impermissible malapportionment).

97. *See* Eistreicher, *Platonic Guardians of Democracy: John Hart Ely's Role for the Supreme Court in the Constitution's Open-Texture*, 56 N.Y.U. L. Rev. 547, 565 (1981) (judicial review of voting procedures requires imposition of substantive values).

98. *See, e.g.*, Gideon v. Wainwright, 372 U.S. 335 (1963) (requiring appointment of counsel for every indigent accused of a felony).

99. Miranda v. Arizona, 384 U.S. 436 (1966).

100. J. Ely, *supra* note 5, at 124–125.

101. *Id.*, at 75, 103.

102. J. Choper, *supra* note 1, at 9–10.

103. *See* Eistreicher, *supra* note 97, at 575 ("No . . . claim can be made that judicial intervention in support of minority groups is necessarily consistent with, or particularly supportive of, representative democracy").

104. For example, Ely's theory of "virtual representation"—J. Ely, *supra* note 5, at 82–87, 100–101—adds a new element to the definition of democracy because it requires effective representation of all groups in society. While I agree with this addition to the definition, it nevertheless is a limitation on the principle of majority rule with which Ely begins; it replaces the strictly procedural definition of democracy with a substantive one.

105. *See* Westen, *The Empty Idea of Equality*, 95 Harv. L. Rev. 537 (1982). Although a number of commentators have challenged Westen's conclusion that the concept of equality should be banned from legal or moral discourse—*id.*, at 542—none of them has challenged his premise that all discussions of equality require the use of other substantive values. *See* Burton, *Comment on 'Empty Ideas': Logical Positivist Analysis of Equality and Rules*, 91 Yale L. J. 1136 (1982); Chemerinsky, *In Defense of Equality: A Reply to Professor Westen*, 81 Mich. L. Rev. 575 (1983); D'Amato, *Is Equality a Totally Empty Idea?* 81 Mich. L. Rev. 600 (1983).

106. J. Ely, *supra* note 5, at 256 n. 92; *see also* M. Perry, *supra* note 5, at 153 (determining whether distinctions are the result of prejudice or legitimate differences require substantive judgments).

107. *See* Baker, *Neutrality, Process and Rationality: Flawed Interpretations of Equal Protection*, 58 Texas L. Rev. 1029, 1041 (1980); Tribe, *supra* note 84, at 1076. All who challenge a law arguably constitute a minority that opposes a decision by the majority. *See* J. Choper, *supra* note 1, at 76. The courts need substantive criteria to determine which minorities deserve judicial protection.

108. *See* discussion accompanying notes 110–131, *infra* (all theories seeking to reconcile majority rule and judicial review fail).

109. As Maltz remarks: "[T]he exercise of judicial review is fundamentally inconsistent with the practice of electorally accountable government. This fact does not condemn the practice; one can still argue that the abandonment of democratic principles leads to a better governed nation. But unless one is willing to forthrightly take this position, any defense of noninterpretive review is doomed to failure." Maltz, *Murder in the Cathedral: The Supreme Court as Moral Prophet*, 8 U. Dayton L. Rev. 623, 631 (1983); *see also* Burt, *supra* note 76, at 485 n. 93 (Perry's "basic error is in seeking to legitimize judicial review by identifying principles for hierarchically ranking the relative authority of judicial and majoritarian institutions. He has distinguished company in this regard; it has been the dominant theme of constitutional law scholarship at least since James Bradley Thayer"); Brest, *supra* note 23, at 1063.

110. *See, e.g.*, R. Berger, *supra* note 3; Bork, *supra* note 3; Rehnquist, *supra* note 3.

111. 5 U.S. (1 Cranch) 137 (1803).

112. The inherent ambiguity of history as a basis for constitutional interpretation is discussed in Chapter 3, text accompanying notes 26–37, *infra*.

113. *See* H. L. A. Hart, *The Concept of Law* 125 (1961): H. Kelman, *The Pure Theory of Law* 349 (1970) ("Even the most detailed command must leave to the individual executing the command some discretion. Hence every law-applying act is only partly determined by the law and partly undetermined"). The inherent discretion in decision making is discussed in Chapters 3 and 6, *infra*.

114. Saphire, *supra* note 7, at 765 (presenting the originalist argument, attributed to Raoul Berger, that the Framers' intent should be followed because the Framers intended that it be followed).

115. A. Bickel, *supra* note 21, at 1; *see also* Perry, *Interpretivism, Freedom of Expression, and Equal Protection*, 42 Ohio St. L. J. 261, 266 (1981) (The text of the Constitution is equivocal even with regard to originalist judicial review).

116. *See, e.g.*, J. Choper, *supra* note 1, at 423 nn. 7–8; 2 W. Crosskey, *Politics and the Constitution in the History of the United States* 1008–1046 (1953) (arguing that the Framers did not intend judicial review); Monaghan, *The Constitution Goes to Harvard*, 13 Harv. Civ. Rights-Civ. Lib. L. Rev. 117, 125 (1978) (noting that it is "increasingly doubtful that any conclusive case can be made one way or the other. It is an understatement to say that the Framers lacked clarity in their thinking").

117. M. Perry, *supra* note 5, at 74; Jesse Choper observes that "[w]hatever indications may be gleaned from intention or text on the issue of whether the Court should possess the power of judicial review, these sources afford virtually no assistance whatever on the related question of the form and scope of judicial review; or whether . . . the Court should assume a stance of activism or restraint." Choper, *supra* note 1, at 423, n. 7–8.

118. Kay, *Preconstitutional Rules*, 42 Ohio St. L. J. 187, 193 n. 22 (1981) ("It is anomalous to argue . . . that recourse to the intention of the Framers of the Constitution is required . . . [as] demonstrated from a review of the Framers' intention"); Monaghan, *Our Perfect Constitution*, 56 N.Y.U. L. Rev. 353, 383 n. 177 (1981).

119. Simon, *The Authority of the Constitution and Its Meaning: A Preface to a Theory of Constitutional Interpretation*, 58 S. Cal. L. Rev. 603, 645 (1985). In Chapter 4, I develop the contention that a normative theory must be developed to justify any method of interpretation, including originalism. *See* Chapter 4, text accompanying notes 11–47, *infra*.

120. Judge Learned Hand wrote this famous phrase: "For myself it would be most irksome to be ruled by a bevy of Platonic guardians, even if I knew how to choose them, which I assuredly do not." L. Hand, *The Bill of Rights* 73 (1958).

121. Larry Alexander states this well: "Why should the framers, but not the Supreme Court, have the authority to bind us to value judgments not endorsed by contemporary political bodies?" Alexander, *supra* note 66, at 454 n. 29.

122. *See, e.g.*, Bork, *supra* note 3, at 3 ("Society consents to be ruled undemocratically within defined areas by certain enduring principles believed to be stated in, and placed beyond the reach of majorities, by the Constitution"); Lupu, *supra* note 75, at 590 ("Interpretivists, echoing Hamilton in the Federalist Papers, argue that the consent requirements are satisfied in the exercise of judicial review on grounds of enforcement of values which 'the people' have enshrined in the constitutional text").

123. Lerner, *The Constitution and Court as Symbols*, 46 Yale L. J. 1290, 1296 (1937).

124. Paul Brest writes: "Even if the adopters freely consented to the Constitution . . . this is not an adequate basis for continuing fidelity to the founding document, for their consent cannot bind subsequent generations. We did not adopt the Constitution and those who did are dead and gone." Brest, *The Misconceived Quest for the Original Understanding*, 60 B. U. L. Rev. 204, 225 (1980).

125. The ratification of a constitutional amendment requires approval from two thirds of both houses of Congress and three quarters of the states. U.S. Const. art. V.

126. Maltz, *Some New Thoughts on an Old Problem: The Role of the Intent of the Framers in Constitutional Theory*, 63 B. U. L. Rev. 811, 821–822 (1983). (emphasis omitted).

127. Levy, *Judicial Review, History and Democracy: An Introduction*, in *Judicial Review and the Supreme Court* 1, 12 (L. Levy ed. 1967) (people implicitly consented to the Constitution by not changing it); Choper, *supra* note 5, at 810, 848 (implicit consent to judicial review).

128. Brest, *supra* note 124, at 236 ("If inaction can be taken as tacit consent to anything—a problematic assumption in any case—it is to the Court's decisions, including its nonoriginalist decisions").

129. Constitutional amendments have overturned Supreme Court decisions on only four occasions. The Eleventh Amendment overturned the holding of Chisholm v. Georgia, 2 U.S. (2 Dall.) 419 (1793); the Fourteenth Amendment overturned, in part, the holding in Scott v. Sandford, 60 U.S. (19 How.) 393 (1856); the Sixteenth Amendment overturned the holding in Pollock v. Farmers' Loan & Trust Co., 157 U.S. 429 (1895); and the Twenty-sixth Amendment overturned Oregon v. Mitchell, 400 U.S. 112 (1970).

130. 5 U.S. (1 Cranch) 137 (1803).

131. For example, Grano, a contemporary originalist, argues that without judicial review there would be "constitutional anarchy." Grano, *supra* note 4, at 5.

132. Bork, *supra* note 3, at 7.

133. Van Alstyne, *Interpreting this Constitution: The Unhelpful Contributions of Special Theories of Judicial Review*, 35 U. Fla. L. Rev. 209, 229 (1983).

134. In Chapter 5, I discuss how constitutional issues are left to the political process under the political question doctrine and the generalized grievance standing doctrine. *See* Chapter 5, text accompanying notes 75–89, *infra*.

135. *See, e.g.*, Goldwater v. Carter, 444 U.S. 996, 1003 (1979) (mem.) (plurality opinion concluding that the constituionality of a president's rescission of a treaty is a political question); A. D'Amato & R. O'Neill, *The Judiciary and Vietnam* 51–58 (1972) (description of cases dealing with challenges to the constitutionality of the Vietnam War and the political question doctrine); Tigar, *Judicial Power, the Political Question Doctrine, and Foreign Relations*, 17 U.C.L.A. L. Rev. 1135, 1142 (1970).

136. For a discussion of the importance of the recognition power, *see* H. Finer, *The Presidency: Crisis and Regeneration* 91 (1960).

137. The Supreme Court described the relationship between removal and Johnson's impeachment in Myers v. United States, 272 U.S. 52 (1926); *see also* Corwin, *Tenure of Office and the Removal Power under the Constitution*, 27 Colum. L. Rev. 353 (1927).

138. United States v. Nixon, 418 U.S. 683 (1974); for a discussion of the importance of the release of the tapes in Nixon's decision to resign, *see* T. White, *Breach of Faith* (1975).

CHAPTER 2

1. Some scholars use a much more specific definition of *interpretation* that includes a stipulation of the proper interpretive methodology. For example, Walter Benn Michaels defines *interpretation* as a process of determining the intent of the author. Michaels writes: "I want to argue that any interpretation of the Constitution that really is an interpretation of the Constitution is always and only an interpretation of what the Constitution originally meant." Michaels, *A Response to Perry and Simon*, 58 S. Cal. L. Rev. 673, 673 (1985); *see also* Michaels, *Against Formalism*, in *The State of the Language* 410–420 (L. Michaels & C. Ricks eds. 1980).

I reject Michaels' definition of *interpretation* because it begs the key methodological question of how decision makers should give meaning to a text. In the first section of Chapter 4 I respond to Michaels directly and argue that there the term *interpretation* does not inherently require any particular approach; that the debate between originalism and nonoriginalism cannot be won by stipulation. *See* Chapter 4, text accompanying notes 11–37, *infra*.

2. Larry Simon states this question and explains its importance in Simon, *The Authority of the Constitution and Its Meaning: A Preface to a Theory of Constitutional Interpretation*, 58 S. Cal. L. Rev. 603 (1985).

3. Monaghan, *Our Perfect Constitution*, 56 N.Y.U. L. Rev. 353, 383–384 (1981) (emphasis omitted).

4. Religious texts are obeyed because they are believed to communicate God's will, and interpretation is a process of applying God's instructions to particular situations. *See generally* Garet, *Comparative Normative Hermeneutics: Scripture, Literature, Constitution*, 58 S. Cal. L. Rev. 237 (1985).

5. Simon, *The Authority of the Framers of the Constitution: Can Originalist Interpretation Be Justified?* 73 Cal. L. Rev. 1482 (1985).

6. *See, e.g.*, Civil Rights Act of 1964, 42 U.S.C. §§2000a–2000h (1982) (prohibiting discrimination in public accommodations, education, and employment).

7. For example, tort law is developing to protect employees against wrongful termination by their employers. *See* Klare, *The Public/Private Distinction in Labor Law*, 130 U. Pa. L. Rev. 1358, 1362–1363 (1982); Stone, *Corporate Vices and Corporate Virtues: Do Public/Private Distinctions Matter?* 130 U. Pa. L. Rev. 1441, 1481 n. 143 (1982) (citing to cases limiting wrongful terminations).

8. Legislatures could enact laws that contain provisions making their change more difficult in the future. For example, a law might stipulate that it can be overridden only by a two-thirds vote of a future legislature. In this way, a statute resembles a constitution. It also poses questions similar to those raised about constitutions, such as, What authority does this legislature have to bind future legislatures?

9. *See, e.g.*, Lerner, *Constitution and Court as Symbols*, 46 Yale L. J. 1290, 1296 (1937); A. Miller, *Democratic Dictatorship* 41 (1981) (the Constitution as a "sacred document").

10. *See* Attanasio, *Everyman's Constitutional Law: A Theory of the Power of Judicial Review*, 72 Geo. L. J. 1665, 1711 (1984); Lerner, *supra* note 9, at 1295–1296; Schechter, *The Early History of the Tradition of the Constitution*, 9 Am. Pol. Sci. Rev. 707 (1915).

11. L. Tribe, *American Constitutional Law* 9 (1978).

12. G. Wood, *The Creation of the American Republic, 1776–1787* 379 (1969).

13. *See, e.g.*, Carter, *Constitutional Adjudication and the Indeterminate Text: A Preliminary Defense of an Imperfect Muddle*, 94 Yale L. J. 821, 861 (1985); L. Levy, *Judgments: Essays on American Constitutional History* 5–13 (1972); F. McDonald, *A Constitutional History of the United States* (1982) (describing desire for a separation of powers and for a constitution as a way of limiting the possibility of despotic rule).

14. *See, e.g.*, 1, 2 W. Crosskey, *Politics and the Constitution in the History of the United States* (1953); J. Fiske, *The Critical Period of American History* (1916); A. Kelly & W. Harbison, *The American Constitution: Its Origin and Development* 97, 103–104 (1976); H. P. Hood & Co. v. DuMond, 336 U.S. 525 (1949) (describing economic events that led to the drafting of the Constitution).

15. The Declaration of Independence cites these as among the abuses by the king of England against the colonists. *See* H. Lee, *The Story of the Constitution* 123–124 (1932) (describing abuses of bills of attainder and ex post facto clause).

16. *See* C. Miller, *The Supreme Court and the Uses of History* 45–46 (1969); Home Building & Loan Ass'n v. Blaisdell, 290 U.S. 398 (1934) (describing purpose behind the contract clause).

17. *See* 1 B. Schwartz, *The Bill of Rights: A Documentary History* 435–620 (1971) (describing opposition to ratification of the Constitution based on the absence of a Bill of Rights); F. McDonald, *supra* note 13.

18. *See* C. Beard, *An Economic Interpretation of the Constitution of the United States* (1929); *see also* R. Brown, *Charles Beard and the Constitution: A Critical Analysis of 'An Economic Interpretation of the Constitution'* (1956).

19. The analogy to Ulysses and the concept of precommitment are drawn from J. Elster, *Ulysses and the Sirens: Studies in Rationality and Irrationality* (1979). The story of Ulysses is from Homer's *Odyssey, Book XII* (Harper Colophon ed. 1985).

20. J. Elster, *supra* note 19, at 36. Tribe describes the phenomenon of precommitment in different terms, using the "parable of the pigeons." L. Tribe, *supra* note 11, at 10. Tribe describes an experiment in which pigeons acted to foreclose temptation to help their long-term interests. *Id.*, at 10, citing Ainslie, *Impulse Control in Pigeons*, 21 J. Exper. Ann. Behav. 485 (1974) ("Pigeons seem capable of learning to bind their 'own future freedom of choice' in order to reap the rewards of acting in ways that would elude them under the pressures of the moment"). Tribe explains how the Constitution can be understood as a mechanism to insulate some matters from majoritarian pressures. L. Tribe, *supra* note 11, at 10.

21. J. Elster, *supra* note 19, at 37.

22. *See, e.g.*, Schenck v. United States, 249 U.S. 47 (1919); Debs v. United States, 249 U.S. 211 (1919); Abrams v. United States, 250 U.S. 616 (1919) (convictions for speech activities during World War I); Dennis v. United States, 341 U.S. 494 (1951); Scales v. United States, 367 U.S. 203 (1961) (convictions for speech activities during the McCarthy era).

These examples demonstrate that courts are, at best, an imperfect check against the pressures of the majority. I argue in subsequent chapters that they are the best check society has, although they, too, fail at times.

23. In Chapter 1, I criticized the originalists for justifying their theory by claiming that the people have consented to the text of the Constitution but not to non-originalist decision making. *See* Chapter 1, text accompanying notes 22–26, *supra*. I, therefore, am not arguing that the existence of the Constitution is justified because people now consent to it because, as I argued in Chapter 1, silence cannot be taken as consent to a document that

requires the efforts of a super-majority to bring about change. However, it should be noted that my criticism is not directed at consent theories generally nor am I arguing that it is illegitimate to justify the existence of a Constitution by consent theories. My point is a much more limited one that consent of the majority cannot be established by silence when the majority (defined as 51 percent) would be impotent to bring about change.

24. *See, e.g.*, R. Dworkin, *Taking Rights Seriously* (1977); *cf.*, Moore, *Moral Reality*, 1982 Wis. L. Rev. 1061; Moore, *A Natural Law Theory of Interpretation*, 58 S. Cal. L. Rev. 277 (1985); M. Perry, *The Constitution, the Courts, and Human Rights* 101–114 (1982) (arguing from a moral realist perspective that there are correct moral values); Wellington, *Common Law Rules and Constitutional Double Standards: Some Notes on Adjudication*, 83 Yale L. J. 221 (1973); Simon, *supra* note 5, at 1505–1508 (describing deep consensus theories of rights).

25. Dworkin, *supra* note 24, at xi.

26. For an excellent argument against rights theories, *see* Tushnet, *An Essay on Rights*, 62 Texas L. Rev. 1363 (1984).

27. For an excellent argument against the existence of the norm of equality, *see* Westen, *The Empty Idea of Equality*, 95 Harv. L. Rev. 537 (1982); *see also*, Chemerinsky, *In Defense of Equality: A Reply to Professor Westen*, 81 Mich. L. Rev. 575 (1983); Greenawalt, *How Empty is the Idea of Equality?*, 83 Colum. L. Rev. 1167 (1983); Karst, *Why Equality Matters*, 17 Ga. L. Rev. 245 (1983).

28. The fullest exposition of Rawls's theory is found in J. Rawls, *A Theory of Justice* (1971). Other theorists develop social contract theories that also might be used to justify continued governance under a constitution. *See* P. Riley, *Will and Political Legitimacy: A Critical Exposition of Social Contract Theory in Hobbes, Locke, Rousseau, Kant, and Hegel* 8 (1982); J. Simmons, *Moral Principles and Political Obligations* 57 (1979).

29. Rawls, *supra* note 28, at 11–22.

30. *Id.*, at 137–138.

31. *Id.*, at 137 (''Indeed, the parties are presumed to know whatever general facts affect the choice of the principles of justice'').

32. Boynton, *The Season of Fiction Is Over: A Study of the Original Position in John Rawls' A Theory of Justice*, 15 Osgoode Hall L. J. 215, 238 (1977).

33. There is voluminous literature critiquing Rawls. A particularly impressive collection of essays is found in N. Daniels, *Reading Rawls* (1980), including, Nagel, *Rawls on Justice*, at 1–16; Dworkin, *The Original Position*, at 17–19; Fisk, *History and Reason in Rawls' Moral Theory*, at 53–80.

34. Fisk, *supra* note 33, at 53–80.

35. The Critical Legal Studies movement has been instrumental in pointing out how legal thought and doctrine always has ideological presuppositions. For a collection of essays illustrating this, *see* D. Kairys, *The Politics of Law: A Progressive Critique* (1982).

36. For example, Mark Tushnet attacks the liberal premise that the welfare of the individual is the most important concern for society and that individual rights should be the basis for jurisprudence. *See, e.g.*, Tushnet, *supra* note 26.

37. Chemerinsky, *The Price of Asking the Wrong Question: An Essay on Constitutional Scholarship and Judicial Review*, 62 Texas L. Rev. 1207, 1231 (1984).

38. For example, historians have documented that the Framers of the Fourteenth Amendment intentionally wrote the amendment in broad language to enhance its chances of ratification. *See* Kelly, *The Fourteenth Amendment Reconsidered*, 54 Mich. L. Rev. 1049, 1080, 1086 (1956).

39. Simon, *supra* note 2, at 615 ("Studies show that there is broad consensus among Americans on the abstract principles thought to be fundamental values of American society"); C. Elder & R. Cobb, *The Political Uses of Symbols* 119 (1983); D. Devine, *The Political Culture of the United States* 179–230 (1972).

40. Prothro & Grigg, *Fundamental Principles of Democracy: Agreement and Disagreement*, 22 J. Politics 276, 285–286 (1960).

41. H. McCloskey & A. Brill, *Dimensions of Tolerance: What Americans Believe about Civil Liberties* (1983).

42. *Id.*, at 39.

43. *Id.*, at 39.

44. *Id.*, at 39.

45. McCloskey and Brill test their proposition that there is general agreement to the Constitution but no agreement as to specific meanings, with examples from virtually every part of the Bill of Rights. *Id.*, at 136–170 (due process); 171–231 (privacy rights). Other studies confirm the McCloskey and Brill findings. *See, e.g.*, M. Edelman, *Politics as Symbolic Action* 5 (1971); C. Elder & R. Cobb, *supra* note 39, at 119; D. Devine, *supra* note 39, at 179–230.

46. C. Elder & R. Cobb, *supra* note 39, at 33 (describing the distinction between condensation and referential symbols); R. Pranger, *Action, Symbolism and Order* 168–176 (1968) (discussing types of political symbols); *cf.* M. Eliade, *The Two and the One* 20 (1965) (describing religious symbols that convey many different meanings).

47. *See* A. Etzioni, *Modern Organizations* 52 (1964) ("[t]he subjects accept a ruling as justified because it agrees with a set of more abstract rules which they consider legitimate, and from which the ruling is 'derived' ").

48. *See* C. Elder & R. Cobb, *supra* note 39, at 101; D. Easton, *A Systems Analysis of Political Life* 300 (1965); A. Miller, *Social Change and Fundamental Law: America's Evolving Constitution* 349 (1979) (Constitution as preserving fundamental values in times of social stress). *But see* Levinson, *The Constitution in American Civil Religion*, 1979 Sup. Ct. Rev. 123 (arguing that the Constitution's ambiguity might undercut its unifying function).

49. Grey, *The Constitution as Scripture*, 37 Stan. L. Rev. 1, 3 (1984).

50. Attanasio, *supra* note 10, at 1711; *see also* A. Miller, *supra* note 9, at 41–43.

51. Lerner, *supra* note 9, at 1295–1296, 1298.

52. R. Williams, *American Society: A Sociological Interpretation* (1951), quoted in Levinson, *supra* note 48, at 124.

53. *See* D. Beetham, *Max Weber and the Theory of Modern Politics* 122 (1974).

54. *Id.*, at 122.

55. *See, e.g.*, Levinson, *supra* note 48, at 125; Lerner, *supra* note 9, at 1295; Grey, *supra* note 49, at 3 (describing the Constitution as a source of national unity); Loewenstein, *The Value of Constitutions in Our Revolutionary Age*, in *Constitutions and Constitutional Trends Since World War II* (A. Zurcher ed.) 220 (1951) (symbolic value of constitutions).

56. L. Tribe, *Constitutional Choices* 26 (1985).

57. *Developments in the Law: The Interpretation of State Constitutions*, 95 Harv. L. Rev. 1324, 1353, 1355 (1982); P. Kauper, *The State Constitution: Its Nature and Purpose* 13 (1971).

58. *Development in the Law*, *supra* note 57, at 1353 (frequency of amendment of state constitutions); E. Cornwell, *State Constitutional Conventions* 5 (1975) (frequency of amendment and "wholesale" revisions of state constitutions); A. Sturm, *The Development*

of American State Constitutions, 12 Publius 57, 58–59, 75–76 (1982) (frequency of total revisions of state constitutions).

59. L. Tribe, *supra* note 56, at 289 n. 43. Nor is this a new point. *See* Long, *Tinkering with the Constitution*, 24 Yale L. J. 573 (1915): "The federal constitution has so far been a fairly stable document. It has never been revised as a whole, and has been changed by amendment in only a few particulars. It has happily escaped the fate that has befallen the constitutions of the states. Not only are they subject to constant change, but they have long since ceased to be constitutions in a true sense. Instead of embodying broad general propositions of fundamental permanent law, they now exhibit the prolixity of a code and consist largely of mere legislation. No one now entertains any respect for a state constitution. It has little more dignity than an ordinary act of the legislature."

60. I. Duchacek, *Power Maps: Comparative Politics of Constitutions* 5 (1973) ("[A] constitution is a chart of channels and courses open to political authorities for identifying and solving the major problems and stresses which confront their national community"); Casper, *Guardians of the Constitution*, 53 S. Cal. L. Rev. 773, 779 (1980) (use of constitutional principles in times of "social, psychological, and cultural strain").

61. *See* Bruff, *Legislative Formality, Administrative Rationality*, 63 Texas L. Rev. 207, 216 (1984); R. Axelrod, *The Evolution of Cooperation* 7–10 (1984) (describing the "prisoner's dilemma problem"—that given uncertainty about the conduct of others, individuals will act to benefit themselves to the detriment of others).

62. James M. Buchanan and Gordon Tullock have used public choice theory to explain why a constitution is desirable as a way of restraining individuals acting in their self-interest and of maximizing society's welfare. Their classic book *The Calculus of Consent: Logical Foundations of Constitutional Democracy* (1962) develops, with economic theory and mathematical proofs, support for my conclusions about the desirability of a constitution as a unifying device.

63. C. Elder & R. Cobb, *supra* note 39, at 118.

64. *See* J. Buchanan & G. Tullock, *supra* note 62, at 81–84 (describing why it is rational to have a constitution).

65. *See, e.g.*, Tushnet, *supra* note 26, at 1371 ("[F]undamental indeterminacy makes it impossible to connect that abstract right . . . to any particular outcome"); Moore, *The Semantics of Judging*, 54 S. Cal. L. Rev. 151, 181–202 (1981) (discussing problems in interpreting language, including ambiguity, metaphors, vagueness, and open texture); McCulloch v. Maryland, 17 U.S. (4 Wheat.) 316, 414–415 (1819) (inherent indeterminacy of language).

66. E. McWhinney, *Constitution-Making: Principles, Process, Practice* 9–10 (1981); *see generally* H. L. A. Hart, *The Concept of Law* 125 (1961); H. Kelman, *The Pure Theory of Law* 349 (1970) (inevitability of discretion in applying general rules to particular situations).

67. Undoubtedly, much of current constitutional scholarship has been preoccupied with searching for ways of limiting judicial discretion and finding methods of decision making that yield determinate results in particular cases. In Chapter 6, I argue that this search is futile—that discretion is inherent in constitutional decision making and that no model can provide determinacy.

68. M. Cappelletti & W. Cohen, *Comparative Constitutional Law: Cases and Materials* 11 (1979) (describing constitutionalism as a Western phenomenon); *see* Geck, *Judicial Review of Statutes: A Comparative Survey of Present Institutions and Practices*, 51 Cornell L. Q. 250, 250–251 (1966) (describing increase in number of nations with con-

stitutions since World War II); Friedrich, *The Political Theory of the New Democratic Constitutions*, in *Constitutions and Constitutional Trends Since World War II* 13–35 (A. Zurcher ed. 1955) (increasing number of nations relying on written constitutions to limit government).

69. These certainly are not the only two countries that might be examined. For instance, Canada recently, in 1982, adopted a Charter of Rights, which is closely patterned after the U.S. Bill of Rights. However, it contains a clause that allows Parliament and the provinces to enact legislation exempt from the charter (section 33 permits this). Canada's Charter of Rights is thus a constitution in a very different sense than the U.S. Constitution that has as a primary feature its "entrenchment"—its difficulty of change.

70. *See* Jalowicz, *The Judicial Protection of Fundamental Rights under English Law*, in *The Cambridge—Tilburg Law Lectures* 5 (B. Markesinis & J. Willems eds. 1980): "The United Kingdom, of which England forms a part, has no written constitution and there are no codes. . . . There is no legislative statement of constitutionally protected rights, there is not even much legislative statement of general principle such as is found in a continental code, and it is still rare—it was formerly unknown—for legal reasoning to take as its starting point the right of an individual with a view to deciding whether or not that right has been infringed."

71. A. Dicey, *Introduction to the Study of the Law of the Constitution* 40 (1960); J. Jaconelli, *Enacting a Bill of Rights* 12 (1980); Ackerman & Charney, *Canada at the Constitutional Crossroads*, 34 U. Toronto L. J. 117, 118 (1984).

72. Jalowicz, *Fundamental Guarantees in Civil Litigation: England*, in *Fundamental Guarantees of the Parties in Civil Litigation* 123–124 (M. Cappelletti & D. Talon eds. 1973).

73. *Id.*, at 132; Jalowicz, *supra* note 70, at 5.

74. Jalowicz, *supra* note 72, at 132.

75. A. Dicey, *supra* note 71, at 43.

76. N. Johnson, *In Search of a Constitution: Reflections on State and Society in Britain* 30, 32 (1977).

77. *Id.*, at 197–198; J. Jaconelli, *supra* note 71, at vii. For a discussion of the development of the Canadian Constitution, *see* Ackerman & Charney, *supra* note 71; Schwartz, *General National Agreement: The Legal Sanction for Constitutional Reform in Canada*, 6 Queens L. J. 5132 (1981).

78. N. Johnson, *supra* note 76, at 33, 35.

79. Schwarzschild, *Book Review, Variations on an Enigma: Law in Practice and Law on the Books in the USSR*, 99 Harv. L. Rev. 685, 688 (1986) ("Although the Soviet system is governed by law, its law differs fundamentally from common law and from Western European civil law. Its essential and distinguishing characteristic is that while ordinary citizens and subordinate officials are subject to the law, the state itself is above the law—an unlimited dictatorship").

80. O. Ioffe & P. Maggs, *Soviet Law in Theory and Practice* 2 (1983).

81. W. Butler & P. Maggs, *The Soviet Legal System: Fundamental Principles and Historical Commentary* 89 (3d ed. 1977); *see also* W. Kulski, *The Soviet Regime: Communism in Practice* 144 (1963).

82. W. Butler & P. Maggs, *supra* note 81, at 86–89.

83. Schwarzschild, *supra* note 79, at 689.

84. Soviet Const. of 1977 art. 39, quoted in Schwarzschild, *supra note 79, at 689.*

85. *See* text accompanying notes 39–44, *supra*.

CHAPTER 3

1. T. Cooley, *A Treatise on the Constitutional Limitations Which Rest Upon the Legislative Powers of the States of the American Union* 124 (Carrington's 8th ed. 1927).

2. South Carolina v. United States, 199 U.S. 437, 448 (1905).

3. 17 U.S. (4 Wheat.) 415 (1819).

4. Bennett, *'Mere Rationality' in Constitutional Law: Judicial Review and Democratic Theory*, 67 Calif L. Rev. 1049, 1094 (1979).

5. *See, e.g.*, Van Alstyne, *Interpreting This Constitution: The Unhelpful Contributions of Special Theories of Judicial Review*, 35 U. Fla. L. Rev. 209, 229 (1983) (importance of limiting constitutional decisions to what is clearly required in the text or intended by the Framers).

6. *See, e.g.*, Munzer & Nickel, *Does the Constitution Mean What It Always Meant?* 77 Colum. L. Rev. 1029, 1029 (1977) ("The Constitution has remained vital largely because its provisions have proved adaptable to the changing needs of a developing society"); Sandalow, *Judicial Protection of Minorities*, 75 Mich. L. Rev. 1162, 1185 (1977) (constitutional law understood as the expression of evolving social norms).

7. Sandalow, *Constitutional Interpretation*, 79 Mich. L. Rev. 1033, 1060–1061 (1981) (agreement as to need for mechanism to change the Constitution).

8. I. Duchacek, *Power Maps: Comparative Politics of Constitutions* 210 (1973).

9. *Id.*, at 210.

10. *Id.*, at 210.

11. *Id.*, at 210.

12. *Id.*, at 210 (example of Morocco's constitution, which provides that Islam is the official religion).

13. *See* Moore, *The Semantics of Judging*, 54 S. Cal. L. Rev. 151, 181–202 (1981) (discussing ambiguity, vagueness, metaphors, and open texture as preventing literal following of language).

14. *See, e.g.*, Levinson, *Law and Literature* 60 Texas L. Rev. 373, 391 (1982); Miller, *The Critic as Host*, 3 Critical Inq. 439 (1977) (inevitable indeterminacy of interpretation).

15. Levinson, *What Do Lawyers Know (and What Do They Do with Their Knowledge)?: Comments on Schauer and Moore*, 58 S. Cal. L. Rev. 441, 449 (1985).

16. S. Fish, *Is There a Text in This Class?* 327 (1980).

17. McCulloch v. Maryland, 17 U.S. (4 Wheat.) 316, 414–415 (1819).

18. *See, e.g.*, Smith v. California, 361 U.S. 147, 157 (1959) (Black J., concurring).

19. Fiss, *Objectivity and Interpretation*, 34 Stan. L. Rev. 739, 743 (1982).

20. U.S. Const. art I, §8. The commerce clause of the Constitution is extremely important in that it is the basis for almost all national economic regulation. From 1887 to 1937, the Supreme Court limited the federal government's regulatory power by narrowly interpreting the commerce clause. *See, e.g.*, Carter v. Carter Coal Co., 298 U.S. 238 (1936); Schechter Poultry Corp. v. United States, 295 U.S. 495 (1935); United States v. E. C. Knight Co., 156 U.S. 1 (1895). Since 1937 the Supreme Court has interpreted the commerce clause broadly, allowing Congress expansive authority to regulate the economy. *See, e.g.*, United States v. Darby, 312 U.S. 100 (1941); Wickard v. Filburn, 317 U.S. 111 (1942); Katzenback v. McClung, 379 U.S. 294 (1964).

21. *See, e.g.*, Schechter Poultry Corp. v. United States, 295 U.S. 495 (1935); Railroad Retirement Board v. Alton R. R., 295 U.S. 330 (1935).

22. *See* 1 W. Crosskey, *Politics and the Constitution in the History of the United States* 51, 74–80 (1953).

23. *See, e.g.*, Carter v. Carter Coal Co., 298 U.S. 238 (1936); Schechter Poultry Corp. v. United States, 295 U.S. 495 (1935); United States v. E. C. Knight Co., 156 U.S. 1 (1895).

24. Brest, *The Misconceived Quest for the Original Understanding*, 60 B.U. L. Rev. 204, 207 (1980).

25. *See, e.g.*, R. Berger, *Government by Judiciary: The Transformation of the Fourteenth Amendment* (1977); Bork, *Neutral Principles and Some First Amendment Problems*, 47 Ind. L. J. 1 (1971); Rehnquist, *The Notion of a Living Constitution*, 54 Texas L. Rev. 693 (1976).

26. Wofford, *The Blinding Light: The Uses of History in Constitutional Interpretation*, 31 U. Chi. L. Rev. 502, 508–509 (1964).

27. J. Ely, *Democracy and Distrust: A Theory of Judicial Review* 17 (1980); Dworkin, *The Forum of Principle*, 56 N.Y.U. L. Rev. 469, 481 (1981) (noting that "we have no fixed concept of a group intention that makes what the Framers intended simply a matter of historical fact").

28. *See, e.g.*, Arrow, *A Difficulty in the Concept of Social Welfare*, 58 J. Pol. Econ. 328 (1950); *see also* A. Feldman, *Welfare Economics and Social Choice Theory* 178–195 (1980); *cf.* Easterbrook, *Ways of Criticizing the Court*, 95 Harv. L. Rev. 802 (1982) (applying Arrow's Impossibility Theorem to Supreme Court decision making).

29. Dworkin, *supra* note 27, at 477 ("[T]here are no, or very few, relevant collective intentions, or perhaps only collective intentions that are indeterminate rather than decisive one way or the other"); Saphire, *Judicial Review in the Name of the Constitution*, 8 U. Dayton L. Rev. 745, 778 (1983) ("There is no such thing as a concrete and knowable intent of the framers—at least when intent is defined as the collective, conscious, and subjective state of mind of at least a majority of the persons who voted to adopt and ratify the Constitution").

30. Shaman, *The Constitution, the Supreme Court, and Creativity*, 9 Hastings Const. L. Q. 257, 267 (1982).

31. Youngstown Sheet & Tube Co. v. Sawyer, 343 U.S. 579, 634 (1952) (Jackson, J., concurring).

32. W. Crosskey, *supra* note 22, at 1008–1028.

33. Van Alstyne, *supra* note 5, at 234.

34. R. Collingwood, *The Idea of History* 218–219 (1946); *see also* E. Carr, *What Is History* 16–24 (1964).

35. Florovsky, *The Study of the Past*, in *Ideas of History* 351, 352 (R. Nash ed. 1969).

36. *See* Brest, *supra* note 24; Shaman, *supra* note 30.

37. *See* Carter, *Constitutional Adjudication and the Indeterminate Text: A Preliminary Defense of an Imperfect Muddle*, 94 Yale L. J. 821, 862 (1985) (ability to have "value-free" interpretation of parts of the Constitution dealing with the structure of government); Grano, *Judicial Review and a Written Constitution in a Demoratic Society*, 28 Wayne L. Rev. 1, 20 (1981) (avoiding subjectivity requires following original intent). In Chapter 6 I more fully argue that discretion and subjectivity are impossible, and in the last section of Chapter 4, I respond specifically to Carter (text accompanying notes 106–122).

38. The distinction between *concepts* and *conceptions*, and its relevance for interpretation, is developed in R. Dworkin, *Taking Rights Seriously* 134–136 (1977) (arguing that vague constitutional clauses represent "concepts" that each generation infuses with

meaning through translation into particular "conceptions"). The concept/conception distinction is discussed in detail in the last section of Chapter 4.

39. *See, e.g.*, Brest, *supra* note 24, at 221 (noting that under originalism "Congress could not regulate any item of commerce or any mode of transportation that did not exist in 1789; the first amendment would not protect any means of communication not known then"); *see generally* Miller & Howell, *The Myth of Neutrality in Constitutional Adjudication*, 27 U. Chi. L. Rev. 661, 683 (1960) (Framers' intent cannot govern a totally different world).

40. *See, e.g.*, Crosskey, *supra* note 22; C. Warren, *The Making of the Constitution* 85 (1928); 1 G. Bancroft, *History of the Formation of the Constitution of the United States* 250–252 (1882); Stern, *That Commerce Which Concerns More States than One*, 47 Harv. L. Rev. 1335, 1344 (1934).

41. A. MacIntyre, *After Virtue: A Study in Moral Theory* 10 (1981).

42. *See, e.g.*, Bradwell v. State, 83 U.S. (16 Wall.) 130 (1873) (upholding state prohibition of practice of law by women); Goesart v. Cleary, 335 U.S. 464 (1948) (upholding law preventing women from being bartenders except in bars owned by their husbands or fathers); M. Gruberg, *Women in American Politics: An Assessment and Sourcebook* (1960).

43. For example, the Supreme Court has used the equal protection clause to protect women—*see, e.g.*, Reed v. Reed, 404 U.S. 71 (1971); illegitimate children—*see, e.g.*, Levy v. Louisiana, 391 U.S. 68 (1968); aliens—*see, e.g.*, Graham v. Richardson, 403 U.S. 365 (1971); and individuals with mental handicaps—*see, e.g.*, City of Cleburne v. Cleburne Living Center, 105 S.Ct. 3249 (1985).

44. *See, e.g.*, Griswold v. Connecticut, 381 U.S. 479 (1965) (right to privacy prevents state from prohibiting use of contraceptives by married couples); Roe v. Wade, 410 U.S. 113 (1973) (right to privacy prevents state from prohibiting abortion during first two trimesters of pregnancy).

45. Chisholm v. Georgia, 2 U.S. (2 Dall.) 419 (1793).

46. *See* C. Jacobs, *The Eleventh Amendment and Sovereign Immunity* (1972); Fletcher, *A Historical Interpretation of the Eleventh Amendment: A Narrow Construction of an Affirmative Grant of Jurisdiction Rather than a Prohibition Against Jurisdiction*, 35 Stan. L. Rev. 1033 (1983); Gibbons, *The Eleventh Amendment and State Sovereign Immunity: A Reinterpretation*, 83 Colum. L. Rev. 1889 (1983); Field, *The Eleventh Amendment and Other Sovereign Immunity Doctrines: Part I*, 126 U. Pa. L. Rev. 515 (1977).

CHAPTER 4

1. *See, e.g.*, R. Berger, *Government by Judiciary: The Transformation of the Fourteenth Amendment* 410 (1977); Bork, *Neutral Principles and Some First Amendment Problems*, 47 Ind. L. J. 1, 6 (1971); Rehnquist, *The Notion of a Living Constitution*, 54 Texas L. Rev. 693, 695–699 (1977).

2. *See* discussion in Chapter 2. Also, the indeterminacy of all forms of decision making is discussed in more detail in Chapter 6.

3. *See, e.g.*, Van Alstyne, *Interpreting This Constitution: The Unhelpful Contributions of Special Theories of Judicial Review*, 35 U. Fla. L. Rev. 209, 234–235 n. 66 (1983) (changes should be by amendment); Berger, *G. Edward White's Apology for Judicial Activism*, 63 Texas L. Rev. 367, 372 (1984) ("The Framers did not leave us in the

dark in this score; by Article Five, they confided the power to amend to the people, not to the judges'').

4. Bork, *supra* note 1, at 8.

5. Van Alstyne, *supra* note 3.

6. United States v. Butler, 297 U.S. 6, 62 (1936); Van Alstyne argues in favor of this approach to constitutional interpretation in Van Alstyne, *supra* note 3, at 225, 231.

7. Van Alstyne, *supra* note 3, at 229.

8. *See* Trimble v. Gordon, 430 U.S. 762, 777 (1977) (Rehnquist, J., dissenting) (arguing that the Fourteenth Amendment only was intended and only should protect racial minorities).

9. Almost all commentators agree that virtually every decision in the last quarter of a century protecting individual liberties cannot be justified under an originalist methodology. *See, e.g.*, M. Perry, *The Constitution, the Courts, and Human Rights* 2 (1982); J. Choper, *Judicial Review and the National Political Process* 137 (1980).

10. Moore, *A Natural Law Theory of Interpretation,* 58 S. Cal. L. Rev. 279, 357 (1985).

11. *See, e.g.*, Michaels, *Response to Perry and Simon*, 58 S. Cal. L. Rev. 673, 673 (1985) (constitutional interpretation only occurs if the Court follows the original intent).

12. Simon, *The Authority of the Framers of the Constitution: Can Originalist Interpretation Be Justified?* 73 Calif. L. Rev. 1482, 1487 (1985); *see also* Perry, *The Authority of the Text, Tradition, and Reason: A Theory of Constitutional Interpretation*, 58 S. Cal. L. Rev. 551, 576 (1985) (no particular approach can claim authoritative status).

13. Monaghan, *Our Perfect Constitution*, 56 N.Y.U. L. Rev. 353, 374–375 (1981).

14. *See* Bennett, *The Mission of Moral Reasoning in Constitutional Law*, 58 S. Cal. L. Rev. 649, 649 (1985) (''There is no doubt that language can be construed without reference to the author's intention in using it'').

15. Michaels, *supra* note 11, at 673.

16. *Id.*, at 673.

17. Perry, *supra* note 12, at 572 n. 68.

18. Simon, *The Authority of the Constitution and Its Meaning: A Preface to a Theory of Constitutional Interpretation*, 58 S. Cal. L. Rev. 603, 620 (1985).

19. *See, e.g.*, S. Fish, *Is There a Text in This Class?* 268–292 (1980).

20. Melvin, *Judicial Activism: The Violation of an Oath*, 27 Cath. L. Rev. 283, 284 (1982).

21. *Id.*, at 284.

22. Perry, *supra* note 12, at 588; Eakin v. Rauh, 12 S. & R. 330, 340 (Pa. 1825) (Gibson, J., dissenting) (all government officers take oath of office); Jackson, *Veto Message*, 2 *Messages and Papers of the Presidents* (Richardson ed. 1896) 576, 581–583 (''each public officer . . . takes an oath to support the Constitution'').

23. Berger, *supra* note 3, at 372. The argument that the existence of the amendment process justifies originalism is addressed at text accompanying notes 45–48, *infra*.

24. Bork, *The Impossibility of Finding Welfare Rights in the Constitution*, 1979 Wash. U. L. Q. 695, 697.

25. Kay, *Preconstitutional Rules*, 42 Ohio St. L. J. 187, 193 n. 22 (1981) (''It is anomalous to argue . . . that recourse to the intention of the Framers of the Constitution is required . . . [as] demonstrated from a review of the Framers' intention''); Monaghan,

supra note 13, at 383 n. 177 ("bootstrapping" to say that the courts must follow the Framers' intent because the Framers wanted their intent to be followed).

26. National Mut. Ins. Co. v. Tidewater Transfer Co., 337 U.S. 582, 646 (1949) (Frankfurter, J., dissenting); R. Dworkin, *Taking Rights Seriously* 135–136 (1977); Moore, *supra* note 10, at 394.

27. Lynch, *Book Review, Constitutional Law as Moral Philosophy*, 84 Colum. L. Rev. 537, 546 (1984).

28. *See, e.g.*, P. Sigmund, *Natural Law In Political Thought* 98 (1971) ("It is well known that the Declaration of Independence was based on the natural rights philosophy of John Locke"); Z. Chaffee, *How Human Rights Got into the Constitution* 12 (1952) ("[T]he opening paragraphs of the Declaration of Independence relied on the natural rights of all men everywhere"); B. Bailyn, *The Ideological Origins of the American Revolution* 77–78 (1968) (importance of natural rights philosophy); C. Mullett, *Fundamental Law and the American Revolution, 1760–1776* 17 (1933) (importance of natural law).

29. The drafters of the Constitution did not include a Bill of Rights because they believed that the enumeration of rights was unnecessary. *See* L. Levy, *Judgements: Essays on American Constitutional History* 14–15 (1972); L. Tribe, *American Constitutional Law* 3 n.7 (1978).

30. *See* Clinton, *Judges Must Make Law: A Realistic Appraisal of the Judicial Function in a Democratic Society*, 67 Iowa L. Rev. 711, 734 (1982).

31. Powell, *The Original Understanding of Original Intent*, 98 Harv. L. Rev. 886, 948 (1985).

32. *See* Brest, *The Fundamental Rights Controversy: The Essential Contradictions of Normative Constitutional Scholarship*, 90 Yale L. J. 1063, 1090 (1981) ("There is no reason to suppose that the adopters of the Fourteenth Amendment intended its provisions to be interpreted by Berger's strict intentionalist canons. . . . Thus, fidelity to their intentions may require an interpreter to eschew detailed inquiry into the adopters' particular views").

33. J. Ely, *Democracy and Distrust: A Theory of Judicial Review* 3 (1980); Bork, *supra* note 1, at 3–4.

34. 313 U.S. 299 (1941).

35. *Id.*, at 315–316.

36. 290 U.S. 398 (1934).

37. *Id.*, at 435.

38. Brown v. Board of Education, 347 U.S. 483 (1954).

39. 383 U.S. 663 (1966).

40. Miranda v. Arizona, 384 U.S. 436, 531 (1966) (White, J., dissenting).

41. Powell, *supra* note 31, at 948.

42. J. Choper, *supra* note 9, at 423 nn. 7–8; 2 W. Crosskey, *Politics and the Constitution in the History of the U.S.* 1008–1046 (1953) (arguing that the Framers did not intend judicial review); Monaghan, *The Constitution Goes to Harvard*, 13 Harv. Civ. Rights-Civ. Lib. L. Rev. 117, 125 (1978) (noting that it is "increasingly doubtful that any conclusive case can be made one way or the other. It is an understatement to say that the framers lacked clarity in their thinking").

43. *See, e.g.*, Calder v. Bull, 3 U.S. (3 Dall.) 386, 388 (1798); Fletcher v. Peck, 10 U.S. (6 Cranch) 87, 135, 139, 143 (1810); Terrett v. Taylor, 13 U.S. (9 Cranch) 43, 52 (1815) (decisions based on natural law); *see also* Currie, *The Constitution in the Supreme Court: 1789–1801*, 48 U. Chi. L. Rev. 819, 844 (1981) (willingness of judges during early

part of nineteenth century to exercise "judicial discretion" to protect principles of natural justice).

44. *See, e.g.*, M. Perry, *supra* note 9, at 2; J. Choper, *supra* note 9, at 137 (modern protection of rights based on nonoriginalism).

45. Shaman, *The Constitution, the Supreme Court, and Creativity*, 9 Hastings Const. L. Q. 257, 258 (1982).

46. For a discussion of the importance of presumption in the resolution of controversies, *see* J. Patterson & D. Zarefsky, *Contemporary Debate* (1982); Whately, *Presumption and Burden of Proof*, in *Readings in Argumentation* 26–29 (J. Anderson & P. Dovre eds. 1968).

47. *See* Monaghan, *Taking Supreme Court Opinions Seriously*, 39 Md. L. Rev. 1 (1979); Monaghan, *supra* note 42 at 130; Munzer & Nickel, *Does the Constitution Mean What It Always Meant?* 77 Colum. L. Rev. 1029, 1032 (1977) (stating that a "great deal of doctrinal and social disruption would result if one were to turn back the clock").

48. The right of privacy could not be justified under literalism (the text does not mention it), originalism (the Framers did not intend to protect it), or process-based theories (it is a substantive value and not related to fair procedure).

49. It is tempting to try to make an originalist-type argument that the Constitution includes not only what the Framers intended but also the gloss that has been added by subsequent Supreme Court decisions. *See, e.g.*, Dames & Moore v. Regan, 453 U.S. 654, 680–682 (1981); Youngstown Sheet & Tube Co. v. Sawyer, 343 U.S. 579, 610–611 (1952) (Frankfurter, J., concurring) (gloss on Constitution adds to its meaning). Because the Court has frequently embraced nonoriginalism—*see* cases discussed at notes 33–42, *supra*—this method could be viewed as part of the Constitution. This, however, is an unsatisfactory way to decide constitutional theory because what has been done previously does not indicate what is best normatively.

50. Berger, *supra* note 3, at 372; Melvin, *supra* note 20, at 284.

51. Melvin, *supra* note 20, at 284.

52. The Eleventh Amendment overturned the holding of Chisholm v. Georgia, 2 U.S. (2 Dall.) (419 (1793); the Fourteenth Amendment overturned, in part, the holding of Scott v. Sandford, 60 U.S. (19 How.) 393 (1857); the Sixteenth Amendment overturned the holding in Pollock v. Farmers Loan & Trust Co., 157 U.S. 429 (1895); and the Twenty-sixth Amendment overturned Oregon v. Mitchell, 400 U.S. 112 (1970).

53. *See* Carter, *Constitutional Adjudication and the Indeterminate Text: A Preliminary Defense of an Imperfect Muddle*, 94 Yale L. J. 821, 843 (1985) (Carter espouses an originalist philosophy to the parts of the Constitution dealing with the structure of government; *see id.*, at 861–862.). Carter recently clarified his thesis in *The Right Questions in the Creation of Constitutional Meaning*, 66 B. U. L. Rev. 71 (1986). In this essay, he says that he did not mean to imply in his earlier article advocacy for originalism. Carter recently wrote that "the interpretive visions of the document's authors are relatively unimportant to my scheme." *Id.*, at 76.

54. Saphire, *Judicial Review in the Name of the Constitution*, 8 U. Dayton L. Rev. 745, 796–797 (1983).

55. *Id.*, at 796–797 (the Framers "would have understood Article II to exclude women from presidential eligibility"); L. Tribe, *supra* note 29, at 1060.

56. Quoted in M. Gruberg, *Women in American Politics* 4 (1960), quoted in L. Tribe, *supra* note 29, at 1060 n. 2.

57. In fact, an originalist cannot escape this conclusion by asserting that the courts

could duck the issue by declaring it to be a political question. The electoral college would be compelled to refuse to elect a female as president or vice president because such an election would violate their oath to uphold the Constitution.

58. After all, the failure of the states to ratify the equal rights amendment indicates that a constitutional amendment to ensure equal treatment of women, even in the limited area of presidential elections, is not ensured of passage.

59. In fact, the purpose of the Fourteenth Amendment, as reflected in its language, was to restrict state governments. There was no indication of a desire to limit the federal government.

60. *See, e.g.*, Bolling v. Sharp, 347 U.S. 497, 499 (1971) (applying equal protection concepts to the federal government under the due process clause of the Fifth Amendment); Buckley v. Valeo, 424 U.S. 1, 93 (1976) ("Equal protection analysis in the Fifth Amendment is the same as that under the Fourteenth Amendment").

61. *See* Maltz, *Some New Thoughts on an Old Problem: The Role of the Intent of the Framers in Constitutional Theory*, 63 B. U. L. Rev. 811, 850 (1983) (Bolling v. Sharp, applying equal protection to the federal government, is totally inconsistent with the Framers' intent).

62. Incumbents were not about to vote themselves out of office by redistricting the legislatures. For this reason, Chief Justice Earl Warren described the reapportionment cases as the most important decisions during his tenure on the Court. *See The Warren Court: An Editorial Preface*, 67 Mich. L. Rev. 219 (1968). *See* Baker v. Carr, 369 U.S. 186 (1962) (holding reapportionment claims to be justiciable); Reynolds v. Sims, 377 U.S. 533 (1964) (declaring one person/one vote to be constitutionally required by the equal protection clause).

63. *See, e.g.*, Duncan v. Louisiana, 391 U.S. 145 (1968) (trial by jury incorporated by the Fourteenth Amendment and applies to the states); Gideon v. Wainwright, 372 U.S. 335 (1963) (right to counsel incorporated by the Fourteenth Amendment and applies to the states); Mapp v. Ohio, 367 U.S. 643 (1949) (exclusionary rule incorporated by the Fourteenth Amendment and applies to the states); Fiske v. Kansas, 274 U.S. 380 (1927) (First Amendment incorporated by the Fourteenth Amendment and applies to the states).

64. For a discussion of why the political process would not have desegregated the schools, *see* text accompanying notes 66–71 in this chapter.

65. Although there has been some protection of rights through statutes, such as the Civil Rights acts, there are many areas where the only protection has come through Court decisions. *See* Chemerinsky, *Rethinking State Action*, 80 Nw. L. Rev. 503, 518–519 (1985) (describing areas where the only protection of rights is through the Court). Even in areas where there are statutes protecting rights, it is highly unlikely that the statutes would have passed if they required two-thirds approval of both houses of Congress, let alone ratification by three quarters of the states.

66. *See* C. Woodward, *The Strange Career of Jim Crow* 7 (1966) (describing how segregation reflected belief in the inferiority of blacks); *see also* Brown v. Board of Education, 347 U.S. 483 (1954) (school segregation based on assumption of inferiority of blacks); Loving v. Virginia, 388 U.S. 1 (1967) (antimiscegenation statutes reflect assumption of inferiority of blacks).

67. *See* J. Bass, *Unlikely Heroes* 148 (1981): "The political realities [facing the Kennedy administration in acting on civil rights] was having to deal with Congress at a time when the seniority system was at its peak and dominated by Southern Democrats committed to the defense of segregation, either because of their conviction or their perception

of political reality at home." For a vivid description of the resistance to desegregation, *see* W. Manchester, *The Glory and The Dream: A Narrative History of America, 1932–1972* 799–810 (1974).

68. *New York Times*, March 12, 1956, at 19, col. 2 (the "Southern Declaration of Independence").

69. For a review of state laws segregating southern and border state schools, *see* R. Kluger, *Simple Justice* (1978).

70. Cahn, *Jurisprudence*, 30 N. Y. U. L. Rev. 150, 156 (1955).

71. *See* Chemerinsky, *Controlling Inherent Presidential Power: Providing a Framework for Judicial Review*, 56 S. Cal. L. Rev. 863 (1983) (describing areas of presidential decision making where the Constitution and Congress are silent).

72. *See, e.g.*, Nebraska Press Association v. Stuart, 427 U.S. 539 (1976) (First Amendment limits on prior restraints used to preserve defendant's right to fair trial).

73. Justice Rehnquist has argued that the Fourteenth Amendment was intended only to protect racial minorities and it should not be used to safeguard any other group. *See* Trimble v. Gordon, 430 U.S. 762, 777–786 (1977) (Rehnquist, J., dissenting).

74. *See, e.g.*, Meyer v. Nebraska, 262 U.S. 390 (1923); Pierce v. Society of Sisters, 268 U.S. 510 (1925); Moore v. City of East Cleveland, 431 U.S. 494 (1977) (decisions protecting family autonomy under the Fourteenth Amendment).

75. McCulloch v. Maryland, 17 U.S. (4 Wheat.) 316, 414–415 (1819).

76. Long, *Tinkering with the Constitution*, 24 Yale L. J. 573 (1915).

77. L. Tribe, *Constitutional Choices* 289 n. 43 (1985); *see also Developments in the Law: The Interpretation of State Constitutions*, 95 Harv. L. Rev. 1324, 1353–1356 (1982).

78. For an excellent description of the social and intellectual commitment to laissez-faire principles at the end of the nineteenth century, *see* A. Paul, *The Conservative Crisis and the Rule of Law: Attitudes of the Bar and Bench, 1887–1895* (1976).

79. *See, e.g.*, Allgeyer v. Louisiana, 165 U.S. 578 (1895); Lochner v. New York, 198 U.S. 45 (1905) (cases striking down state laws as violating freedom of contract).

80. G. Gunther, *Constitutional Law* 453 (11th ed. 1985) ("[D]uring the Lochner era . . . nearly 200 regulations were struck down"); *see also* P. Murphy, *The Constitution in Crisis Times 1918–1969* 63 (1972) (between 1920 and 1930 almost 140 laws were held unconstitutional).

81. *See, e.g.*, L. Tribe, *American Constitutional Law* 446–449 (1978) (describing economic and political pressures that brought an end to Lochnerism).

82. The Supreme Court's decision in West Coast Hotel v. Parrish, 300 U.S. 379 (1937), marked an end to the Court's protection of economic substantive due process; and the Court's decision in NLRB v. Jones & Laughlin Steel Corp., 301 U.S. 1 (1937), marked an end to the Court's restrictive interpretation of Congress's powers under the commerce clause.

83. 305 U.S. 337 (1938).

84. 339 U.S. 629 (1950).

85. 339 U.S. 637 (1950).

86. 347 U.S. 483 (1954). For an excellent history of the school desegregation litigation leading up to Brown v. Board of Education, *see* R. Kluger, *supra* note 69.

87. *See, e.g.*, Mayor of Baltimore v. Dawson, 350 U.S. 877 (1955) (beaches); Gayle v. Browder, 352 U.S. 903 (1956) (buses); Holmes v. Atlanta, 350 U.S. 879 (1955) (golf

courses); New Orleans City Park Improvement Association v. Detiege, 358 U.S. 54 (1958) (parks).

88. Johnson v. Virginia, 373 U.S. 61 (1963).

89. *See, e.g.*, A. Wildavsky, *Incrementalism* (1972).

90. But the argument can be made that incremental changes legitimized those opposing segregation and substantial incremental change is unlikely to occur. *See, e.g.*, J. Hochschild, *The New American Dilemma: Liberal Democracy and School Desegregation* (1984); Freeman, *Legitimizing Racial Discrimination Through Anti-Discrimination Law: A Critical Review of Supreme Court Doctrine*, 62 Minn. L. Rev. 1049 (1978).

91. Chief Justice Marshall, in McCulloch v. Maryland, 17 U.S. (4 Wheat.) 316 (1819), described the Constitution in these terms. ("Its nature, therefore, requires that only its great outlines should be marked, its important objects designated").

92. *See* Chemerinsky, *supra* note 71, at 871–872.

93. Powell, *supra* note 31, at 913.

94. Brest, *The Misconceived Quest for the Original Understanding*, 60 B. U. L. Rev. 204, 205 (1980).

95. *Id.*, at 205.

96. R. Dworkin, *supra* note 26, at 134–136.

97. *Id.*, at 134.

98. Munzer & Nickel, *supra* note 47, at 1037.

99. Simon, *supra* note 12, at 1517.

100. *See, e.g.*, Strauder v. West Virginia, 100 U.S. 303, 307 (1880) (Fourteenth Amendment's purpose is to prevent discrimination against blacks).

101. *See, e.g.*, Slaughterhouse Cases, 83 U.S. (16 Wall.) 36, 71 (1873) (Fourteenth Amendment's purpose is to ensure freedom for former slaves).

102. *See, e.g.*, Korematsu v. United States, 323 U.S. 214 (1944) (equal protection clause applies to discrimination on the basis of race or national origin).

103. *See, e.g.*, United States v. Carolene Products Co., 304 U.S. 144, 152–153 n. 4 (1938) (describing Fourteenth Amendment's protection of insular minorities).

104. *See, e.g.*, F. S. Royster Guano Co. v. Virginia, 253 U.S. 412, 415 (1920); Perry, *Modern Equal Protection: A Conceptualization and an Appraisal*, 79 Colum. L. Rev. 1023, 1068–1069 (1979); Tussman & tenBroek, *The Equal Protection of the Laws*, 37 Calif. L. Rev. 341, 344 (1949).

105. Tushnet, *Following the Rules Laid Down: A Critique of Interpretivism and Neutral Principles*, 96 Harv. L. Rev. 781, 791 (1983).

106. Brest, *supra* note 32, at 1092 ("The fact is that all adjudication requires making choices among the levels of generality on which to articulate principles and all such choices are inherently non-neutral").

107. *See* Monaghan, *supra* note 13, at 378 (describing process of "conceptualizing original intent at a level of abstraction that, in effect, removes it as an institutional constraint").

108. In fact, the Supreme Court in Brown v. Board of Education explicitly stated that changes in the importance of education and the development of free public education made the Framers' intent of limited relevance. 347 U.S. 483 (1954).

109. Bork, *supra* note 1, at 14 (defending Brown on the grounds that the Fourteenth Amendment "was intended to enforce a core idea of black equality against government discrimination").

110. *See* Bennett, *Objectivity in Constitutional Law*, 132 U. Pa. L. Rev. 445, 462 n. 54

(1984) (describing how Bork manipulates the level of generality to achieve particular results).

111. During the 1950s, originalists attacked the school desegregation decisions with all the fervor that has been applied to *Roe v. Wade*. It is telling that as society has come to accept the wisdom and necessity of these decisions, the methodological objections to them have disappeared and originalists find *Brown* the hardest example for them to deal with. For originalist arguments criticizing the *Brown* decision, *see, e.g.*, Cook, *School Segregation Decisions: Opposing the Option of the Supreme Court*, 42 A. B. A. J. 313 (1956); Crownover, *Segregation Cases: A Deliberate and Dangerous Exercise of Power*, 42 A. B. A. J. 727 (1956); Sanders, *Implications of the Segregation Decisions*, 4 La. B. J. 93 (1956).

112. L. Lusky, *By What Right?: A Commentary on the Supreme Court's Power to Revise the Constitution* 21 (1975); *see also* Linde, *Judges, Critics, and the Realist Tradition*, 82 Yale L. J. 227, 254 (1972).

113. Tushnet, *supra* note 105, at 793, 802.

114. Perry, *supra* note 12, at 599.

115. *Id.*, at 599.

116. Bennett, *supra* note 110, at 457; Lynch, *supra* note 27, at 547 ("An inquiry into whether the drafters— let alone the ratifiers—of the fourth amendment would have considered the electronic interception of telephone signals to be similar to a writ of assistance, if only they had known about the role of telephonic communications in modern society is a manifest absurdity: to give Madison enough information about contemporary society and technology to answer the question intelligently would be to transform him from Madison the framer to Madison our contemporary and thus to deny him of the ability to speak the framer's intent").

117. M. Perry, *supra* note 9, at 37–60 [no functional justification exists for non-interpretive review in separation of powers cases, *id.*, at 60]; Carter, *Constitutional Adjudication and the Indeterminate Text, supra* note 53, at 861–862. Carter has recently written that he did not mean to advocate originalism for the political Constitution. Carter, *The Right Questions in the Creation of Constitutional Meaning, supra* note 53, at 71, 74. Carter, however, continues to argue for a more limited role for the Court in separation of powers cases as compared to individual liberties cases. Carter writes: "My goal . . . is to construct a constitutional safe harbor, a place where adjudication will be possible through an ordered application of interpretive rules to a text and its history. The political Constitution strikes me as the obvious place to build, at least if we want an edifice that will stand. Were the courts somehow above the political fray rather than an integral part of it, finding narrowing hermeneutical methods would perhaps be less important. But if the work of the judiciary is, as I have suggested, a vital part of the system of checks and balances, then rendering that system as concrete as can be is plainly indispensable." *Id.*, at 76. Thus, although Carter disavows any reliance on the Framers' intent, he continues to advocate a different interpretive method for the political Constitution than for individual rights. Although the text focuses on Carter's first article where the claim seemed to be directly for originalism, the arguments also apply to his most recent essay because I question whether it makes sense to use different methods of interpretation for varying parts of the Constitution.

118. Carter, *Constitutional Adjudication and the Indeterminate Text, supra* note 53, at 861.

119. *See* text accompanying notes 11–22, *supra* (arguing that originalism cannot be

asserted to be correct and must be demonstrated to be desirable on the basis of a normative theory)

120. Carter, *Constitutional Adjudication and the Indeterminate Text, supra* note 53, at 861.

121. Carter, *Constitutional Adjudication and the Indeterminate Text, supra* note 53, at 861.

122. *See* discussion accompanying notes 54–56, *supra*; Saphire, *supra* note 54, at 796–797.

123. *See* Chemerinsky, *supra* note 71, at 866 (defining such situations as presenting questions of inherent presidential power and discussing the frequency of such questions arising).

124. Youngstown Sheet & Tube Co. v. Sawyer, 343 U.S. 579 (1952).

125. Goldwater v. Carter, 444 U.S. 996 (1979).

126. Train v. City of New York, 420 U.S. 35 (1975): Louisiana *ex rel.* Guste v. Brinegar, 388 F. Supp. 1319 (D. D. C. 1975); National Council of Community Mental Health Centers, Inc. v. Weinberger, 361 F. Supp. 897, 901 (D. D. C. 1973).

127. United States v. Nixon, 418 U.S. 683 (1974).

128. There were numerous challenges to the constitutionality of the Vietnam War. For a description of these cases, *see* A. D'Amato & R. O'Neill, *The Judiciary and Vietnam* 51–58 (1972); Henken, *Vietnam in the Courts of the United States: Political Questions*, 63 Am. J. Int'l L. 284, 284–289 (1969); Sugarman, *Judicial Decisions Concerning the Constitutionality of United States Military Activity in Indo-China: A Bibliography of Court Decisions*, 13 Colum. J. Transn'l L. 470, 470–476 (1974).

129. *See, e.g.*, Chadha v. Immigration and Naturalization Service, 462 U.S. 919 (1983).

130. Carter, *Constitutional Adjudication and the Indeterminate Text, supra* note 53, at 861.

131. *Id.*, at 861–862.

132. *Id.*, at 861–862.

133. I developed this argument in Chapter 3, in the text accompanying notes 13–31.

134. *See* R. Collingwood, *The Idea of History* (1946); Florovsky, *The Study of the Past*, in *Ideas of History* (R. Nash ed. 1969); E. Carr, *What Is History* 16–22 (1964) (history is always a process of interpretation). I developed this argument in Chapter 3, in the text accompanying notes 32–35.

CHAPTER 5

1. Thomas Jefferson, letter to Abigail Adams, September 11, 1804, 8 *The Writings of Thomas Jefferson* 310 (Ford ed. 1897).

2. Andrew Jackson, *Veto Message*, 2 *Messages and Papers of the Presidents* 576, 581–583 (Richardson ed. 1896).

3. 31 U.S.C.A. §3351–3556 (West. Supp. 1985).

4. The CICA permits a potential or actual bidder for a government contract who disputes the terms or award of a government contract to challenge the procurement of the contract by filing a protest with the comptroller general. The filing of a protest freezes, or stays, the award of any action until the comptroller general makes a decision on the protest or the agency head certifies in writing that there are "urgent and compelling" circum-

stances that require the immediate award of the contract. *See* 31 U. S. C. A. 3553 (West Supp. 1985).

5. The General Accounting Office is a congressional agency that primarily performs investigations of government operations. The comptroller general, the highest ranking official, is appointed by the president. For a discussion of the role and duties of the comptroller general, *see* Ameron, Inc. v. U.S. Army Corps of Engineers, 787 F.2d 875 (3rd Cir. 1986) (upholding the constitutionality of the CICA); *see also* Bowsher v. Synar, 106 S.Ct. 3181 (1986) (ruling on the constitutionality of the Gramm-Rudman Balanced Budget and Emergency Deficit Control Act based on the role of the comptroller general).

6. 20 *Weekly Compilations of Presidential Documents* 1027 (July 18, 1984).

7. *Procedures Governing Implementation of Certain Unconstitutional Provisions of the CICA of 1984*, Office of Management and Budgeting Bulletin 85–88 (1985), quoted in Ameron, Inc. v. U. S. Army Corps of Engineers, 610 F. Supp. 750, 754 (D. C. N. J. 1985).

8. *Constitutionality of GAO's Bid Protest Function*, Hearings before a Subcomm. of the House Comm. on Government Operations, 99th Cong., 1st Sess., 301, 318 (1985) (testimony of D. Lowel Jensen, acting deputy attorney general).

9. Ameron, Inc. v. U.S. Army Corps of Engineers, 610 F. Supp. 754 (D. C. N. J. 1985).

10. *New York Times*, May 21, 1985, at A–26 (letter of Attorney General Edwin Meese).

11. *New York Times*, May 15, 1985, at B–10.

12. *New York Times*, June 4, 1985, at A–14.

13. Meese, "The Law of the Constitution: A Bicentennial Lecture," Tulane University Citizens Forum on the Bicentennial of the Constitution, October 21, 1986, at 11.

14. *See* A. D'Amato & R. O'Neill, *The Judiciary and Vietnam* 51–58 (1972); Henken, *Vietnam in the Courts of the United States: Political Questions*, 63 Am. J. Int'l. L. 284, 284–289 (1969); Sugarman, *Judicial Decisions Concerning the Constitutionality of United States Military Activity in Indo-China: A Bibliography of Court Decisions*, 13 Colum. J. Trans'l L. 470, 470–476 (1974). *See, e.g.*, Holtzman v. Schlesinger, 484 F. 2d 1307, 1309 (3rd Cir.), *cert. denied*, 416 U.S. 936 (1973); DeCosta v. Laird, 471 F.2d 1146, 1147 (2d Cir. 1973); Sarnoff v. Connally, 457 F.2d 809, 810 (9th Cir. 1972) (declaring question of the constitutionality of the Vietnam War to be a political question).

15. Sanchez-Espinoza v. Regan, 568 F. Supp. 596 (D. D. C. 1983), *aff'd* 770 F.2d 202 (D. C. Cir. 1985); Ramirez deArellano v. Weinberger, 568 F. Supp. 1236 (D. D. C. 1983), *aff'd on other grounds*, 724 F.2d 143 (D. C. Cir. 1983) (dismissing challenges to U.S. policy in Nicaragua as a political question).

16. 5 U.S. (1 Cranch) 137, 177 (1803).

17. 418 U.S. 683 (1974).

18. *Id.*, at 703–705.

19. *Id.*, at 713.

20. *Id.*, at 709.

21. There are several "abstention doctrines"—rules for when federal courts should abstain from deciding a case even though they have jurisdiction. *See, e.g.*, Railroad Comm'n of Texas v. Pullman Co., 312 U.S. 496 (1941); Louisiana Power & Light Co. v. Thibodaux, 360 U.S. 25 (1959); Colorado River Water Conservation Dist. v. United States, 424 U.S. 800 (1976). The Supreme Court, however, has emphasized that the abstention doctrines are limited exceptions to a general rule that "there is a virtually

unflagging obligation of the federal courts to exercise the jurisdiction given them.'' Colorado River Water Conservation Dist. v. United States, 424 U.S., at 817.

22. Cohens v. Virginia, 19 U.S. (6 Wheat), 264, 404 (1821); *see also* Wilcox v. Consolidated Gas Co., 212 U.S. 19, 39–40 (1909).

23. Richardson v. Ramirez, 418 U.S. 24 (1974) (upholding the constitutionality of disenfranchising ex-felons).

24. Comment, *Confronting the Conditions of Confinement: An Expanded Role for the Courts in Prison Reform*, 12 Harv. Civ. Rights-Civ. Lib. L. Rev. 367, 386 (1980) (''[T]he improvement of prison living conditions is not an issue likely to engender widespread political support. States have limited financial resources, the public is increasingly alarmed about crime, and a disproportionate number of criminals come from socioeconomic groups which themselves lack political power. Legislators and executive officials therefore have few but humanitarian incentives to finance improvements in prison conditions''). *See also* Frug, *The Judicial Power of the Purse*, 126 U. Pa. L. Rev. 715, 718, 723 (1978).

25. *See* M. Perry, *The Constitution, the Courts, and Human Rights* 146–162 (1982) (describing the importance of nonoriginalist review in such cases).

26. The notion that likes should be treated alike is thought to stem from Aristotle and be the basis of formal equality and justice. *See* Plato, *The Republic* VIII 558 (B. Jowett trans. 1892); P. Polyviou, *The Equal Protection of the Laws* 7 (1980); H. L. A. Hart, *The Concept of Law* 153–163 (1961).

27. *See* Ashwander v. United States, 297 U.S. 288, 346 (1936) (Brandies, J., concurring) (describing circumstances under which federal courts should avoid ruling on constitutional questions).

28. *See, e.g.*, Brest, *Who Decides?*, 58 S. Cal. L. Rev. 661, 663 (1985) (''Judges do not represent constituents; they should decide each case on its own terms and not engage in the 'logrolling' or 'horsetrading' that characterizes other political decision-making'').

29. 1 A. de Tocqueville, *Democracy in America* 103 (Bradley ed. 1945).

30. Fiss, *The Forms of Justice* 93 Harv. L. Rev. 1, 10 (1979).

31. Wellington, *Common Law Rules and Constitutional Double Standards: Some Notes on Adjudication*, 83 Yale L. J. 221, 246–247 (1973).

32. *See, e.g.*, Moore, *Moral Reality*, 1982 Wis. L. Rev. 1061; Moore, *A Natural Law Theory of Interpretation*, 58 S. Cal. L. Rev. 279 (1985).

33. *See, e.g.*, Simon, *The Authority of the Framers of the Constitution: Can Originalist Interpretation Be Justified?* 73 Calif. L. Rev. 1482, 1505–1510 (1985).

34. *See, e.g.*, Conkle, *The Legitimacy of Judicial Review in Individual Rights Cases: Michael Perry's Constitutional Theory and Beyond*, 69 Minn. L. Rev. 587, 629–637 (1985) (arguing for tradition as a basis for judicial decision making); J. Ely, *Democracy and Distrust: A Theory of Judicial Review* 60–63 (1980) (describing and critiquing tradition as a basis for decisions).

35. A. Bickel, *The Least Dangerous Branch* 26 (1962).

36. *See, e.g.*, Marshall v. Weinberger, 103 S.Ct. 843, 851 n.4 (1983); Capp. v. Naughton, 414 U.S. 141, 149–150 (1973); Rochin v. California, 342 U.S. 165, 169 (1952).

37. Although the Congress publishes legislative histories and the president issues official statements, there is no obligation that either of these branches decide solely on the merits or on the basis of arguments and reasoning. Purely political decisions are accepted and expected from the political branches of government.

38. *See generally* Bennett, *Objectivity in Constitutional Law*, 132 U. Pa. L. Rev. 445,

479 (1984) (describing requirement for written opinions as primary constraint upon judiciary); *The Speeches of the Right Honorable Edmund Burke on the Impeachment of Warren Hastings* 200–201 (H. G. Bohn ed. 1901) (need for judiciary to give reasons for its decisions); Radin, *The Requirement of Written Opinions*, 18 Calif. L. Rev. 486 (1930) (requirement in state constitutions and common law for written opinions).

39. White, *The Evolution of Reasoned Elaboration: Jurisprudential Criticism and Social Change*, 59 Va. L. Rev. 279, 299 (1973); *see also* Dewey, *Logical Method and the Law*, 10 Cornell L. Q. 17, 24 (1924) (importance of judicial statements of reasons for decisions); Karst, *Legislative Facts in Constitutional Litigation*, 1960 Sup. Ct. Rev. 75, 75–76 ("[U]nexplained decisions tend to substitute judicial fiat not only for the rule of a democratic majority but also for the rule of law").

40. Golding, *Principled Decision-Making and the Supreme Court*, 63 Colum. L. Rev. 35, 40–41 (1963); Wechsler, *Towards Neutral Principles of Constitutional Law*, 73 Harv. L. Rev. 1, 19 (1959).

41. *See* Braden, *The Search for Objectivity in Constitutional Law*, 57 Yale L. J. 571, 576 (1948) (describing decision rules as limits on judicial powers); Bennett, *supra* note 38, at 479 (describing requirement for justification as limit on judicial power).

42. Many have suggested that judicial decisions are merely public rationalizations for hunches. *See, e.g.*, W. Douglas, *The Court Years* 8 (1980); J. Frank, *Law and the Modern Mind* 148 (1930); Hutcheson, *The Judgment Intuitive; The Function of Hunch in Judicial Decision*, 14 Cornell L. Q. 274 (1929).

43. R. Wasserstrom, *The Judicial Decision* 25–30 (1961). Ely criticizes decisions based on moral analysis by saying that they come down to a statement of: "We like Rawls, you like Nozick. We win 6–3." J. Ely, *supra* note 34, at 58. The reason this is undesirable is not because Rawls's theory is an impermissible basis for determining constitutional values but because the Court should give reasons for its conclusions and should justify its adherence to a particular theory.

44. Spann, *Expository Justice*, 131 U. Pa. L. Rev. 585, 598 (1983).

45. Dewey, *supra* note 39, at 24.

46. *See, e.g.*, L. Festinger, *A Theory of Cognitive Dissonance* (1957); G. Miller & M. Burgoon, *New Techniques of Persuasion* 61 (1973); Aronson, *Dissonance Theory: Progress and Problems*, in *Theories of Cognitive Consistency: A Sourcebook* 24 (Abelson ed. 1968).

47. 347 U.S. 483 (1954).

48. Roe v. Wade, 410 U.S. 113 (1973); Doe v. Bolton, 410 U.S. 179 (1973).

49. *See* Erskine & Siegel, *Civil Liberties and the American Public* 31 J. of Social Issues 13, 19–21 (1975) (shift in public opinion on controversial questions like school desegregation and abortion because of Supreme Court decisions); Combs, *The Supreme Court as a National Policy-Maker: A Historical and Legal Analysis of School Desegregation*, 8 So. U. L. Rev. 197, 229 (1982) (Court as catalyst for changes in public opinion on school desegregation); F. Way, *Liberty in the Balance: Current Issues in Civil Liberties* 19 (1976) (describing changes in opinion on school desegregation because of Court's decisions).

50. For a discussion of the benefits of the adversary system as a method of dispute resolution, *see* Fuller, *The Adversary System*, in *Talks on American Law* (H. Berman ed. 1961); Simon, *The Ideology of Advocacy*, 1978 Wis. L. Rev. 30; M. Frankel, *Partisan Justice* (1980); M. Freedman, *Lawyer's Ethics in an Adversary System* (1975).

51. *See* Maltz, *Some Thoughts on the Death of Stare Decisis in Constitutional Law*,

1980 Wis. L. Rev. 467, 494–496 (listing cases in which the Supreme Court has reversed itself).

52. *See, e.g.*, United States v. Darby, 312 U.S. 100 (1941); NLRB v. Jones & Laughlin Steel Corp., 301 U.S. 1 (1937).

53. Betts v. Brady, 316 U.S. 455 (1942); Gideon v. Wainwright, 372 U.S. 335, 339 (1963).

54. 410 U.S. 113, 163–164 (1973).

55. 384 U.S. 436 (1966).

56. 395 U.S. 444 (1969).

57. 413 U.S. 15 (1973).

58. 403 U.S. 602 (1971).

59. Garcia v. San Antonio Metropolitan Transit Authority, 105 S.Ct. 1005 (1985).

60. National League of Cities v. Usery, 426 U.S. 833 (1976).

61. Garcia v. San Antonio Metropolitan Transit Authority, 105 S.Ct., at 1011–1020.

62. Moore, *A Natural Law Theory of Interpretation*, *supra* note 32, at 371–372.

63. Goodhart, *Determining the Ratio Decidendi of a Case*, 40 Yale L. J. 161, 169 (1930).

64. *See* Dewey, *supra* note 39, at 24; Greenawalt, *Discretion and the Judicial Decision: The Elusive Quest for the Fetters that Bind Judges*, 75 Colum. L. Rev. 359, 383–384 (1975).

65. *See* Moore, *A Natural Law Theory of Interpretation*, *supra* note 32, at 393–396 (describing moral reality as it applies in interpreting constitutional texts).

66. M. Perry, *supra* note 25, at 102.

67. *Id.*, at 115.

68. Wellington, *supra* note 31, at 284.

69. *See, e.g.*, Conkle, *supra* note 34, at 629–637 (arguing for tradition as a basis for judicial decision making; J. Ely, *supra* note 34, at 60–63 (1980) (describing and critiquing tradition as a basis for decisions).

70. G. White, *Patterns in American Legal Thought* 160 (1978); Simon, *supra* note 33, at 1505–1510.

71. Lynch, *Constitutional Law as Moral Philosophy*, 84 Colum. L. Rev. 537, 550 (1984).

72. *See* Carter, *Constitutional Adjudication and the Indeterminate Text: A Preliminary Defense of an Imperfect Muddle*, 94 Yale L. J. 821, 855–858 (1985) (describing clarity of many constitutional provisions and the relative lack of interpretive questions under them).

73. United States v. Nixon, 418 U.S. 683 (1974). James St. Clair, in defending Nixon, argued to the Supreme Court that the president has equal authority to interpret the Constitution and determine the scope of executive privilege. *See Transcript of Oral Arguments in United States v. Nixon*, 60–61 (1974); L. Jaworski, *The Right and the Power* 194 (1976).

74. For example, The Grand Jury investigating the Watergate cover-up did not indict Richard Nixon because they were unsure whether they could indict a sitting President, *Id.*, at 99–103.

75. 418 U.S. 166 (1974).

76. *Id.*, at 179.

77. 418 U.S. 208 (1974).

78. *Id.*, at 227.

79. 102 S.Ct. 752 (1982).

80. *Id.*, at 765.

81. *Id.*, at 767.

82. For an originalist argument that standing is not a constitutionality required limit on judicial power, *see* Berger, *Standing to Sue in Public Actions: Is It a Constitutional Requirement?* 78 Yale L. J. 816, 827 (1969).

83. *See* Gladstone, Realtors v. Village of Bellwood, 441 U.S. 91, 100 (1979); Warth v. Seldin, 422 U.S. 490, 501 (1976) (generalized grievance doctrine is prudential, not constitutional).

84. *See* L. Tribe, *American Constitutional Law* 71–73 (1978) (political question doctrine leaves matter to other branches to decide); Henken, *Is There a Political Question Doctrine?* 85 Yale L. J. 597 (1976).

85. Marbury v. Madison, 5 U.S. (1 Cranch) 137, 165–166, 170 (1803).

86. *See, e.g.*, Goldwater v. Carter, 444 U.S. 996 (1979); Little v. Barreme, 6 U.S. (2 Cranch) 177 (1804); *see generally* Tigar, *Judicial Power, the 'Political Question Doctrine,' and Foreign Relations*, 17 U.C.L.A. L. Rev. 1135 (1970).

87. 444 U.S. 996 (1979).

88. *Id.*, at 1003.

89. *See* A. D'Amato & R. O'Neill, *supra* note 13, at 51–58; Henken, *Vietnam in the Courts of the United States: Political Questions*, 63 Am. J. Int'l L. 284, 284–289 (1969); Sugarman, *Judicial Decisions Concerning the Constitutionality of United States Military Activity in Indo-China: A Bibliography of Court Decisions*, 13 Colum. J. Trans'l L. 470, 470–476 (1974). *See, e.g.*, Holtzman v. Schlesinger, 484 F.2d 1307, 1309 (3rd Cir.), *cert. denied*, 416 U.S. 936 (1973); DeCosta v. Laird, 471 F.2d 1146, 1147 (2d Cir. 1973); Sarnoff v. Connally, 457 F.2d 809, 810 (9th Cir. 1972) (declaring question of the constitutionality of the Vietnam War to be a political question).

90. *See, e.g.*, Luther v. Borden, 48 U.S. (7 How.) 1 (1849) (holding that disputes involving the "republican form of government clause" present a political question).

91. *See, e.g.*, Coleman v. Miller, 307 U.S. 433 (1939) (dispute over process of ratifying constitutional amendments poses a political question).

92. J. Choper, *Judicial Review and the National Political Process* 263, 298 (1980). Choper also argues that questions of federalism should be left to the political process.

93. *Id.*, at 263.

94. *See* Youngstown Sheet & Tube Co. v. Sawyer, 343 U.S. 579 (1952) (declaring unconstitutional presidential seizure of steel mills).

95. *See, e.g.*, Train v. City of New York, 420 U.S. 35 (1975) (invalidating presidential impoundment of funds on statutory grounds); Louisiana *ex rel.* Guste v. Brinegar, 388 F. Supp. 1319, 1325 (D. D. C. 1975) (declaring presidential impoundment of funds to be unconstitutional); Local 2677, Am. Fed'n of Gov't Employees v. Phillips, 358 F. Supp. 60, 75 (D. D. C. 1973) (declaring unconstitutional presidential impoundment of funds).

96. Youngstown Sheet & Tube Co. v. Sawyer, 343 U.S. 579 (1952) 594 (Frankfurter, J., concurring).

97. *See* Miller, *An Inquiry into the Relevance of the Intentions of the Founding Fathers, With Special Emphasis Upon the Doctrine of Separation of Powers*, 27 Ark. L. Rev. 583, 600 (1973).

98. Gewirtz, *The Courts, Congress, and Executive Policy-Making: Notes on Three Doctrines*, 40 Law & Contemp. Probs. 46, 79 (1976); *see also* A. Miller, *Presidential Power in a Nutshell* 29–30 (1977).

99. Gewirtz, *supra* note 98, at 79.

100. 5 U.S. (1 Cranch) 137, 165–166 (1803).

101. 369 U.S. 186, 211 (1961) (emphasis added).

102. Goldwater v. Carter, 444 U.S. 996, 1007 (1979) (Brennan, J., dissenting).

103. *See, e.g.*, United States v. Curtiss-Wright Export Corp., 299 U.S. 304, 315–316 (1936) (arguing that the president has special expertise and therefore greater powers in the area of foreign affairs); *but see* Lofgren, *United States v. Curtiss-Wright Export Corporation: A Historical Reassessment*, 83 Yale L. J. 1 (1973) (challenging the reasoning and holding in Curtiss-Wright).

104. *See, e.g.*, L. Tribe, *Constitutional Choices* 22–23 (1985) (arguing that the constitutional amendment process is properly regarded as a political question); *but see* Dellinger, *The Legitimacy of Constitutional Change: Rethinking the Amendment Process*, 97 Harv. L. Rev. 386 (1983).

105. Quoted in L. Tribe, *supra* note 104, at 23.

106. *Id.*, at 22; Coleman v. Miller, 307 U.S. 433 (1939).

107. The history of the ratification of the Fourteenth Amendment is reviewed in Coleman v. Miller, 307 U.S. 433 (1939).

108. In other words, a distinction should be drawn between deference and abdication. Certainly, the Court should be deferential, especially in questions involving amendments to overturn the Court's decisions. This, however, does not require total judicial abdication.

109. J. Choper, *supra* note 92, at 260–379 (arguing for judicial restraint in reviewing separation of powers questions).

110. *See* A. Bickel, *The Supreme Court and the Idea of Progress* 94 (1970) (Court risks its credibility when it intervenes too much); Bickel, *The Passive Virtues*, 75 Harv. L. Rev. 40 (1961) (arguing for judicial restraint to preserve judicial credibility).

111. J. Choper, *supra* note 92, at 139–140 ("[T]he Court's public prestige and institutional capital [are] exhaustible"); A. Bickel, *supra* note 110, at 94–95 ("[T]here is a natural quantitative limit to the number of major, principled interventions the Court can permit itself. . . . A Court unmindful of this limit will find that more and more of its pronouncements are unfulfilled promises, which will ultimately discredit and denude the functions of constitutional adjudication").

112. Choper argues that the Court should reserve its decisions for individual rights cases. J. Choper, *supra* note 92, at 60–84.

113. 343 U.S. 579 (1952).

114. 418 U.S. 683 (1974).

115. For example, the credibility of the federal judiciary was enhanced by the courts' role in the Watergate scandal. *See* Frankel, *Book Review*, 43 U. Chi. L. Rev. 874, 874 (1976).

116. Tigar, *supra* note 86, at 1142.

117. J. Choper, *supra* note 92, at 56 (describing instances of presidential disobedience to judicial rulings).

CHAPTER 6

1. *See* Simon, *The Authority of the Constitution and Its Meaning: A Preface to a Theory of Constitutional Interpretation*, 58 S. Cal. L. Rev. 603, 606 (1985) (the search for ways of constraining justices has been the preoccupation of constitutional scholarship throughout the century).

2. Bennett, *Objectivity in Constitutional Law*, 132 U. Pa. L. Rev. 445, 447 (1984); *see, e.g.*, Solem v. Helm, 103 S.Ct. 3001, 3022 (1983) (Burger, C. J., dissenting) ("Today's conclusion by five justices . . . is nothing other than a bald substitution of individual subjective moral values for those of the legislature").

3. *See* R. Berger, *Government by Judiciary: The Transformation of the Fourteenth Amendment* (1977); Bork, *Neutral Principles and Some First Amendment Problems*, 47 Ind. L. J. 1 (1971); Rehnquist, *The Notion of a Living Constitution*, 54 Texas L. Rev. 693 (1976).

4. Bork, *supra* note 3, at 6.

5. Carter, *Constitutional Adjudication and the Indeterminate Text: A Preliminary Defense of an Imperfect Muddle*, 94 Yale L. J. 821, 826 (1985) (describing position of liberal critics such as Tushnet); *see also* Tushnet, *A Note on the Revival of Textualism in Constitutional Theory*, 58 S. Cal. L. Rev. 683, 685 (1985); Tushnet, *Darkness on the Edge of Town: The Contributions of John Hart Ely to Constitutional Theory*, 89 Yale L. J. 1037, 1057 (1980).

6. *See, e.g.*, Tushnet, *Following the Rules Laid Down: A Critique of Interpretivism and Neutral Principles*, 96 Harv. L. Rev. 781 (1983); Tushnet, *The Dilemmas of Liberal Constitutionalism*, 42 Ohio St. L. J. 411 (1981); Tushnet, *Darkness on the Edge of Town*, *supra* note 5, at 1057.

7. Simon, *supra* note 1, at 606.

8. The term *literalism* for this theory comes from Robert Bennett. *See* Bennett, *'Mere Rationality' in Constitutional Law: Judicial Review and Democratic Theory*, 67 Calif. L. Rev. 1049, 1089 (1979). Paul Brest refers to this theory as "textualism." Brest, *The Misconceived Quest for the Original Understanding*, 60 B.U. L. Rev. 204, 206 (1980).

9. United States v. Butler, 297 U.S. 1, 62 (1936); *see also* Van Alstyne, *Interpreting This Constitution: The Unhelpful Contributions of Special Theories of Judicial Review*, 35 U. Fla. L. Rev. 209, 229, 231 (1983).

10. *See, e.g.*, *In re* Winship, 397 U.S. 358, 377–378 (1970) (Black, J., dissenting); Griswold v. Connecticut, 381 U.S. 479, 508–509, 520–521 (1965) (Black, J., dissenting); Rochin v. California, 342 U.S. 165, 174 (1952) (Black, J., concurring); H. Black, *A Constitutional Faith* 33–34 (1968).

11. Brest, *supra* note 8, at 204; Raoul Berger is a classic example of an originalist. *See* R. Berger, *supra* note 3, at 408; *see also* Rehnquist, *supra* note 3, at 694–695 (acknowledging that the Constitution may apply to cases not foreseen by the Framers but criticizing the view that the Court should "substitute some other set of values for those which may be derived from the language and intent of the framers").

12. *See* Munzer & Nickel, *Does the Constitution Mean What It Always Meant?* 77 Colum L. Rev. 1029, 1030 (1977); Brest, *supra* note 8, at 204.

13. Home Building & Loan Ass'n v. Blaisdell, 290 U.S. 398, 453 (1934) (Sutherland, J., dissenting).

14. Brest terms this theory "moderate originalism." Brest, *supra* note 8, at 205 (stating that "moderate originalism . . . [is] more concerned with the adopters' general purpose than with their intentions in a very precise sense"). It is distinct from originalism because originalism limits constitutional interpretation to what the Framers intended, whereas conceptualism allows consideration of modern circumstances in interpretation. Undoubtedly, under originalism, the Framers' intent can be stated at many different levels of abstraction. The distinction between originalism and conceptualism, therefore, is not always clear. Ultimately, the difference is that originalism is based on the belief that the

meaning of the Constitution is static, but conceptualism endorses the view that the precise meaning of the Constitution shifts over time. For a full discussion of conceptualism, *see* Chapter 4, *supra*, text accompanying notes 86–102.

15. R. Dworkin, *Taking Rights Seriously* 134–136 (1977) (drawing the distinction between concepts and conceptions; arguing that vague constitutional clauses represent "concepts" that each generation infuses with meaning through translation into particular "conceptions").

16. A variation of the conceptualist approach is to ask "[w]hat results would the drafters have intended had they been confronted with the problems and context of today's world?" L. Lusky, *By What Right? A Commentary on the Supreme Court's Power to Revise the Constitution* 21 (1975). This might be thought of as a separate approach, termed "transposition." *See* Tushnet, *Following the Rules Laid Down*, *supra* note 6, at 793, 802. For a discussion of transposition, *see* Chapter 4, *supra*, text accompanying notes 101–105.

17. I believe that cultural values theories are indistinguishable from "open-ended modernism" because both allow judges to decide what values are sufficiently important as to be worthy of constitutional protection. However, advocates of cultural values theories see them as a constraint on judicial decision making. *See, e.g.*, Conkle, *The Legitimacy of Judicial Review in Individual Rights Cases: Michael Perry's Constitutional Theory and Beyond*, 69 Minn. L. Rev. 587 (1985) (arguing for tradition as an alternative to judges deciding cases based on their own values). I reject the view that these theories constrain the Court because I believe almost anything can be said to be part of the "natural law," "traditions," or the "deep consensus." *See* text accompanying notes 40–47, *infra*, this chapter.

18. *See, e.g.*, Lupu, *Untangling the Strands of the Fourteenth Amendment*, 77 Mich. L. Rev. 981, 985, 1040–1041 (1979) (determining fundamental values through examination of historical traditions); Conkle, *supra* note 17, at 626–637.

19. G. White, *Patterns of American Legal Thought* 160 (1978); *see also* Simon, *The Authority of the Framers of the Constitution: Can Originalist Interpretation Be Justified?* 73 Calif. L. Rev. 1482, 1505–1510 (1985) (constitutional interpretation based on "deeply layered consensus").

20. Ely reviews these theories in J. Ely, *Democracy and Distrust: A Theory of Judicial Review* 63–69 (1980). For an example of a theorist believing constitutional interpretation should be based on natural law principles, *see* Moore, *A Natural Law Theory of Interpretation*, 58 S. Cal. L. Rev. 279, 393–396 (1985). For an example of a theorist arguing for constitutional interpretation based on moral consensus, *see* Wellington, *Common Law Rules and Constitutional Double Standards: Some Notes on Adjudication*, 83 Yale L. J. 221, 284 (1973).

21. J. Ely, *supra* note 19, at 73–75 (describing view that constitutional interpretation should be process bound rather than substantive).

22. *Id.*, at vii, 73–77.

23. *See* Chapter 1, *supra*, text accompanying notes 81–109.

24. J. Ely, *supra* note 19, at 48.

25. Dworkin, *Is Law a System of Rules?* in *Essays on Legal Philosophy* 44–45 (R. Summers ed. 1968).

26. *See* Bennett, *supra* note 2, at 447 (describing what it means for judges to decide cases based on their personal interests).

27. *See* Tammado, *Legal Formalism and Formalistic Devices of Juristic Thinking*, in *Law and Philosophy* 316 (S. Hook ed. 1964); H. L. A. Hart, *The Concept of Law* 126

(1961); N. MacCormick, *Legal Reasoning and Legal Theory* 21–22 (1978) (describing legal formalism).

28. For an excellent discussion of problems in interpreting language literally, *see* Moore, *The Semantics of Judging*, 54 S. Cal. L. Rev. 151, 181–202 (1981) (discussing ambiguity, metaphors, vagueness, and open-texture as problems of interpretation).

29. McCulloch v. Maryland, 17 U.S. (4 Wheat.) 316, 414–415 (1819).

30. U.S. Const. Art. I, §8.

31. McCulloch v. Maryland, 17 U.S. (4 Wheat.) 316, 414–415 (1819) (discussing meaning of the necessary and proper clause in art. I, §8).

32. H. L. A. Hart, *supra* note 27, at 129–132.

33. *Id.*, at 132.

34. M. Perry, *The Constitution, the Courts, and Human Rights* ix (1982).

35. For example, the Supreme Court has held that the Eleventh Amendment's limitation on state liability in federal court is modified by the Fourteenth Amendment. Fitzpatrick v. Bitzer, 427 U.S. 445 (1976).

36. People v. Castro, 113 Ill. App. 3d 265, 270, 446 N.E.2d 1267, 1271 (1983); this case is discussed in Levinson, *What Do Lawyers Know (and What Do They Do With Their Knowledge)? Comments on Schauer and Moore*, 58 S. Cal. L. Rev. 441, 450 (1985).

37. *See* Wofford, *The Blinding Light: The Uses of History in Constitutional Interpretation*, 31 U. Chi. L. Rev. 502, 508–509 (1964); J. Ely, *supra* note 19, at 17; *see also* discussion in Chapter 3, *supra*, text accompanying notes 26–34.

38. *See* Arrow, *A Difficulty in the Concept of Social Welfare*, 58 J. Pol. Econ. 328 (1950); *see also* A. Feldman, *Welfare Economics and Social Choice Theory* 178–195 (1980); *cf.* Easterbrook, *Ways of Criticizing the Court*, 95 Harv. L. Rev. 802 (1982) (applying Arrow's Impossibility Theorem to the Supreme Court).

39. *See* Alexander, *Modern Equal Protection Theories: A Metatheoretical Taxonomy and Critique*, 42 Ohio St. L. J. 3, 7 (1981); Brest, *The Fundamental Rights Controversy: The Essential Contradictions of Normative Constitutional Scholarship*, 90 Yale L. J. 1063, 1092 (1981); *see also* the discussion in Chapter 4, *supra*, text accompanying notes 86–100.

40. *See* discussion in Chapter 4, *supra*, text accompanying notes 90–94.

41. Brest, *supra* note 39, at 1092.

42. *Id.*, at 1092.

43. G. White, *supra* note 20, at 160. Wellington is one of the most prominent advocates of this approach. *See, e.g.*, Wellington, *supra* note 19, at 284.

44. For an excellent criticism of these theories, describing their inability to constrain judges, *see* J. Ely, *supra* note 19, at 48–69. I recognize that natural law theories often are not based on a particular culture's values and hence it is perhaps wrong to place them under the label "cultural value theories." Yet, I do so here because natural law, like tradition and consensus, are possible sources of values for judicial decision makers that are not based on the text of the Constitution or the Framers' intent. Hence, these sources, albeit quite different, share an important common characteristic.

45. *Id.*, at 50.

46. Bradwell v. Illinois, 83 U.S. (16 Wall.) 130, 141 (1873) (Bradley, J., concurring).

47. G. Wills, *Inventing America* xiii (1978), *quoted in* J. Ely, *supra* note 19, at 60.

48. J. Ely, *supra* note 19, at 69.

49. Radin, *Cruel Punishment and Respect for Persons; Super Due Process for Death*, 53 S. Cal. L. Rev. 1143, 1176 & n.109 (1980).

50. Wellington, *supra* note 19, at 67. *See also* Simon, *supra* note 20, at 1505–1510 (describing interpretation based on "deeply layered consensus").

51. J. Ely, *supra* note 19, at 67.

52. *See, e.g.*, Tribe, *The Puzzling Persistence of Process-Based Constitutional Theories*, 89 Yale L. J. 1063, 1067 (1980) (criticizing process-based theories because of their failure to deal with substantive constitutional provisions); *see also* discussion in Chapter 1, *supra*, text accompanying notes 85--88.

53. E. Levi, *An Introduction to Legal Reasoning* 1–2 (1961); *see also* J. Stone, *The Province and Function of Law: A Study in Jurisprudence* 8–9 (1950).

54. *See* Roberts v. United States Jaycees, 104 S.Ct. 3244 (1984); Linder, *Freedom of Association after Roberts v. United States Jaycees*, 82 Mich. L. Rev. 1878 (1985).

55. *See, e.g.*, Runyon v. McCrary, 427 U.S. 160 (1976); Bob Jones University v. United States, 103 S.Ct. 2017 (1983). For an excellent discussion of the tension between freedom of association and other social values, such as equality, *see* Marshall, *Discrimination and the Right of Association*, 81 Nw.U. L. Rev. 68 (1986).

56. *See, e.g.*, Nebraska Press Ass'n v. Stuart, 427 U.S. 539 (1976).

57. For an excellent discussion of the tension between the establishment clause and the free exercise clause, and a proposed solution, *see* Marshall, *Solving the Free Exercise Dilemma: Free Exercise as Expression*, 67 Minn. L. Rev. 545 (1983).

58. Nowak, *Resurrecting Realist Jurisprudence: The Political Bias of Burger Court Justices*, 17 Suffolk L. Rev. 549, 616 (1983).

59. M. Perry, *supra* note 34, at 111, 123.

60. Miller, *Judicial Activism and American Constitutionalism: Some Notes and Reflections*, in XX *Nomos* 333, 349 (J. Pennock & J. Chapman eds. 1979).

61. *See* Conkle, *supra* note 17, at 615 ("The requirement of principled explanation . . . derives from the more fundamental proposition that courts adjudicating constitutional cases, must render judicial decisions, not legislative ones").

62. J. Frank, *Law and the Modern Mind* 21 (1930).

63. *See* B. Bailyn, *The Ideological Origins of the American Revolution* 273–280 (1967); G. Wood, *The Creation of the American Republic* 151 (1969) (describing distrust of those in power as inspiring the structure of American government).

64. A. Bickel, *The Least Dangerous Branch* 28 (1962).

65. See R. Berger, *Government by Judiciary: The Transformation of the Fourteenth Amendment* (1977) (criticizing excessive judicial activism under the Fourteenth Amendment).

66. *See* Lochner v. New York, 198 U.S. 45 (1905) (invalidating maximum hours legislation for bakers). The decision is symbolic of the period from the late nineteenth century until 1937, during which the Court overturned needed federal and state social legislation. *See L. Tribe, American Constitutional Law* 434–436 (1978) (discussing use of the term "Lochner era").

67. *See* L. Tribe, *supra* note 66, at 446–449.

68. Ely, *Democracy and the Right to Be Different*, 56 N.Y.U. L. Rev. 397, 402 (1981).

69. Monaghan, *Commentary*, 56 N.Y.U. L. Rev. 525, 533 (1981).

70. Shaman, *The Constitution, the Supreme Court, and Creativity*, 9 Hastings Const.

L. Q. 257, 278 (1982) ("The Court has made its mistakes, including a few egregious ones, but so have the other branches of government").

71. Fiss, *The Forms of Justice*, 93 Harv. L. Rev. 1, 10 (1979).

72. For a discussion of the general failure of state governments to protect constitutional rights adequately, *see* Neuborne, *The Myth of Parity*, 90 Harv. L. Rev. 1105 (1977).

73. L. Tribe, *supra* note 66, at 13.

74. *See* R. Dworkin, *supra* note 15, at 130 (noting the argument that "because judges will often, by misadventure, produce unjust decisions they should make no effort to produce just ones"). Some commentators have argued that, overall, the Court has done well in protecting basic rights. *See, e.g.*, M. Perry, *supra* note 34, at 117; Wasby, *Arrogation of Power Accountability: Judicial Imperialism Revisited*, 65 Judicature 209, 210 (1981).

75. Originalists argue that Brown v. Board of Education was wrongly decided because the Framers did not intend to desegregate schools. *See, e.g.*, R. Berger, *supra* note 3, at 117–133.

76. Originalists oppose a judicially created right of privacy. *See, e.g.*, Bork, *supra* note 3, at 8–9.

77. Earlier, in Chapter 5, I discussed why it was unlikely that the legislature would have produced numerous key reforms, such as desegregating the South, reapportioning legislatures, or protecting the rights of criminal defendants. *See* Chapter 5, *supra*, text accompanying notes 21–30.

78. 60 U.S. (19 How.) 393 (1857) ("No one, we presume, supposes that any change in public opinion or feeling . . . should induce the Court to give to the words of the Constitution a more liberal construction in their favor than they were intended to bear when the instrument was framed and adopted").

79. *See* discussion in Chapter 4, *supra*, text accompanying notes 49–53.

80. *See* T. Dye & H. Ziegler, *The Irony of Democracy* (2d ed. 1980) (describing how government officials, including judges, represent elites).

81. *See* A. Paul, *The Conservative Crisis and the Rule of Law: Attitudes of Bar and Bench, 1887–1895* (1960) (describing prevailing support for laissez-faire ideology at the end of the nineteenth century).

82. *The Federalist No. 78*, at 490 (A. Hamilton) (B. Wright ed. 1961).

83. J. Choper, *Judicial Review and the National Political Process* 56 (1980).

84. Dahl, *Decision-Making in a Democracy: The Supreme Court as a National Policy-Maker*, 6 J. Pub. L. 279, 284–285 (1957).

85. *See* H. Simon, *Administrative Behavior* 110–153 (1957); Sarbin & Allen, *Role Theory*, in *Handbook of Social Psychology* 488–558 (G. Lindsay ed. 1968).

86. *See* Kelman, *Three Processes of Social Influence*, in *Current Perspectives in Social Psychology* 454 (E. Hollander & R. Hunt eds. 1973); Reeder, Donahue & Biblarz, *Conceptions of Self and Others*, in *Society and Self* 69 (B. Stoodley ed. 1962).

87. *See* discussion in Chapter 5, *supra*, text accompanying notes 37–71.

88. Bennett, *supra* note 2, at 479.

89. *Id.*, at 484.

90. 2 U.S. (2 Dall.) 419 (1793).

91. 60 U.S. (19 How.) 393 (1857).

92. 157 U.S. 429 (1895).

93. 400 U.S. 112 (1970).

94. *See, e.g.*, Carter, *supra* note 5, at 842–844; J. Choper, *supra* note 83.

95. R. Dworkin, *supra* note 15, at 148.

96. 323 U.S. 214 (1944).

97. Report of the Commission on Wartime Relocation and Internment of Civilians, *Personal Justice Denied* (1982); M. Grodzins, *Americans Betrayed* (1949); Dembitz, *Racial Discrimination and the Military Judgment*, 45 Colum. L. Rev. (1945); Rostow, *The Japanese American Cases: A Disaster*, in the *Sovereign Perspective* 193 (1962).

98. *See, e.g.*, Chemerinsky, *Ending the Dual System of American Public Education: The Urgent Need for Legislative Action*, 32 DePaul L. Rev. 77 (1982); Sedler, *Metropolitan Desegregation in the Wake of Milliken—On Losing Big Battles and Winning Small Wars*, 1975 Wash. U. L. Q. 535.

99. I recognize, however, that the Supreme Court's decisions can legitimize undesirable practices. For instance, the Korematsu decisions approved the relocation of Japanese Americans and put the judiciary's stamp of approval on the action. When I say that it is almost as if the judiciary did not exist at all, I am speaking of this in terms of whether the action would have occurred.

100. 60 U.S. (19 How.) 393 (1857).

CHAPTER 7

1. Shaman, *The Constitution, the Supreme Court, and Creativity*, 9 Hastings Const. L. Q. 257, 259 (1982).

2. Clinton, *Judges Must Make Law: A Realistic Appraisal of the Judicial Function in a Democratic Society*, 67 Iowa L. Rev. 711, 734–736 (1982).

3. Shaman, *supra* note 1, at 260.

4. Calder v. Bull, 3 U.S. (3 Dall.) 386 (1790).

5. 3 U.S. (3 Dall.), at 388; *see also* Grey, *Do We Have an Unwritten Constitution?* 27 Stan. L. Rev. 703 (1975); Grey, *The Origins of the Unwritten Constitution*, 30 Stan. L. Rev. 843 (1978).

6. Fletcher v. Peck, 10 U.S. (6 Cranch) 87 (1810).

7. *Id.*, at 135, 139, 143; *see* Shaman, *supra* note 1, at 260.

8. 60 U.S. (19 How.) 393 (1857).

9. *See* P. Finkelman, *An Imperfect Union: Slavery, Federalism and Comity* (1981); R. Cover, *Justice Accused* (1975).

10. Shaman, *supra* note 1, at 260.

11. *See, e.g.*, C. Cook, *The American Codification Movement: A Study of Antebellum Legal Reform* (1979); R. Cover, *supra* note 9, at 131 (describing the demise of natural law theories).

12. *See, e.g.*, Carter v. Carter Coal Co., 298 U.S. 238 (1936); A. L. A. Schechter Poultry Corp. v. United States, 295 U.S. 495 (1935); United States v. E. C. Knight Co., 156 U.S. 1 (1895) (view that there is a zone of activities reserved to the states).

13. 22 U.S. (9 Wheat.) 1 (1824).

14. *See, e.g.*, Carter v. Carter Coal Co., 298 U.S. 238 (1936); A. L. A. Schechter Poultry Corp. v. United States, 295 U.S. 495 (1935); Railroad Retirement Board v. Alton R. R., 295 U.S. 330 (1935); Hammer v. Dagenhart, 247 U.S. 251 (1918); United States v. E. C. Knight Co., 156 U.S. 1 (1895).

15. *See, e.g.*, Carter v. Carter Coal Co., 298 U.S. 238 (1936); A. L. A. Schechter Poultry Corp. v. United States, 295 U.S. 495 (1935); United States v. E. C. Knight Co., 156 U.S. 1 (1895).

16. *See, e.g.*, A. L. A. Schechter Poultry Co. v. United States, 295 U.S. 495 (1935); Railroad Retirement Board v. Alton R. R., 295 U.S. 330 (1935).

17. *See, e.g.*, Hammer v. Dagenhart, 247 U.S. 251 (1918) (declaring unconstitutional a congressional law excluding from interstate commerce the products of child labor).

18. *See* 1, 2 W. Crosskey, *Politics and the Constitution in the History of the United States* (1953).

19. 165 U.S. 578 (1897).

20. 262 U.S. 390, 399 (1923).

21. *Id.*, at 399.

22. 268 U.S. 510, 535 (1925).

23. *See, e.g.*, Coppage v. Kansas, 236 U.S. 1 (1915); Adair v. United States, 208 U.S. 161 (1908); Lochner v. New York, 198 U.S. 45 (1905); Allgeyer v. Louisiana, 165 U.S. 578 (1897) (decisions striking down state economic regulations as a violation of substantive due process).

24. G. Gunther, *Constitutional Law* 453 (11th ed. 1985) ("[D]uring the Lochner era . . . nearly 200 regulations were struck down").

25. *See, e.g.*, NLRB v. Jones & Laughlin Steel Corp., 301 U.S. 1 (1937); United States v. Darby, 312 U.S. 100 (1941); Wickard v. Filburn, 317 U.S. 111 (1942) (narrowly construing congressional commerce power and invalidating federal regulations).

26. *See, e.g.*, West Coast Hotel v. Parrish, 300 U.S. 379 (1937); United States v. Carolene Products Co., 304 U.S. 144 (1938); Williamson v. Lee Optical Co., 348 U.S. 483 (1955) (minimal protection of economic liberties under the due process clause of the Fourteenth Amendment).

27. The judiciary's position of deference to the political process as to economic matters, but active protection of civil liberties and "insular minorities," was articulated in the famous footnote in United States v. Carolene Products Co., 304 U.S. 144, 152–153 n. 4 (1938).

28. *See* Betts v. Brady, 316 U.S. 455 (1942) (the Constitution does not require the provision of counsel to indigent defendants in state proceedings); overruled by Gideon v. Wainwright, 372 U.S. 335, 339 (1963).

29. *See* Wolfe v. Colorado, 338 U.S. 25 (1949) (the Constitution does not require the exclusion of illegally obtained evidence in state proceedings); overruled by Mapp v. Ohio, 367 U.S. 643, 653–655 (1961) (the exclusionary rule applies to states).

30. *See, e.g.*, Lemon v. Kurtzman, 403 U.S. 602 (1971) (articulating test for determining whether aid to parochial schools violates the First Amendment); Committee for Public Education v. Regan, 444 U.S. 646 (1980) (invalidating several forms of aid to parochial schools); Engel v. Vitale, 370 U.S. 421 (1962) (invalidating school prayer).

31. *See, e.g.*, Shapiro v. Thompson, 394 U.S. 618, 630 (1969) (protecting the right to travel but declaring "[W]e have no occasion to ascribe the source of this right"); United States v. Guest, 363 U.S. 745, 758 (1966) (protecting the right to travel but declaring "that right finds no explicit mention in the Constitution").

32. *See, e.g.*, Roe v. Wade, 410 U.S. 113 (1973) (right to privacy includes a woman's choice of whether to terminate a pregnancy); Griswold v. Connecticut, 381 U.S. 479 (1965) (right to privacy includes a married couple's use of contraceptives); *see* Bork, *Neutral Principles and Some First Amendment Problems*, 47 Ind. L. J. 1, 8–9 (1971) (text of Constitution does not protect privacy and Framers did not intend such protection).

33. *See* Fairman, *Does the Fourteenth Amendment Incorporate the Bill of Rights?: The*

Original Understanding, 2 Stan. L. Rev. 5 (1949) (arguing that the Framers of the Fourteenth Amendment did not intent to apply the Bill of Rights to the states).

34. *See, e.g.*, Harper v. Board of Elections, 383 U.S. 663, 669 (1966) (concept of equal protection changes over time); Brown v. Board of Education, 347 U.S. 483, 491–492 (1954) (cannot look to world as it existed when the Fourteenth Amendment was ratified in determining its meaning); McCullum v. Board of Education, 334 U.S. 203, 237–238 (1948) (irrelevancy of Framers' intent to decide question of what is secular and what is sectarian); United States v. Classic, 313 U.S. 315–316 (1941) (Framers' intent not determinative in constitutional interpretation).

35. *See, e.g.*, Conkle, *The Legitimacy of Judicial Review in Individual Rights Cases: Michael Perry's Constitutional Theory and Beyond*, 69 Minn. L. Rev. 587, 588 (1985) (expansive nonoriginalist review "would undermine . . . [the Court's] fragile legitimacy [and] . . . the Court's constitutional decisions would face all-but-certain popular repudiation"); *see also* J. Choper, *Judicial Review and the National Political Process* 55–59 (1980); A. Bickel, *The Least Dangerous Branch* 201–268 (1962) (the importance of the Court acting to preserve its credibility).

36. *See* U. Rosenthal, *Political Order* 110 (1978) (legitimacy gains public acceptance of even unpleasant policies); H. Eckstein, *The Evaluation of Political Performance: Problems and Dimensions* 52, 62 (1971) (importance of legitimacy in gaining compliance); C. Mueller, *The Politics of Communication* 129–130 (1973) (importance of legitimacy).

37. C. Mueller, *supra* note 36, at 130.

38. U. Rosenthal, *supra* note 36, at 110.

39. *See, e.g.*, Conkle, *supra* note 35, at 588 (expansive nonoriginalist review would "undermine [the Court's] fragile legitimacy"); J. Choper, *supra* note 35, at 55–59; A. Bickel, *supra* note 35, at 201–268.

40. *See* J. Choper, *supra* note 35, at 55–59; A. Bickel, *supra* note 35, at 201–268.

41. Conkle, *supra* note 35, at 588.

42. Saphire, *Making Noninterpretivism Respectable: Michael J. Perry's Contribution to Constitutional Theory*, 81 Mich. L. Rev. 781, 796 (1983) ("[A] candid confession of the policymaking nature of noninterpretive review may not only undermine its ability to protect human rights . . . but also may adversely affect its ability to perform its interpretive function").

43. *See, e.g.*, Conkle, *supra* note 35, at 588 (describing the Court's "fragile legitimacy" with no explanation of why it should be perceived as fragile or why public perception of the Court's policy-making role would cause it to lose its legitimacy).

44. Lerner, *The Constitution and the Court as Symbols*, 46 Yale L. J. 1290, 1314 (1937).

45. Gibbons, *Keynote Address*, 56 N.Y.U. L. Rev. 260, 271 (1981).

46. *See, e.g.*, Carter v. Carter Coal Co., 298 U.S. 238 (1936); A. L. A. Schechter Poultry Corp. v. United States, 295 U.S. 495 (1935); Railroad Retirement Board v. Alton R. R., 295 U.S. 330 (1935).

47. For a discussion of the events surrounding the Court packing plan, *see* L. Baker, *Back to Back: The Duel between FDR and the Supreme Court* (1967); R. Jackson, *The Struggle for Judicial Supremacy* (1941); Leuchtenburg, *The Origins of Franklin D. Roosevelt's Court-Packing Plan*, 1966 Sup. Ct. Rev. 347.

48. Sen. Jud. Comm., S. 711, 75th Cong., 1st Sess. 13–14 (1937).

49. *See* McKay, *Judicial Review in a Liberal Democracy*, in *Liberal Democracy*, Nomos XXV, 121, 126 (J. Pennock & J. Chapman eds. 1983).

50. J. Ely, *Democracy and Distrust: A Theory of Judicial Review* 47–48 (1980).

51. *See* C. Mueller, *supra* note 36, at 133–135; Bensman, *Max Weber's Concept of Legitimacy: An Appraisal*, in *Conflict and Control* 42–47 (A. Vidich & R. Glassman eds. 1979); Blau, *Critical Remarks on Weber's Theory of Authority*, 57 Am. Pol. Sci. Rev. 315, 316 (1963).

52. *See* Lane, *The Legitimacy Bias: Conservative Man in Market and State*, in *Legitimation of Regimes* 69 (B. Denitch ed. 1979) (''[F]amiliarity . . . represents a powerful force making for loyalty to a known form of government and a known form of economic behavior. . . . There may be psychological bases for the preference for the familiar'').

53. *See* Lerner, *supra* note 44, at 1294; Grey, *The Constitution as Scripture*, 37 Stan. L. Rev. 1, 3 (1984) (''[I]t has been, virtually from the moment of its ratification, a sacred symbol'').

54. *See* C. Mueller, *supra* note 36, at 135 (positive results increase legitimacy); D. Easton, *A Systems Analysis of Political Life* 208, 278–310 (1965).

55. *See* Lane, *supra* note 52, at 69 (describing familiar practices as a basis for legitimacy).

56. A. Cox, *The Role of the Supreme Court in American Government* 104 (1976).

57. *See, e.g.*, Epstein, *Toward a Revitalization of the Contract Clause*, 51 U. Chi. L. Rev. 703, 736 (1984) (''Why bother with a constitution at all if it is to be rewritten anew in each generation?'').

58. J. Choper, *supra* note 35, at 60–128.

59. J. Ely, *supra* note 50, at 73–180.

60. M. Perry, *The Constitution, the Courts, and Human Rights* 146–162 (1982).

61. 372 U.S. 335 (1963) (Constitution requires provision of counsel to indigents accused of a felony).

62. Reynolds v. Sims, 377 U.S. 533 (1964) (Constitution requires standard of one person/one vote).

Selected Bibliography

Beard, Charles. *An Economic Interpretation of the Constitution*. New York: Macmillan, 1954.

Bennett, Robert. " 'Mere Rationality' in Constitutional Law: Judicial Review and Democratic Theory." 67 *California Law Review* 1049 (1979).

———. "Objectivity in Constitutional Law." 132 *University of Pennsylvania Law Review* 445 (1984).

Berger, Raoul. *Government by Judiciary: The Transformation of the Fourteenth Amendment*. Cambridge: Harvard University Press, 1977.

Bickel, Alexander M. *The Least Dangerous Branch*. Indianapolis: Bobbs-Merrill, 1962.

———. *The Supreme Court and the Idea of Progress*. New York: Harper & Row, 1970.

Black, Charles L. Jr. *The People and the Court*. New York: Macmillan, 1960.

Bobbitt, Phillip. *Constitutional Fate*. New York: Oxford University Press, 1980.

Bork, Robert. "Neutral Principles and Some First Amendment Problems." 47 *Indiana Law Journal* 1 (1971).

Brest, Paul. "The Fundamental Rights Controversy: The Essential Contradictions of Normative Constitutional Scholarship." 90 *Yale Law Journal* 1063 (1981).

———. "The Misconceived Quest for the Original Understanding." 60 *Boston University Law Review* 204 (1980).

———. "The Substance of Process." 42 *Ohio State Law Journal* 131 (1981).

Carter, Stephen. "Constitutional Adjudication and the Indeterminate Text: A Preliminary Defense of an Imperfect Muddle." 94 *Yale Law Journal* 821 (1985).

———. "The Right Questions in the Creation of Constitutional Meaning." 66 *Boston University Law Review* 71 (1986).

Chemerinsky, Erwin. "The Price of Asking the Wrong Question: An Essay on Constitutional Scholarship and Judicial Review." 62 *Texas Law Review* 1207 (1984).

Choper, Jesse H. *The Supreme Court and the National Political Process*. Chicago: University of Chicago Press, 1980.

Conkle, Daniel. "The Legitimacy of Judicial Review in Individual Rights Cases: Michael

Perry's Constitutional Theory and Beyond.'' 69 *Minnesota Law Review* 587 (1985).

Cox, Archibald. *The Role of the Supreme Court in American Government*. New York: Oxford University Press, 1976.

Crosskey, William W. 1, 2 *Politics and the Constitution in the History of the United States*. Chicago: University of Chicago Press, 1953.

Dworkin, Ronald. *Law's Empire*. Cambridge: Harvard University Press, 1986.

———. *Taking Rights Seriously*. Cambridge: Harvard University Press, 1977.

Ely, John H. *Democracy and Distrust: A Theory of Judicial Review*. Cambridge: Harvard University Press, 1980.

Fiss, Owen. ''The Forms of Justice.'' 93 *Harvard Law Review* 1 (1979).

Grey, Thomas. ''Do We Have an Unwritten Constitution?'' 27 *Stanford Law Review* 703 (1975).

Levinson, Sanford. ''The Constitution in American Civil Religion.'' 1979 *Supreme Court Review* 123.

Lupu, Ira. ''Untangling the Strands of the Fourteenth Amendment.'' 77 *Michigan Law Review* 981 (1979).

Lusky, Louis. *By What Right?: A Commentary on the Supreme Court's Power to Revise the Constitution*. Charlottesville: Michie, 1975.

Miller, Arthur S. *The Supreme Court: Myth and Reality*. Westport, Ct.: Greenwood Press, 1978.

———. *Toward Increased Judicial Activism*. Westport, Ct.: Greenwood Press, 1982.

Moore, Michael. ''A Natural Law Theory of Interpretation.'' 58 *Southern California Law Review* 277 (1985).

Perry, Michael. *The Constitution, the Courts, and Human Rights*. New Haven: Yale University Press, 1982.

Rawls, John. *A Theory of Justice*. Cambridge: Harvard University Press, 1971.

Shaman, Jeffrey. ''The Constitution, the Supreme Court, and Creativity.'' 9 *Hastings Constitutional Law Quarterly 257 (1982).*

Shapiro, Martin. The Courts: A Comparative and Political Analysis. Chicago: University of Chicago Press, 1981.

———. *Law and Politics in the Supreme Court*. New York: Free Press, 1964.

Simon, Larry. ''The Authority of the Constitution and Its Meaning: A Preface to a Theory of Constitutional Interpretation.'' 58 *Southern California Law Review* 603 (1985).

———. ''The Authority of the Framers of the Constitution: Can Originalist Interpretation Be Justified?'' 73 *California Law Review* 1482 (1985).

Thayer, James. ''The Origin and Scope of the American Doctrine of Constitutional Law.'' 7 *Harvard Law Review* (1893).

Tribe, Laurence. *American Constitutional Law*. Mineola, NY: Foundation Press, 1978.

———. *Constitutional Choices*. Cambridge: Harvard University Press, 1985.

———. ''The Puzzling Persistence of Process-Based Constitutional Theories.'' 89 *Yale Law Journal* 1063 (1980).

Tushnet, Mark. ''Darkness on the Edge of Town: The Contributions of John Hart Ely to Constitutional Theory.'' 89 *Yale Law Journal 1037 (1980).*

———. *''The Dilemmas of Liberal Constitutionalism.'' 42 Ohio State Law Journal* 411 (1981).

———. ''Following the Rules Laid Down: A Critique of Interpretivism and Neutral Principles.'' 96 *Harvard Law Review* 781 (1983).

Van Alstyne, William. "Interpreting This Constitution: The Unhelpful Contributions of Special Theories of Judicial Review." 35 *University of Florida Law Review* 209 (1983).

Wasserstrom, Richard A. *The Judicial Decision*. Palo Alto: Stanford University Press, 1961.

Wechsler, Herbert. "Towards Neutral Principles of Constitutional Law." 73 *Harvard Law Review* 1 (1959).

Wellington, Harry. "Common Law Rules and Constitutional Double Standards: Some Notes on Adjudication." 83 *Yale Law Journal* 221 (1973).

Index

About the Author

ERWIN CHEMERINSKY is a Professor of Law at the University of Southern California Law Center.

Professor. Chemerinsky has published widely in the area of constitutional law. His articles have appeared in journals such as the *Boston University Law Review*, the *Michigan Law Review*, the *Northwestern Law Review*, the *Southern California Law Review*, and the *Texas Law Review*.

Professor Chemerinsky holds a B.S. degree from Northwestern University and a J.D. from Harvard Law School.